D1197218

B. Moose Peterson

2nd Edition

Magic Lantern Guide to
Nikon Lenses, 2nd Edition

Published in the United States of America by
Silver Pixel Press®
A Tiffen® Company
21 Jet View Drive
Rochester, NY 14624
Fax: (716) 328-5078
www.saundersphoto.com

ISBN 1-883403-63-4

Written by B. Moose Peterson

Printed in Germany by Kösel GmbH, Kempten

Library of Congress Cataloging-in-Publication Data
Peterson, B. (Bruce), 1959-
Nikon lenses / B. Moose Peterson.—2nd ed.
p. cm. — (Magic lantern guides)
ISBN 1-883403-63-4 (pbk.)
1. Photographic lenses—Handbooks, manuals, etc. 2. Nikon camera—Handbooks, manuals, etc. I. Title. II. Series.

TR270.P48 2000 99-38318
771.3'52—dc21 CIP

This book is not sponsored by Nikon, Inc. Information, data, and procedures are correct to the best of the publisher's knowledge; all other liability is expressly disclaimed. Because specifications may be changed by the manufacturer without notice, the contents of the book may not necessarily agree with changes made after publication. Product photographs were supplied by Nikon. All other photographs are by B. Moose Peterson, unless otherwise noted.

Contents

Nikon Lens Terminology 11
AIS Meter Coupling 11
    Manual Lenses 13
Autofocus Lenses 13
    AF-I Autofocusing 16
    AF-S (Silent Wave) Autofocusing 17
Close-Range Correction (CRC) 17
    Rear Focusing 18
D Lens Technology 18
ED Optics 19
Internal Focusing (IF) 20
Nikon Integrated Coatings (NIC) 21
Focal Length and Angle of View 22
Photographic Terminology 23
Caring for Your Nikon Lens 30
Using This Book 31

Fisheyes and Ultra Wides 33
Using the Tools 33
Watch Out for Strays! 34
Flare 35
Vignetting 35
Ultra Wides Make the Subject Pop 38
    Nikkor 6mm f/2.8 39
    Nikkor 8mm f/2.8 41
    Nikkor 15mm f/3.5 43
    Nikkor 16mm f/2.8D AF 45
    Nikkor 18mm f/3.5 46
    Nikkor 20mm f/2.8D AF 48

Wide-Angle and Normal Lenses 51
Using the Tools 51
Proper Handholding Technique 53
    Nikkor 24mm f/2 54
    Nikkor 24mm f/2.8D AF 55

Nikkor 28mm f/1.4D AF 57
Nikkor 28mm f/2 58
Nikkor 28mm f/2.8D AF 59
Nikkor 28mm f/3.5 PC 60
Nikkor 35mm f/1.4 61
Nikkor 35mm f/2D AF 62
Nikkor 35mm f/2.8 PC 64
Nikkor 50mm f/1.2 66
Nikkor 50mm f/1.4D AF 67
Nikkor 50mm f/1.8 AF 67

Telephotos 71
Using the Tools 71
Isolating the Subject 71
Compacting the Scene 72
Flare 72
Handholding Technique 73
Nikkor 85mm f/1.4D AF IF 73
Nikkor 85mm f/1.8D AF 74
Nikkor 105mm f/2D DC AF 76
Nikkor 105mm f/2.5 77
Nikkor 135mm f/2 DC AF 78
Nikkor 180mm f/2.8D ED IF AF 79
Nikkor 200mm f/2 ED IF 89

Super Telephotos 93
Using the Tools 93
Lens Speed 93
Filters 94
Focus Controls 95
Lens Shades 97
Super Telephoto Technique 98
Transportation 98
Nikkor 300mm f/2.8D ED IF AF-S 99
Nikkor 300mm f/4 ED IF AF 101
Nikkor 400mm f/2.8 ED IF 103
Nikkor 400mm f/2.8D ED IF AF-S 104
Nikkor 400mm f/3.5 ED IF 106
Nikkor 400mm f/5.6 ED IF 107
Nikkor 600mm f/4 ED IF 108

Nikkor 600mm f/4D ED IF AF-S 109
Nikkor 600mm f/5.6 ED IF 110

Zooms 113
Using the Tools 113
Variable F/Stop Design 114
Macro Plus Versatility 114
AF-S Zooms 115
Nikkor 17-35mm f/2.8D ED IF AF-S 115
Nikkor 20-35mm f/2.8D AF 117
Nikkor 24-50mm f/3.3-4.5 AF 119
Nikkor 28-70mm f/2.8D ED IF AF-S 130
Nikkor 28-70mm f/3.5-4.5D AF 131
Nikkor 28-105mm f/3.5-4.5D IF 132
Nikkor 28-200mm f/3.5-5.6D IF AF 133
Nikkor 35-70mm f/2.8D AF 134
Nikkor 35-80mm f/4-5.6D AF 136
Nikkor 35-105mm f/3.5-4.5D AF 137
Nikkor 50-300mm f/4.5 ED 137
Nikkor 70-210mm f/4-5.6D AF 138
Nikkor 70-300mm f/4-5.6D ED AF 140
Nikkor 80-200mm f/2.8D ED IF AF-S 141
Nikkor 80-200mm f/4.5-5.6D AF 143
Nikkor 80-400mm f/4.5-5.6D ED VR AF 144
Nikkor 180-600mm f/8 ED 145

Specialty Lenses 147
Using the Tools 147
Nikkor 58mm f/1.2 Noct 147
Nikkor 60mm f/2.8D AF Micro 148
Nikkor 85mm f/2.8D PC Micro 152
Nikkor 105mm f/2.8D AF Micro 155
Nikkor 105mm f/4.5 UV 156
Nikkor 120mm f/4 IF Medical 157
Nikkor 200mm f/4D ED IF AF Micro 158
Nikkor 500mm f/8 Reflex 160
Nikkor 1000mm f/11 Reflex 161
Nikkor 70-180mm f/4.5-5.6D ED AF Micro 162

Teleconverters 165
Using the Tools 165
Nikkor TC-14A 169
Nikkor TC-14B 169
Nikkor TC-14E 172
Nikkor TC-20E 172
Nikkor TC-201 173
Nikkor TC-301 173

"Oldies but Goodies" 175
Nikkor 13mm f/5.6 175
Nikkor 16mm f/2.8 177
Nikkor 55mm f/2.8 Micro 180
Nikkor 105mm f/4 Bellows Lens 181
Nikkor 200mm f/4 IF Micro 182
Nikkor 300mm f/2 ED IF 183
Nikkor 300mm f/2.8 ED IF AF 185
Nikkor 300mm f/4.5 ED IF 187
Nikkor 500mm f/4 P ED IF 188
Nikkor 800mm f/8 ED IF 190
Nikkor 1200mm f/11 ED IF 191
Nikkor 25-50mm f/4 192
Nikkor 35-200mm f/3.5-4.5 193
Nikkor 50-135mm f/3.5 194
Nikkor 75-300mm f/4.5-5.6 AF 196
Nikkor 80-200mm f/4.5 197
Nikkor 200-400mm f/4 ED 199

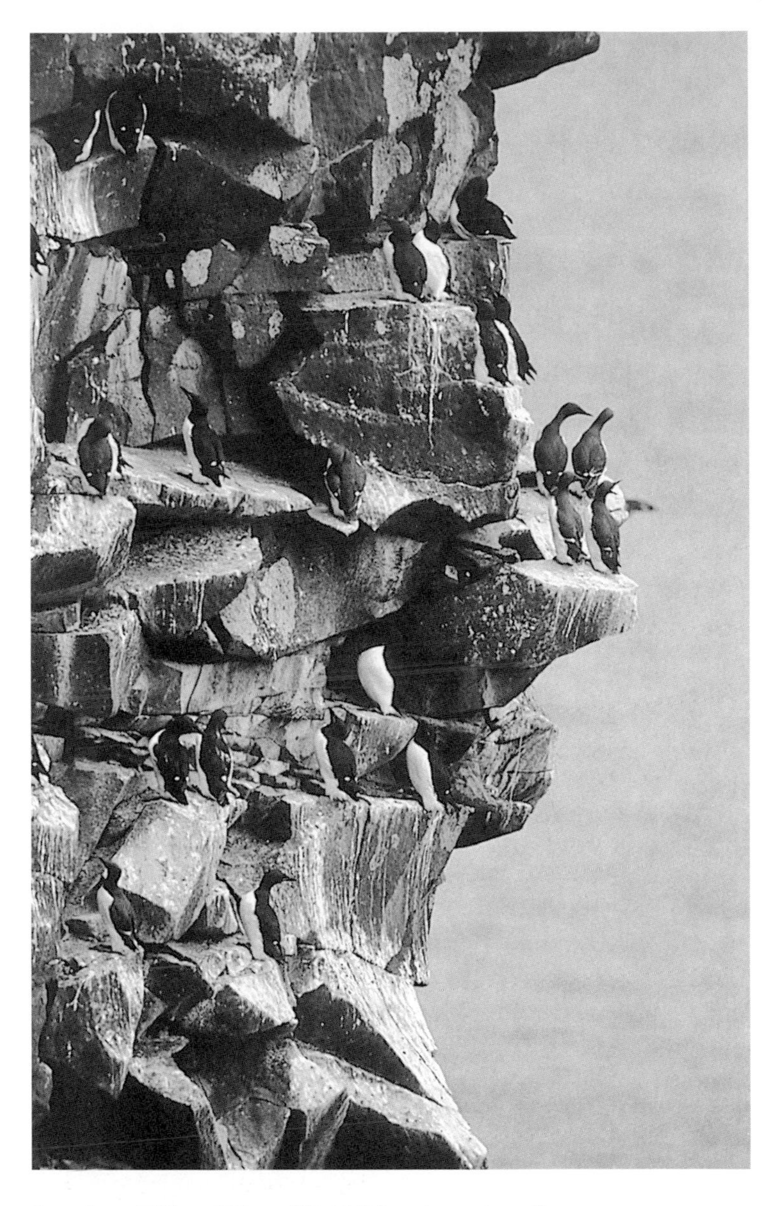

I used my Nikkor 600mm f/4 AF-S lens to capture these common murres (auks) in their rugged habitat on St. Paul Island, in Alaska's Bering Sea.

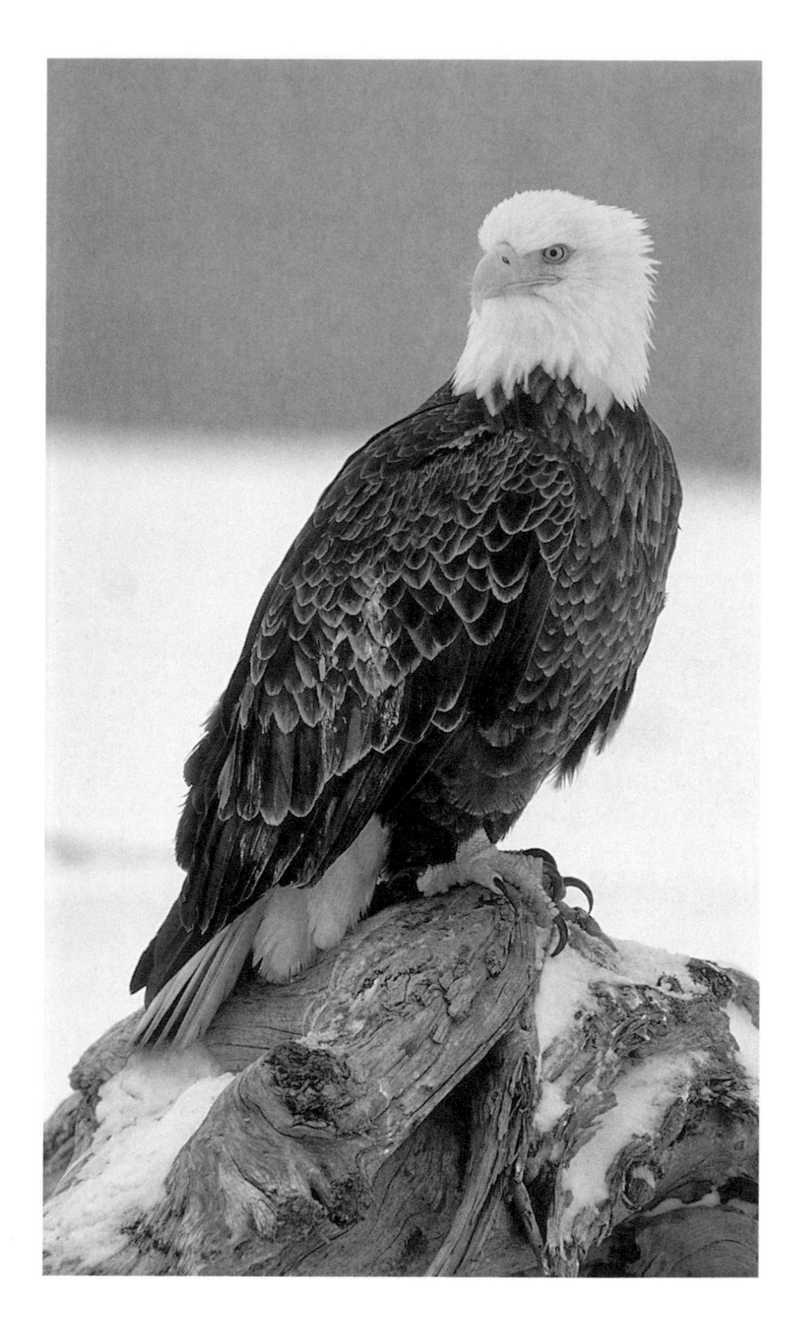

Nikon Lens Terminology

Each lens manufacturer has its own terminology to describe its lenses—and Nikon is no exception. These terms describe either the process by which the lens is manufactured or special attributes particular to that lens. Many of these terms are unique; others are sales tools. But whatever the context, understanding these terms is necessary to be an informed buyer and user of Nikon lenses.

AIS Meter Coupling

In 1982, all Nikkor lenses were converted from AI (automatic maximum indexing) to the AIS (aperture indexing shutter) system of meter coupling. The AIS system allows the camera body to determine the aperture in use, along with the focal length of the attached lens. The aperture is determined simply by a ridge on the rear of the lens' aperture ring; focal length is determined by a small scoop in the lens mounting flange. A small pin in the bayonet mount on the camera body slips into this scoop, thus making Program and Shutter-Priority Automatic Exposure (AE) modes possible. All lenses manufactured since 1982, including autofocus (AF) lenses, are AIS. AF lenses are distinctive enough to eliminate any doubt that they are indeed AIS, but detecting AIS on non-AF lenses is not as clear cut.

With the exception of lenses listed in "Oldies but Goodies," all lenses in this book are current production models. This means they all have AIS (aperture indexing shutter) meter coupling, even though current camera bodies do not rely on it. Some lenses, first introduced in 1959—such as the 105mm f/2.5—have gone through many changes, which have incorporated the newer cosmetics, optics, and, most important, AIS meter coupling.

⇦ Nikkor lenses have been market leaders for many decades. Among the outstanding features Nikon builds into each of its optics are Nikon Integrated Coatings, which assure remarkable contrast, color, and sharpness, as seen in this portrait of a bald eagle.

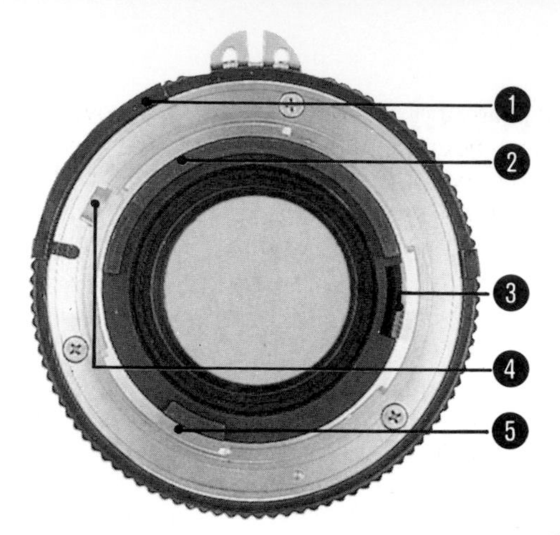

Nikkor Lens with AIS Bayonet Mount

1. Meter coupling ridge
2. Protective collar
3. Auto aperture coupling lever
4. Focal length identification notch
5. Aperture indexing post

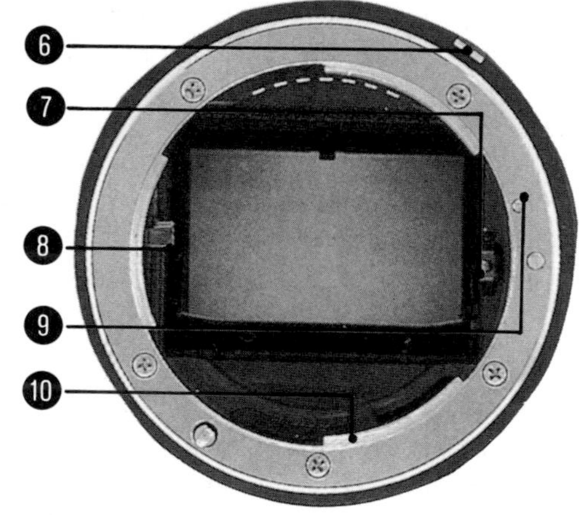

Nikon Camera Lens Mount

6. AIS meter coupling
7. Focal length indicator
8. Aperture stop-down lever
9. Lens mounting flange
10. F bayonet mounting flange

You can determine if a lens is AIS (vs. AI) by examining the aperture ring. The minimum aperture number (the largest number) should be bright orange for *both* the ADR (aperture direct readout) numbers and the main set of aperture numbers (there are a couple of exceptions on lenses privately imported into the United States). If just the main aperture numbers have a bright orange number, chances are it is not an AIS lens. A groove cut out of the back of the lens-mounting flange alone does not necessarily mean it *is* AIS. Some lenses were manufactured as AIS, but older aperture rings lacking the bright orange number were used. In this case, testing the lens on a body with the appropriate modes and seeing if they are activated is the only way of determining if the lens is truly AIS.

Manual Lenses

Manual focus lenses without the bright orange minimum f/stop number are either AI or non-AI. The non-AI system is indicated by the half-moon chrome tab fork attached to the top of the aperture ring. The AI lens also has the non-AI half-moon tab, but in addition has a ridge, on the rear edge of the aperture ring, that engages with a small tab on the camera's lens mount. As these two early versions of meter coupling do not interface with all functions on current camera bodies, they are not described in this book. For a complete, detailed listing and description of every Nikon lens ever manufactured, refer to my *Nikon System Handbook.*

Autofocus Lenses

An AF lens is a lens that can work with an AF camera body and does not require the photographer to turn a focusing ring to focus on the subject. While most current Nikon lenses have AF capability (remember that every AF lens manufactured by Nikon will also operate manually, including those with their own AF motors), over thirty manual lenses continue to be manufactured. These are mainly highly specialized lenses, such as ultra wides and super telephotos. The construction and optical engineering of manual lenses is different from that used in AF lenses. These differences, in most cases, make AF the better option when choosing between the two styles of lenses.

When the first full line of AF lenses was introduced, in 1986, their "plastic" appearance and feel were sharply criticized. The general feeling of photographers was that these lenses would not take the punishment Nikkor optics were well known for withstanding. This perception proved false, however, and many of the original AF lenses are still in heavy use. The materials used in the construction of AF lenses actually give better overall service than do those in the manual lenses they replaced. No lens works well after being dropped or wiped out by a football player crashing into it, but the plastic barrel of the AF lens is usually more forgiving of the occasional bump than the metal barrel of manual lenses. The ability to bounce back rather than acquiring permanent dents, as typically happens with metal barrels, allows AF lenses to continue functioning.

The barrel of the Nikkor lens is really a composite of a number of materials. The majority of AF lenses today have a metal barrel with polycarbonate internal workings; glass-reinforced polycarbonate best describes the outer casing of the barrel, which is internally reinforced with metal where appropriate. Nikon has kept the actual list of components comprising its barrel construction proprietary, so this is an educated approximation.

An important aspect of the barrel is that it does not conduct electricity. With the inclusion of central processing units (CPUs)—the computer—in lens construction, it is important that, if dented, the barrel does not short out the lens' CPU. This same principle is true for camera bodies, which are full of CPUs and electronics that connect the components.

The main difference that sets manual and AF lenses apart cannot be seen externally, however. This difference is internal, where the elements move. The manual lens moves elements around to focus via a helicoid, an oversize nut-and-bolt system. The helicoid is activated by turning the focusing ring, which moves the lens barrel and its attached groups of elements back and forth, thus focusing the image on the film plane. In some older lenses, focusing from infinity to the minimum focusing distance requires turning the lens' focusing ring more than 360°. This is very slow, providing little response to moving subjects. The helicoid is an all-metal unit, requiring a thin layer of special lubricant to function. This same lubricant also made it possible for older zoom lenses to zoom; when a zoom got "loose," the lube had to be replaced, stiffening the zoom action again. The focusing mechanism of an AF lens does not tend to get "looser" with age, as it often does on a manual lens.

AF lenses use what can best be described as a rack-and-pinion system to move the internal elements. In the original AF

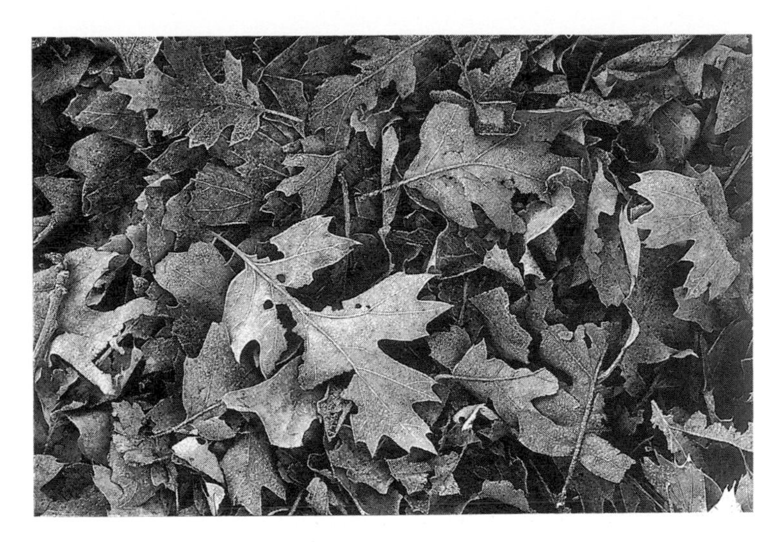

The 105mm f/2.8 micro was the perfect choice for capturing the frost on fallen oak leaves in the High Sierras.

lenses, this system is what made the "tinny" noise so disliked by photographers. The principles remain the same in the newer models, but the noise is gone; AF lenses now have a number of self-lubricating plastic gears and tracks that all rotate with the turn of the focusing ring. This rotation in turn moves the elements riding within the tracks. In some lenses, this system allows elements or element groups to move at different rates due to a change in gear ratios (in manual lenses, they would move as one large group). This has allowed AF lenses, in general, to have closer minimum focusing distances than manual lenses of the same focal length. It has also made them faster to focus, even if focusing them manually.

Even more important, the design of the AF lens creates a lot less mechanical drag, thus requiring a lot less torque from the camera body to focus the lens. An AF motor would have a difficult time trying to focus a helicoid system, with its giant threads and stiff lubricants. The self-lubricating plastic gears and tracks of the AF lens, on the other hand, glide easily, demonstrating how a small coreless motor in a camera or lens can focus a lens. This "looseness"—required to make autofocusing work—is what repelled so many photographers at first. It has been eliminated in all current AF lenses through new, proprietary technologies. This construction also makes AF lenses environmentally friendly. With self-lubricating plastic and other such innovations, AF lenses are able to work in hot and cold environments without their focusing capability becoming looser or tighter. Typically, manual lenses that were used in cold environments had to be stripped down and repacked with special lubes to prevent them from locking up in the cold. Some manual lenses even oozed lube when they got too hot (remember the warning not to keep equipment in the trunk of a car). Neither of these situations are a problem with AF lenses.

AF lenses have CPUs (central processing units) incorporated inside their barrels. These CPUs "talk" to the camera body, communicating a number of photographic facts. A good example of this capability is matrix metering, which can be accomplished only with lenses that have CPUs—which means an AF lens. (The 500mm f/4 P, a manual-focusing lens that incorporates a CPU, is the only exception.) The flash technology of the Nikon F5 and F100 cameras requires the lens' CPU to provide it with distance information. Designated as "D" for distance coding (see "D Lens Technology," below), these lenses, once focused, communicate the subject's distance to the camera's computer.

AF-I Autofocusing

In 1992, the first internal AF motor technology Nikon was to incorporate in its Nikkor AF lens was introduced (a technology, by the way, not believed possible without changing the lens mount). Designated as AF-I, this technology was originally incorporated into two telephoto lenses—the 300mm f/2.8 AF-I and 600mm f/4 AF-I. The motor in the AF-I lens is a coreless motor built on the concept of the AF motor in the F4 camera. The actual workings of the AF-I motor were mostly kept proprietary, even though cutaway drawings of them were found in Nikon literature.

The AF-I motor's CPU connects via contacts on the lens and camera body to the AF sensor in the camera body. The lens receives information from the CPU on which way to rotate for proper focus; with great speed, the AF-I motor moves the elements accordingly. The motor operates from power supplied by the camera's batteries, and can shorten the life of the batteries by half, depending on use. A very important feature of AF-I motors is that they do not require battery power to manually focus. This means they can technically function on any camera body as manual focusing lenses.

AF-S (Silent Wave) Autofocusing

In 1995, Nikon really shocked the photo industry with a completely redesigned internal lens AF motor system. The AF-S, or Silent Wave motor technology, converts "traveling waves" into rotational energy to move the optics for focusing. This motor receives its power from the camera body and its focus input from the camera's AF sensor, and focuses the lens accordingly. The AF motor in the body does none of the autofocusing; only the built-in focus-driving motor in the lens moves the elements.

There are two major benefits to the AF-S motor design and why I think Nikon went with its size and power. Photos of the coreless motor show a cylinder that would have to rest somewhere inside the lens barrel alongside the focusing track, causing the lens barrel to be physically larger in diameter to accommodate the motor. On the other hand, the AF-S motor is circular, with a center opening, permitting the focusing track to reside inside the motor. This allowed the lens barrel diameter to shrink, permitting AF-S lenses that previously were not possible with the AF-I technology (such as the 17-35mm f/2.8 AF-S). This same technology provides faster focusing speed, up to 15% faster with Nikon's latest cameras. The bottom line—AF-S lenses are smaller and faster than their AF-I counterparts.

The AF-S technology was originally introduced with three lenses: 300mm f/2.8 AF-S, 500mm f/4 AF-S, and 600mm f/4 AF-S. In 1999, this lens offering was expanded to seven incredibly fast-focusing lenses with a wide range of focal lengths.

Close-Range Correction (CRC)

The designing of modern lenses is done primarily with computers. Many innovations have resulted from this marriage of the optical engineer's imagination and the computer. Close-range correction (CRC)—an automatic function—is an innovation that is critical to many of today's lens designs. Also referred to as the "floating element" system, CRC was developed to overcome the problem of lenses performing best only at medium focusing range to infinity.

With CRC, the elements automatically shift their position when focused at the lens' minimum focusing distance. This element shift occurs in relation to other elements in the optical formula. Although this shift differs in various lens designs, the principle of minimizing curvature of field at close focusing distances, or flat-field correction, is the same. In wide angles, this means that when focused at or near their minimum focusing distance, corner-to-corner, edge-to-edge sharpness on the film plane is maintained. CRC is also employed in both the 55mm f/2.8 micro and 85mm f/1.4, providing them with the best performance of any lens in their class!

The computer has also been responsible for the design, creation, and manufacture of custom elements. One such design is the aspherical element (the lens' curved surface does not conform to the shape of a sphere). The aspherical element corrects for coma (comet-shaped blurs). For example, if photographing a subject that contains a point light source (such as a light bulb in the photograph), the aspherical element eliminates any flare caused by that light source. The 58mm f/1.2 Noct-Nikkor is the most well-known lens using this unique element, but many of the new AF lenses now incorporate this technology. This same optic design is now used in the 28-80mm f/3.3-4.5 zoom, not to correct for coma, but to reduce the physical size of the lens itself.

Rear Focusing

Rear focusing, at first read, sounds like CRC, but it's not. The principle behind it is to increase focusing speed for AF lenses by dividing the element groups so just the rear element group actually moves to focus. This technology was originally developed with IF lenses, but with computer designs, it can be incorporated in lenses other than those with IF.

D Lens Technology

In 1992, Nikon introduced the first D lenses. "D," which stands for distance-encoder technology, means there is a chip in the lens that transmits subject distance to the camera's computer. This information was originally marketed as needed by the then new N90 flash technology. Later, when the F5 was introduced, D lenses were marketed as a requirement to allow the F5's 3D matrix RGB metering to function correctly. The only way you can tell whether a lens is a D lens is that it is labeled as auch on the lens. There are no other features or tests you can perform to determine whether a lens is a D lens.

ED Optics

In 1977, in conjunction with the introduction of IF optical design (see below) came another breakthrough in optical design and manufacturing. The original two-piece super telephotos typically had to have their apertures closed down to f/11 or f/16 to capture a sharp image. Extra-low dispersion (ED) glass, a proprietary design, changed all of that by directly affecting the way white light bends as it streaks through the lens barrel. The ED glass bends the blue and red bands of light so they focus at the same point on the film plane. This is accomplished even with the lens wide open.

White light is made up of many colors with their associated wavelengths, each bending differently as it passes through the elements of a lens. The blue and red bands of white light (each at different ends of the spectrum—blue the fastest, red the slowest) must be brought into focus at the same point on the film plane for a photograph to be tack sharp when shot wide open. This is exactly what ED glass does: it brings all bands of white light to focus on the same point on the film plane at the same time, even when the lens is wide open. The older, non-ED lenses had to be closed down to achieve the same performance.

With modern technology in optical design and materials, chromatic aberration is usually not a problem in lenses ranging from fisheye to 135mm without ED glass. Beyond this focal length range, though, the blue and red bands of light focus either before or after the film plane, tending to cause "color fringing," or unsharp photographs (also see "diffraction" in Photographic Terminology).

Photographers using older, non-ED telephotos attempted to overcome this problem by closing down the aperture, but this proved only marginally successful. The invention of ED glass solved the problem of color fringing while shooting wide open—and also led to the creation of the fast super telephotos. The introduction of ED glass also made smaller lens designs possible. In addition, because ED glass is not severely affected by heat or cold, focus shift does not occur as in earlier optics. ED glass is hard and scratch resistant, which permits its use in exposed front or rear elements (though, as already noted, the super telephotos of today have dustproof filters in front of these elements).

Nikon has always manufactured its own optical glass; today, more than 200 types of optical glass are being used in Nikon lens construction! Nikon optical engineers create the formulas for the many types of glass manufactured in Nikon factories. This collection of glass is constantly expanding and improving to meet new lens requirements. The introduction of ED glass is a prime example of this.

Internal Focusing (IF)

The first super telephotos manufactured by Nikon were two-part units, with the element groups fitting into a universal focusing unit (which was really an empty tube). These lenses were physically as long as their focal length; a 600mm lens was physically 600 mm long, a 1200 mm lens 1200mm long, and so on. The helicoid in these original telephotos was massive (housed in the focusing unit), with the lens barrel expanding and contracting great physical distances when the lens was focused. This action was required to move the entire front element group (at the end of the focusing tube) either closer or farther away from the film plane. The turning of the focusing ring was so tremendous that focusing on a moving subject was nearly impossible. Three-inch posts were available on most versions to facilitate focusing, as it was so difficult.

Manual telephoto lens design radically changed and improved in 1977 with Nikon's introduction of internal focusing (IF). IF technology basically broke the rules of optical physics, opening up a whole new world in lens design. It differs from helicoid focusing because only the rear element group moves during focusing. The massive front element group never moves, as in the original two-part telephoto versions. This moving of elements is

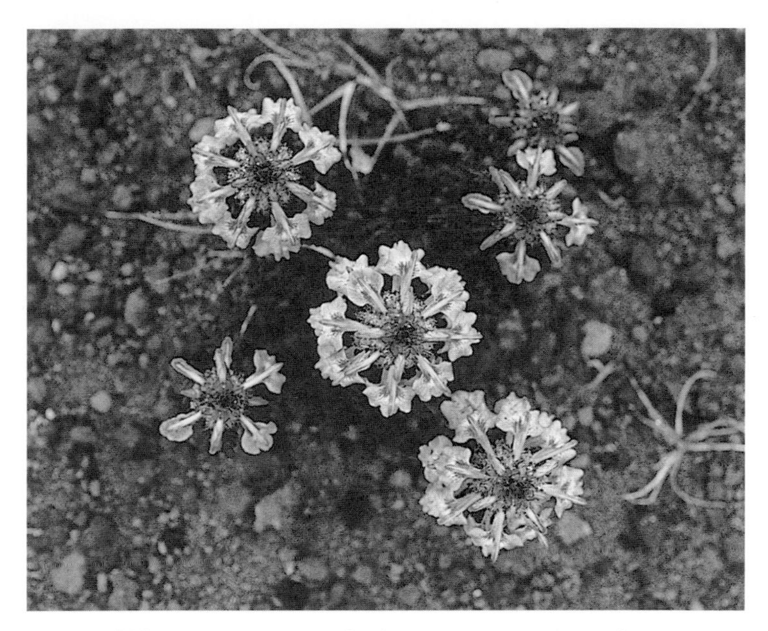

These wildflowers were captured using my 70-180mm AF micro.

done internally; the lens barrel does not need to expand or contract while focusing to move the elements back and forth.

The IF innovation in lens design led to the extremely compact super telephotos of today. It also resulted in benefits such as better balanced lenses, closer minimum focusing distances, and lightweight construction. But probably the biggest benefit is in the speed of focusing possible with IF lenses. A simple and easy roll of the hand over the focusing ring is all that is required to focus an IF lens from infinity to its minimum focusing distance. IF technology is no longer restricted to super telephotos; with new designs in optics, IF technology is being incorporated in many of Nikon's finer optics.

Nikon Integrated Coatings (NIC)

Photography is the art of capturing light. All Nikon optics have coatings applied to their surfaces to aid in the capture of that light. When light passes through ordinary glass, it is reflected, diffracted, and diffused—and all sorts of other things only optical engineers can understand. When this glass was arranged into a grouping, however, as was done in early lens construction, this internal bouncing and absorption of light would lead to poor photographic results. Very early optical designs (before Nikon came to be) were notorious for having problems such as ghost images, flare, and, most of all, poor contrast and color rendition; many photographers, in fact, would only shoot with one lens because switching lenses would lead to different color shifts in the image.

Nikon has always been known for the faithful rendition of color in all its optics no matter what the focal length. In the 1970s, Nikon incorporated various differentiated coatings, called Nikon Integrated Coating (NIC), as an integral part of its lens designs. Lens designers can apply whatever coating or combination of coatings that is required, in whatever number of layers and combinations to whichever element surface necessary, to perfect a lens' performance and permit it to be color corrected. Applied in vacuum chambers, these coatings ensure the remarkable contrast, color, and sharpness that make Nikkor optics legendary! This results in quality that has become world famous as the standard by which all new lens designs are judged.

Focal Length and Angle of View

Focal length and angle of view determine how the subject will be depicted in the photograph, and therefore are two of the most important factors to consider when selecting a lens. Technically speaking, focal length is the distance from the optical center of the lens (the rear nodal point in the optical design) to the film plane (or plane of focus) when the lens is focused at infinity. But most photographers think of focal length only in terms of millimeters, either very little or quite a lot.

A lens with a small focal length has a wide angle of view; these are known as ultra wides and wide angles. For example, the 13mm ultra-wide angle of view is a phenomenal 118°! As focal length increases, the angle of view decreases. Telephoto lenses do not magnify an image as binoculars do; instead, they capture a very narrow angle of view. For example, the 1200mm has a angle of view of just 2°!

Focal length and angle of view (also called picture angle) have a great influence on the background of a photograph. The extreme angle of view of a wide-angle lens encompasses more than the human eye can. To have any effect on the background, a camera with a wide angle would have to be moved a tremendous lateral, physical distance from the subject. The super telephoto, however, with its extremely narrow angle of view, would only need to move inches laterally to radically change the background. This relationship between lens focal length and angle of view to the subject and its background is what dictates the style of a photographer. Understanding this extremely important concept and its application is what separates the great photographers from the rest!

Photographic Terminology

The terms listed and defined in this section are basic to understanding, selecting, and using the right lens for your style of photography. They form the common language of lens knowledge.

Aperture, the opening created by the metal leaf diaphragm near or at the rear of a lens, controls the amount of light that strikes the film. The aperture can prevent vignetting and reduces lens aberrations when applied to optics design. The size of the aperture is communicated in f/stops (see below). The larger the diameter of the aperture, the lower the f-number (e.g., f/2.8). The smaller the diameter, the higher the f-number (e.g., f/32).

Aperture lock allows photographers to lock the aperture in place at its smallest f/stop value. Featured on all current Nikon lenses, it is a convenience for those who shoot in Program mode. In this mode, the aperture must be set at the smallest f/stop, or the camera will not function. The lock prevents accidentally knocking the aperture from this position.

Contrast is the visual difference in brilliance or brightness between different elements in a scene, described as highlights

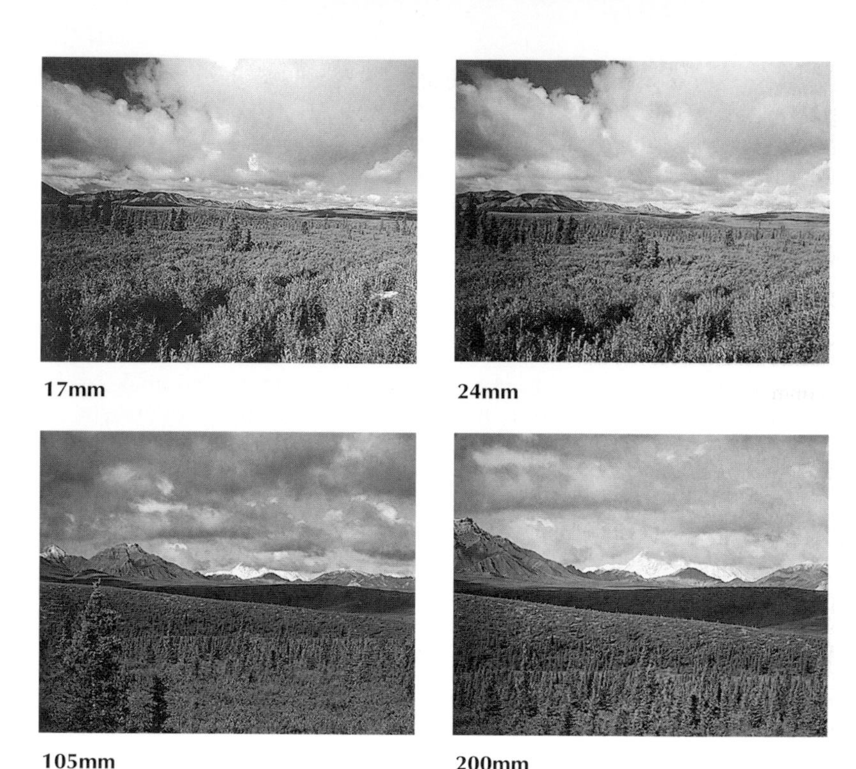
17mm
24mm
105mm
200mm

This series of eight photographs illustrates what happens to image size and angle of view . . .

and shadows, or tonal values; the difference in properly exposing for these determines the range of contrast in the scene. Lens coatings have greatly increased the amount of contrast transmitted by modern lens designs, demanding that photographers have greater skill in exposing film.

Depth of field is a zone of sharpness that falls in front of and behind the subject on which the lens is focused—generally, 1/3 in front of and 2/3 behind the subject. The depth of this zone of focus is dictated by the combination of the focal length of the lens and the f/stop. A general rule of thumb is the smaller the

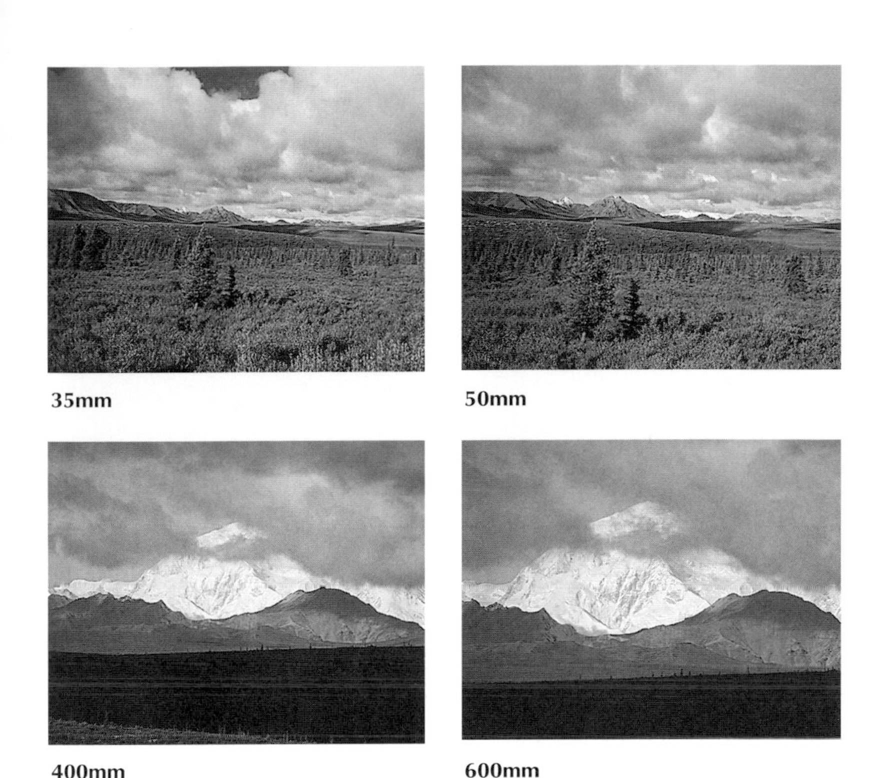

35mm

50mm

400mm

600mm

. . . when the focal length of the lens is changed while the camera position remains constant.

aperture (e.g., f/32), the greater the depth of field; the larger the aperture (e.g., f/2.8), the narrower the depth of field. When working with the 60mm micro at a magnification of 1:1 at f/32, only one inch of depth of field might be attainable, whereas using a 20mm focused at infinity at f/2.8 can capture miles. Each focal length and f/stop combination, focused at various distances, will have a different amount of depth of field. Closing down an aperture to its largest f/stop number (e.g., f/32), however, will not automatically guarantee the sharpest image because of a condition known as diffraction (see below).

Diffraction is the result of light bouncing off the narrow edges of

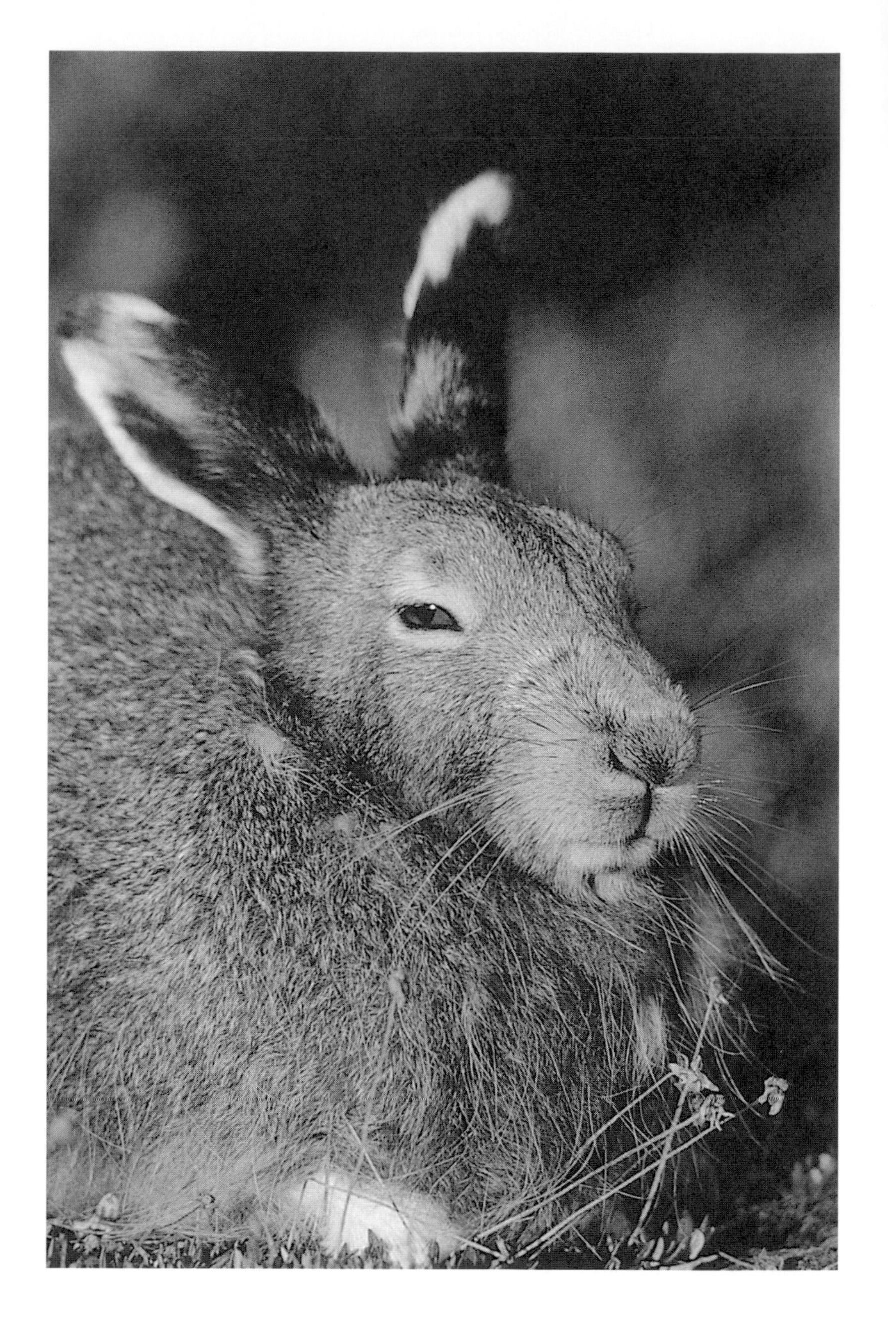

the aperture diaphragm. The extremely small opening created by a lens being closed down completely (e.g., f/32) restricts the light passing through the aperture that is to be focused on the film plane. The light bouncing off the edges of this small opening is diffracted and scattered at the film plane, resulting in an unsharp photograph, a form of color fringing.

Distortion is caused by a lens aberration that does not affect image sharpness but instead alters the physical shape of objects; it can best be thought of as curving a line that in reality is straight. Most distortions are classed as either "barrel" or "pincushion." Barrel distortion means straight lines are bowed out to the edges of the picture frame, occurring most often with wide-angle lenses and wide-angle zooms. Its effects are best seen when using a fish-eye lens. Pincushion distortion is just the opposite of barrel distortion—the lines bow in toward the center of the frame.

Flare is an overall decrease in image contrast and color due to light bouncing off, rather than being transmitted through, a lens surface. This was a common problem in very early optics, as light would bounce off various internal element surfaces while passing through the lens barrel to the film plane. In modern optics, multi-coating prevents this from occurring—except when light strikes or skims across the front lens element, causing textbook flare. A lens shade can eliminate this problem.

Free working distance, a term related to close-up photography, describes the distance between the subject and the front of the lens. This distance, which increases as the focal length of the lens increases, can be an important consideration in the purchase of a micro lens.

F/stop is a fraction indicating the diameter of the aperture (though photographers do not think of it in this way): the "f" is for the focal length of the lens, the slash means "divided by," and

The 600mm f/4 AF-S is the quintessential telephoto in the Nikkor line. It captured this little Arctic hare with such detail that you can see the catchlight in its eye—amazing!

"stop" is a particular f-number. For example, in a 20mm f/2.8, the diameter of the lens aperture when wide open is 20mm divided by 2.8, or 7.1 millimeters. When the same lens is closed down to f/22, the diameter of the aperture is 0.9 millimeter. Calculating this mathematical formula is not important to everyday photography. Aperture and f/stop, though technically different terms, are commonly interchanged; what *is* important is the understanding that they both affect exposure and depth of field.

Ghost images are the green, purple, or violet UFOs (unidentified flare origins) caused by a point light source in a scene. Such images, which are the most common with wide-angle lenses, take the shape of the lens aperture. Ghost images were more common in older optics, before advanced multi-coatings were applied to modern lens design.

Lens aberration describes the minute optical flaws inherent in most lenses. These can be in the form of chromatic aberration, spherical aberration, curvature of field, or distortion.

Lens speed is based on the maximum (largest) aperture of a given lens. Lenses are considered either fast or slow. A 400mm f/2.8 lens is considered fast, because its maximum aperture is f/2.8; a 400mm f/5.6 is considered slow. The focal length is the same, but the maximum aperture is two stops "slower" on the f/5.6 version; thus, "speed" is a relative term, having no actual bearing on the final image. In general, faster lenses are physically much larger and demand a higher price, while slower lenses are smaller and cost less.

Macro is a term used in close-up photography describing a reproduction ratio up to 1:1. This reproduction ratio can be reached by a macro lens being focused to its minimum focusing distance or by the addition of extension tubes moving the lens away from the film plane. Nikkor optics fit this definition, but Nikon refers to its macro lenses as "micro."

The 80-200mm f/2.8D AF-S is optically one of the finest zoom lenses available today. Coupled with the TC-14E, it is a killer combination that allows you to get in close while retaining near-perfect picture quality, as in this shot of a pronghorn. ➪

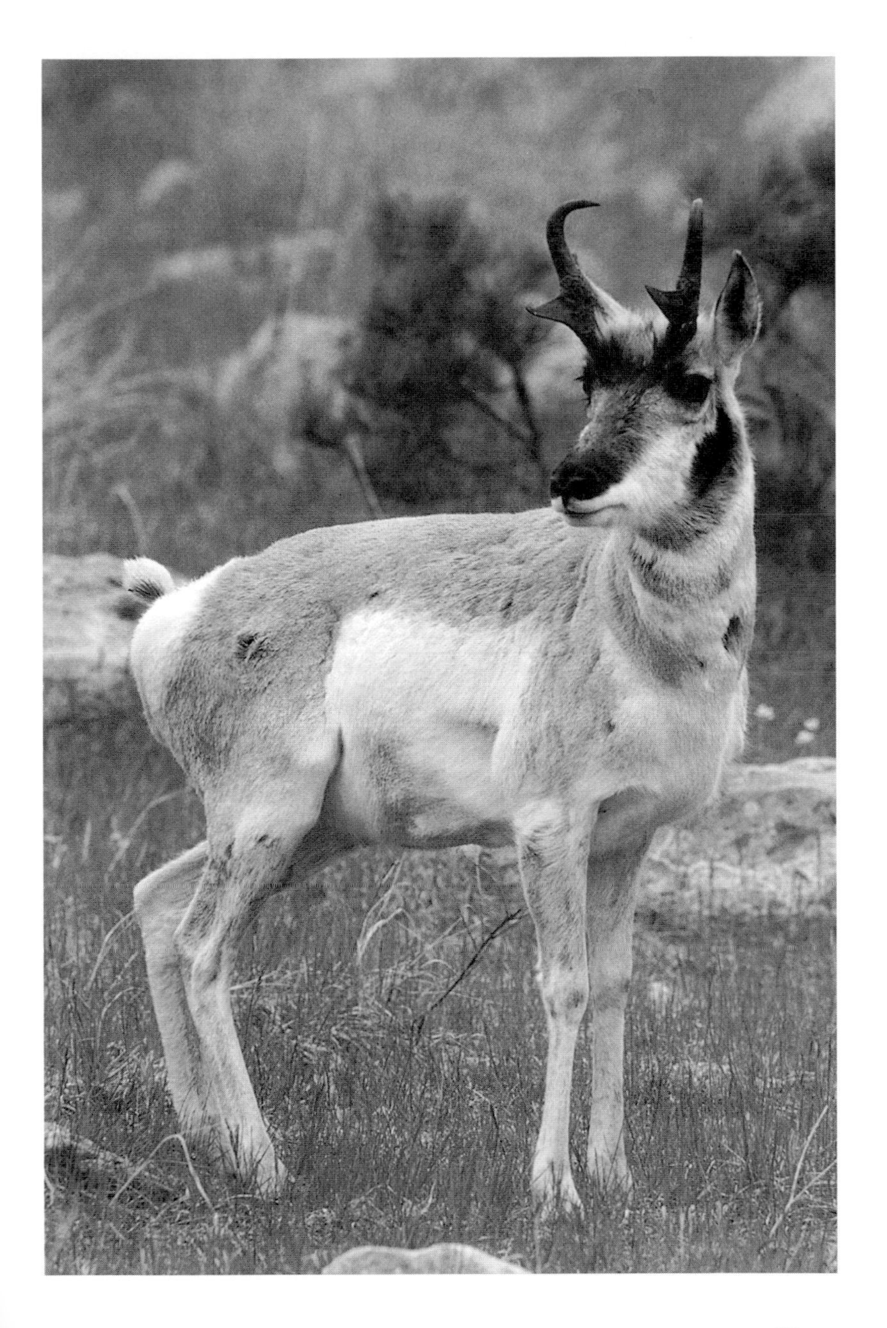

Photomicrography is the process of photographing minute objects with the aid of a microscope. This generally is in the realm of 10:1 to 50:1 or greater.

Reproduction ratio is a term indicating the magnification of a subject in macro photography. This is determined by the size of the subject photographed on the film divided by its actual size. For example, if the subject in real life is one inch long, and it measures physically one inch long on the negative or slide, the reproduction ratio is described as 1:1, or "life size." If the same one-inch subject is only one-half inch long on the film, then the reproduction ratio is 1:2, or one-half life size.

Resolution describes the resolving power (ability to discern minute detail) of a lens and/or film (the two are not related), described in the number of lines per millimeter that can be read from a special, standardized chart. For accurate measurement of a lens' resolution, the film must have greater resolving power than the lens; this is generally the case.

Sharpness describes the ability of a lens to render the fine detail of an object clearly at the film plane. This ability is dependent on a number of factors—contrast, f/stop, and resolution the most dominant.

Caring for Your Nikon Lens

Caring for your Nikon lens is important in maintaining a long life of service. Such attention takes very little time or energy and helps ensure consistent quality and performance. Clean your equipment—camera bodies as well as lenses—after each use, whether this was for just a moment or all day.

Clean the front element as infrequently as possible. When the front or rear element does need cleaning, first blow off the element to remove any large particles that could scratch it; small bulb blowers or canned air can be used. Note that with the introduction of the first ED lenses, Nikon advised not to use canned air, as its cold blast could cause damage. This was in the 1970s, however, before dustproof permanent front elements were used on ED lenses. Fogging the glass with your breath is an excellent, nonabrasive way to clean an element. When you do need to, use lens tissue—the most commonly used material for wiping off a front element.

Normally when an element needs cleaning, it is because something has spotted the glass. In this case, a fluid is often used to remove the spot. If a fluid cleaner is used, be sure to apply it to the lens tissue and not directly to the element, to avoid having the drop flow down the element and into the lens mechanisms or other internal elements.

Cleaning the lens barrel is as important as cleaning the elements. The oil from our palms and the dust that sticks to it on a lens barrel can work its way into the lens. Use a cotton t-shirt to simply wipe down the outside lens barrel after every use. This will prevent any grit from getting into the workings of the lens and causing expensive repair bills.

Using This Book

To get the most out of this book, read it from cover to cover to make sure to get all the information; though some techniques are repeated (for those who target particular lenses), many are mentioned only. This single mention by no means implies that the technique is valid with only the one lens, but was mentioned once only to keep the book from being hundreds of pages; as you read the entire book, all of these techniques will come to light. Only with the knowledge of all of these techniques can every lens in your camera bag be an essential part of your photographic bag of confidence.

The description of lenses in this book pertain to those imported by Nikon USA only. Some variations or special lenses have been created for other smaller markets and were never imported into the United States; I have no firsthand knowledge or use of these lenses, so I'm unable to write about them.

All specifications quoted in this book come from information Nikon USA provided to me. All evaluations are my personal thoughts after using samples and my own equipment. The performance of your equipment might vary, based on a number of factors—including, of course, the photographer.

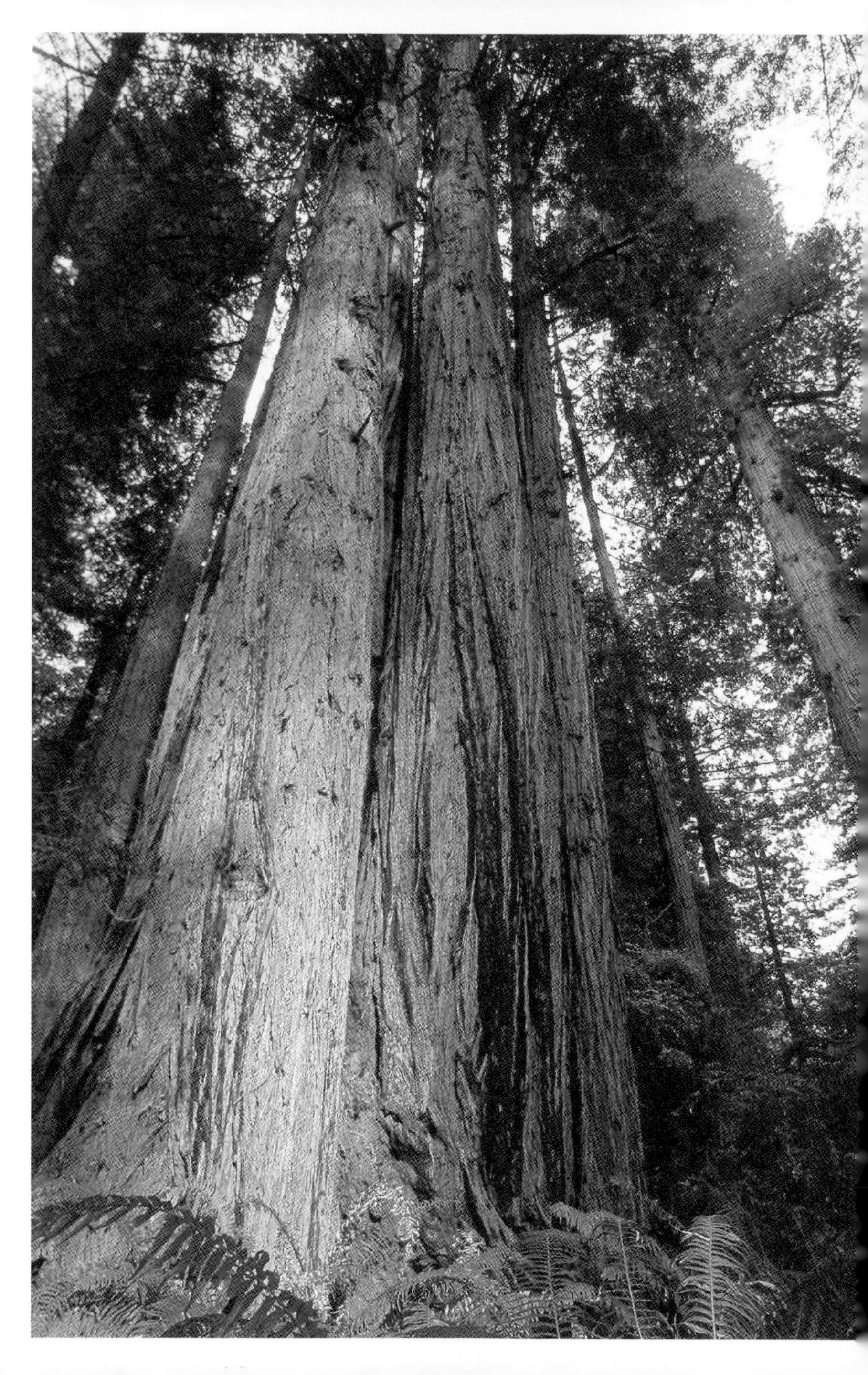

Fisheyes and Ultra Wides

Using the Tools

Lenses are designed with a specific purpose: to solve particular problems faced by photographers in capturing an image on film. The fisheye and ultra-wide lenses are no exception to this rule. What is the purpose of the fisheye, a lens that takes circular photographs?

Since the conception of the fisheye, in 1963, its unique perspective on life has been put to very practical applications. In the '60s, the construction of massive boilers in power plants and thousands of miles of pipelines was taking place. The assembly, welding, and layout of these cylindrical units required the fisheye lens to document the work in progress. The fisheye's ability to cover the entire area of a boiler or pipe in just one photograph made it indispensable in quality control and testing. Meteorologists and astronomers also found the fisheye of tremendous use in their work; some fisheyes, such as the Nikkor 10opmm, were made specifically for them.

The physical size and cost of the 6mm f/2.8 fisheye put it out of range for most photographers. The 8mm f/2.8, though, can be easily handheld and is priced where those who want to explore their world through its curved perspective can. The 16mm f/2.8, which is a full-frame fisheye, has always been popular and resides in many camera bags for those special times when only a fisheye will do the job.

The tremendous angle of view and barrel distortion of fisheyes can make some photographers dizzy when viewing through them. Photographs taken with a fisheye lens are best known by their curved horizon line. This line will be either curved up, giving the illusion of a round planet, or curved down, making it look

This photo of the giant coastal redwoods was shot with the 20mm f/2.8 AF to accentuate their towering majesty as well as add depth to the forest.

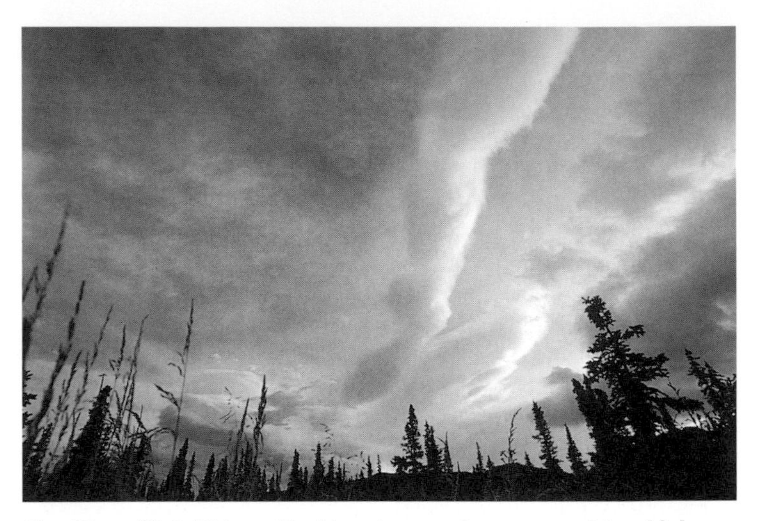

The 18mm f/2.8 AF is an ideal lens to use when you want to add drama to scenic shots. With this in mind, I used it to portray the mysterious presence of a threatening sky over Denali National Park.

as if the photographer had been standing in a giant crater. But if the horizon line is placed directly through the center of the frame, the horizon will not bend at all; only vertical subjects will be curved by the barrel distortion.

Watch Out for Strays!

Some things to be aware of when using fisheyes are tripod legs and the photographer's toes. Because their wide angle of view takes in so much, tilting a fisheye up severely is necessary to exclude your feet and toes when shooting handheld. And with most normal tripods, one if not two tripod legs will appear in the photograph. This can be remedied by using a tripod such as a Benbo® from Tiffen®, which allows the individual positioning of the legs and center column.

When they get their photos back, many photographers see funny brown and black lines near the edges of their image. This is not an optical flaw in the lens, but instead the fingers and camera strap that got into the photograph. Because so much is crammed into the frame, everything is smaller and harder to see through the viewfinder. You must be very careful when using a fisheye—especially the 6mm—to avoid having a branch that is physically behind the lens ending up in the photograph.

Flare

UFOs—unidentified flaring objects—are another concern when using these giant pieces of glass. Because these lenses "see" so much of the world, they tend to see the sun itself. This can cause flare to happen. Flare is the soft effect visible in a photograph resulting from stray light that passes through the lens but is not focused to form the primary image. It can take the shape of blue-green objects streaming through your viewfinder; it also can cause an overall flattening of the image's contrast. Typically, though, flare is displayed as a dark purple aberration in the lower edge of the photograph, a color that is rarely hidden by the colors found in the scene itself.

As for ultra wides, though they usually have built-in shades, they are inadequate for proper lens flare protection most of the time. The easiest and best tool for combatting flare is your hand, using it to block the light striking the front element; in addition, using a camera with 100% viewing will make this process a whole lot easier. With any other camera body, there's a good chance your hand will be in the picture—but that you won't see it. Also be aware that flare can come from other paths and not just directly from the sun. Water, snow, sand, and other highly reflective surfaces can bounce light into the lens, causing flare.

Vignetting

The tremendous coverage of these lenses nearly precludes the use of front element filtration. Vignetting—progressively diminished illumination of the film from the center to the corners—is a common problem, caused when the mount of the filter cuts into the frame. Checking for vignetting requires using a camera with 100% viewing. With the lens attached to the camera, close the lens down to its smallest aperture and depress the depth-of-field

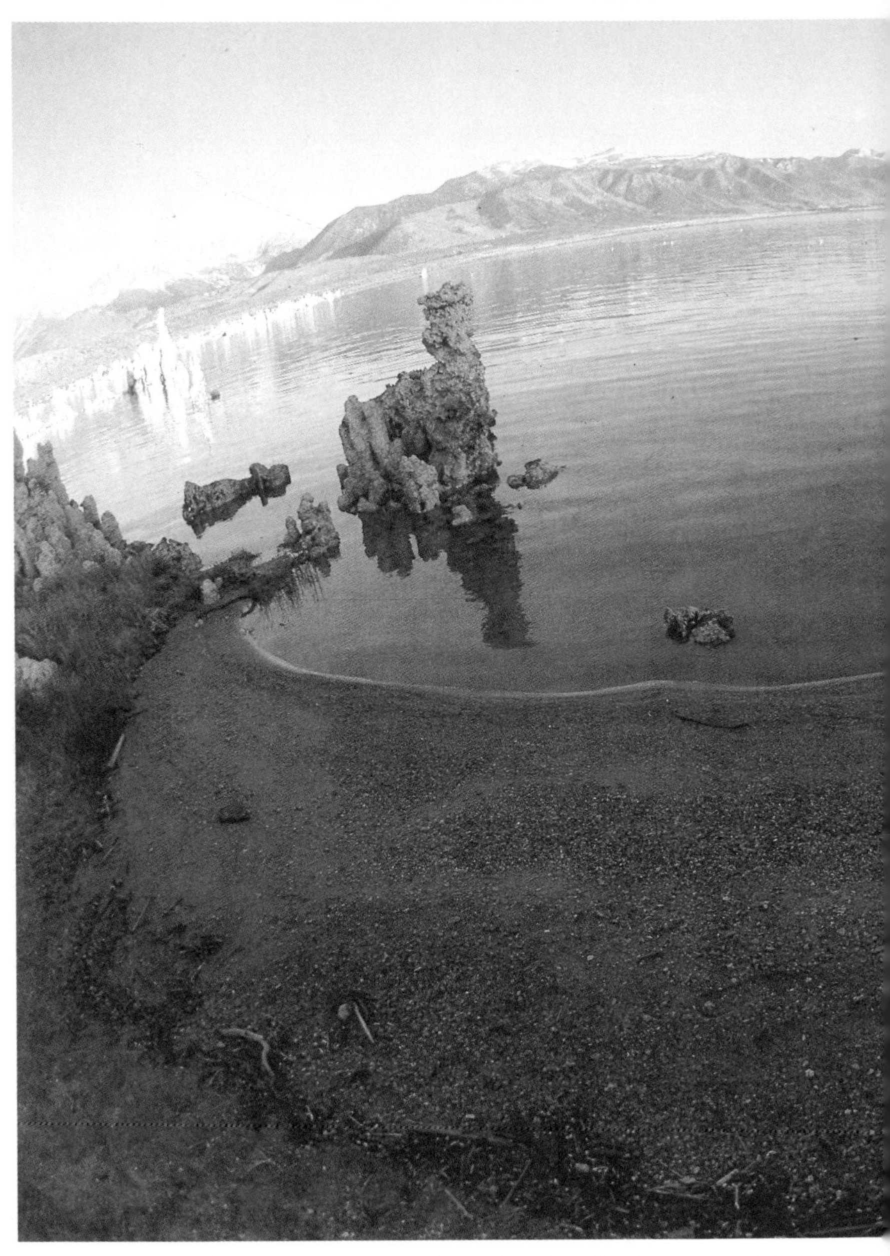

Capturing the expanse of Mono Lake and emphasizing its vastness is best done by curving the earth with the 16mm f/2.8.

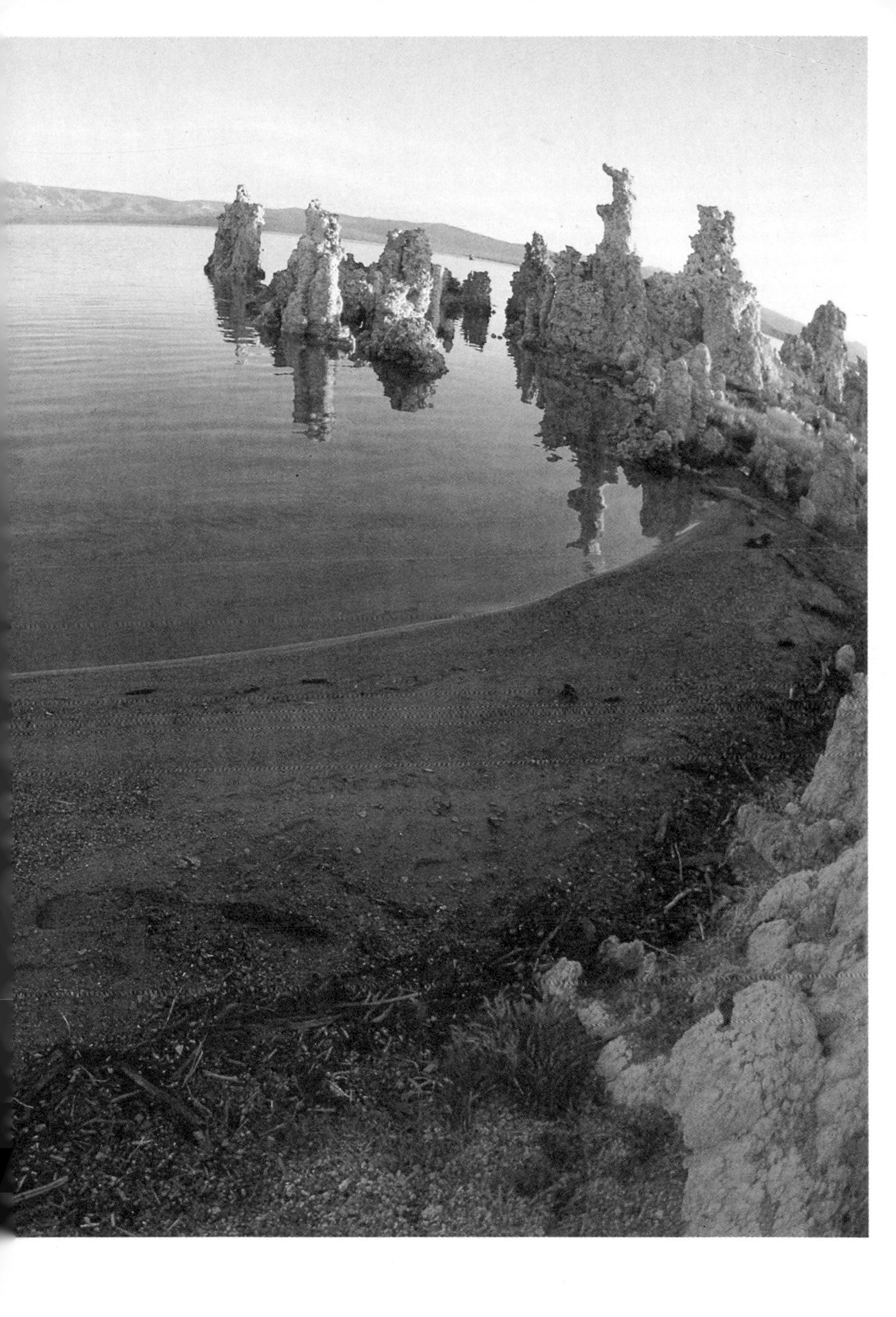

preview button. When no filter is attached, the corners of the picture frame will not darken; this must hold true as well when a filter is attached, or you'll get back images with dark corners. This same test can be performed to check for vignetting with stacked filters, an attached shade, or when using a hand as a shade.

Ultra Wides Make the Subject Pop

Most photographers pigeonhole the ultra-wide lens to scenic duties—which is fine, because ultra wides can capture scenics like no other lens. But the ultra wide's real gift is its tremendous depth of field and the ability to relate elements in a photograph. The best photographs are ones where the subject pops and does not get lost in the wide angle of coverage.

Real talent and skill are required when using ultra wides. Physically moving, whether laterally, up or down, closer or farther from the subject, is the only method of eliminating unwanted objects from the photograph. First seeing and recognizing these unwanted elements and then getting them out of the photograph is the hardest part. With super ultra wides, this is not an easy job, considering you are working with 110° or 118° of coverage. Probably more than any other focal length, a fisheye's and ultra wide's view of our world demands a photographer's undivided scrutiny of the scene for success. They also require imagination in finding subjects—and then in finding solutions to make the subject pop!

It is also essential in using ultra wides that there be a dominant foreground, middle ground, and background to provide the image with visual depth. The formula to success, in fact, when using these lenses is: a strong element in the foreground, the subject in the middle ground, and the background supporting everything.

All of these lenses focus extremely close. My first experience with the 6mm f/2.8, for instance, was in taking a photograph of a grasshopper, which was resting on the front element of the lens with the entire world behind it in focus. Getting physically close to the subject is probably the best way to eliminate unwanted clutter. Because these lenses can focus close and have a huge depth of field, they can be most effective in capturing the grandeur of all they survey.

Nikkor 6mm f/2.8

Original release: 1969
Angle of coverage: 220°
Physical size: 6.7 x 9.3 inches (17 x 23.6 cm)
Weight: 11.5 pounds (5.2 kg)
Filter size: 5 built-in filters
Lens hood: None
M.F.D.: 0.9 foot (0.27 m)
Aperture range: f/2.8-f/22
Unique features: Image diameter 23mm

The front element of the 6mm f/2.8 is 9.3 inches (23.6 cm) across, twice the size of the front element of the 600mm f/4. It comes with a special leather cap that snaps onto the rear of the front element housing, and its lens case is a wooden trunk; its tripod mount is the same size and design as those found on telephoto lenses. If all this does not give you the impression that this lens is huge, maybe the fact that it weighs over 11 pounds will!

Other than an updating of its aperture ring to AIS coupling, the design of the 6mm f/2.8 has not changed since it was first released. This lens can literally "see" behind itself with its 220° of coverage. Because of this, the 6mm has a cantilevered lens stand, which prevents it from being in the photograph. Unlike a typical tripod collar, this one slants back out of the view of the lens.

The lens' angle of view, coupled with its large front element, prohibits the use of any filters over the front element. To provide some filtration, five filters are built into the lens in a turret: the L1a, O56, R60, Y5, and Y48. The L1a is the only filter out of that selection that is usable with color films. Many photographers who own the 6mm have had the stock factory filters removed and custom ones installed for special applications.

This large front element and huge coverage also makes using a lens shade impossible. The backup shades we always have with us—our hands—are also not usable. Cable releases, hands, tripods, and your camera's neck strap can easily wind up in the photograph as well. Avoiding all of these obstacles is a must to create a successful photograph with this marvelous lens.

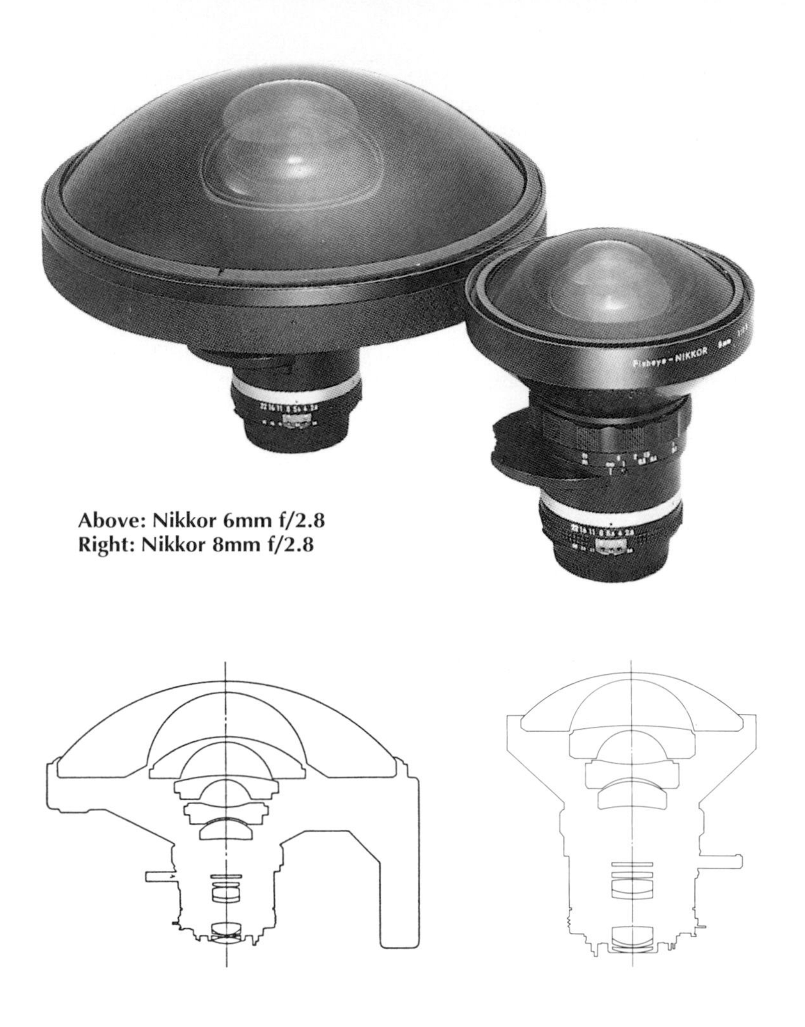

Above: Nikkor 6mm f/2.8
Right: Nikkor 8mm f/2.8

When you're shooting with the 6mm f/2.8, the sun will almost always be in the photograph unless an element in the scene, such as a tree limb, is blocking it. Because of this, the front element must always be kept clean. Any dirt or moisture rings on this element will show up in the photograph as a very bizarre type of flare. So cleaning the front element properly and keeping it clean is very important.

Because of the physical size and weight of the 6mm f/2.8, a heavy-duty tripod and head must be used; this is particularly true because of the contortions that must be made to eliminate unwanted elements, especially feet and tripod legs, and the lens is quite often tilted up to take in less ground. A standard tripod and head would flip over and send itself crashing to the ground. The Benbo 2XL tripod is a natural for this special-application lens because it can be set up in ways dictated by the lens' coverage.

Those looking to buy the 6mm f/2.8 should note that a new lens can be acquired by special order only—and even that is questionable, as we go into the year 2000. Though Nikon does not stock this lens, there are a number of lens rental houses across the country that do stock and rent it. This is the most common way photographers obtain this lens for use.

Nikkor 8mm f/2.8

Original release: 1970
Angle of coverage: 180°
Physical size: 5.0 x 4.8 inches (14 x 12.7 cm)
Weight: 2.4 pounds (1 kg)
Filter size: 5 built-in filters
Lens hood: None
M.F.D.: 1 foot (0.3 m)
Aperture range: f/2.8-f/22
Unique features: Image diameter 23mm

The 8mm f/2.8 is the most practical fisheye to use. The original 7.5mm, 8mm, and 10mm OP (orthographic projection) lenses required the camera's mirror to be locked up, making SLR viewing impossible. They were handholdable, though, because of their small, compact design. The 6mm f/2.8 advanced fisheye lens is SLR viewable, but it is far from handholdable. The current 8mm is the only SLR-viewable, handholdable fisheye Nikon has produced, which accounts for its popularity.

Everything, repeat *everything,* in front of this lens will be in the photograph. The 8mm f/2.8 barrel is physically long enough to permit handholding while keeping the photographer's fingers from being in the photograph. The 8mm f/2.8 has a smaller angle of view than the 6mm f/2.8, but its 180° still takes in enough to require watching out for your toes. Tilting the lens up is the best option for eliminating toes and tripod legs. Using a tripod can still be difficult with the 8mm.

The 8mm f/2.8 has five built-in filters: the L1a, O56, R60, Y5, and Y48. It has an equidistant projection formula, which means that the optics of the lens create no hot spots or vignetting. The exposure is even over the entire 180°. This is important, as a blue sky would otherwise look extremely unnatural—light blue on one side of the frame and dark blue on the other because of the near-total horizon coverage of the 180°. If a polarizer were to be used (though not possible) with the 8mm f/2.8, the equidistant projection formula would render the scene with uneven exposure, as the polarization effect over 180° would not be even.

In Nikon's literature, uses for the 8mm f/2.8 include science and industry. They also include portraiture, which might strike photographers as odd; it might seem as if this lens would turn a subject into Mickey Mouse or Pinocchio. If the subject is centered in the frame—the nose being the dividing line both vertically and horizontally—and the subject is not a great distance from the lens, the subject will be recognizable. If you want to have photographic fun, though, put the subject off center or away from the lens, and watch that nose grow!

The 8mm f/2.8 is great for taking scenic shots. If the scene contains any lines, such as roads or paths, the tremendous depth of focus of the lens and its barrel distortion will give the photograph incredible visual depth. Depicting such subjects as tree canopies is fun with the 8mm f/2.8, as it will capture the tree trunk along with the canopy. As with any wide-angle lens, though, success comes from eliminating the junk. Using a camera that provides 100% viewing and looking carefully at all that is in a scene can make shooting with a fisheye both fun and tremendously rewarding.

The front element must always be kept clean on the 8mm f/2.8. Because the sun will almost always be in the photograph, any dirt or moisture rings on the front element will show up as a very bizarre type of flare, so cleaning the front element properly—and keeping it clean—is very important.

Nikkor 15mm f/3.5

Original release: 1980
Angle of coverage: 110°
Physical size: 3.3 x 3.5 inches (8.4 x 9 cm)
Weight: 22.2 ounces (622 g)
Filter size: 39mm bayonet
Lens hood: Built in
M.F.D.: 1 foot (0.3 m)
Aperture range: f/3.5-f/22
Unique features: Rectilinear, CRC

The 15mm f/3.5 could be considered the baby brother of the 15mm f/5.5 (now discontinued). It is physically smaller than the 13mm f/5.6 (see p. 175 in the chapter on oldies but goodies), making it easier to use. Of all the ultra wides, the 15mm f/3.5 is probably the most commonly owned because of its spectacular angle of view and comparatively modest price.

The 15mm f/3.5 comes with four rear bayonet filters (hidden in the lid of the case), one of which is an A2 (81a). Filtration, such as polarization, is very difficult. Many photographers use large gels held in front of the lens to polarize a scene. Others use them taped to the rear of the lens, but neither are easy solutions. Graduated filters can be used in the front with a little more ease. Using the large, 5 x 5-inch (12.7 x 12.7 cm) filters in front of the element can work, but great care must be taken to avoid flare. Any of these filters placed in front of the lens can catch light—causing, in fact, flare that limits color and contrast; they might also vignette.

Like all ultra wides, the 15mm f/3.5 flares with little provocation. The source of the flare can be a point-light source or bright sun streaming through a canopy of trees. It can also be a reflection off a body of water or from a side window in a room.

The best way to rid the photograph of flare is by simply blocking the light source creating it. The 15mm f/3.5 has a built-in scalloped lens hood, but it is not enough for many situations. Using your hand to block the cause of the flare works great, of course, but this does hinder using the lens handheld. Many photographers use hinged arms to position a small, curved piece of cardboard to

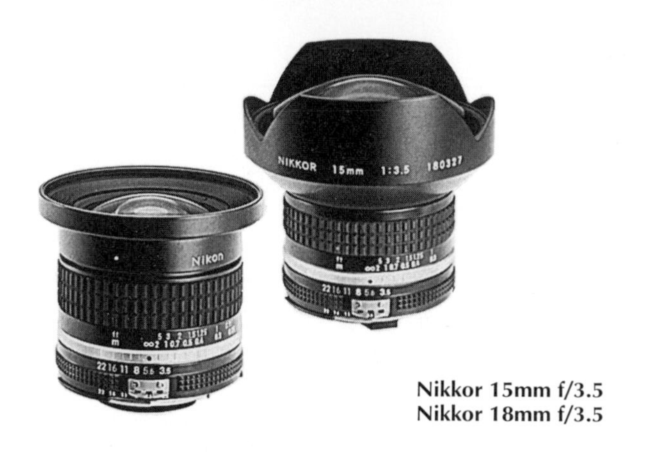

Nikkor 15mm f/3.5
Nikkor 18mm f/3.5

shade the lens. This requires a tripod, but one photographer I know hooked up a small arm to the base of his camera to act as an auxiliary shade, permitting the camera to be handheld.

Finding natural elements in the photograph to block the flare problem is probably the best option. This takes a little talented figuring when you're also trying to compose a photograph. The other option is to physically move laterally the slight distance required to eliminate the flare from the view of the lens. These options, either singly or in combination, will usually solve the flare problem; making the most of them, however, takes practice.

Working with the 15mm f/3.5 is an incredible experience. Many of the great photographs taken with this lens were made at every angle but eye level. Getting down low and pointing up, or getting up high and pointing down, are the most widely used techniques with this lens. Because of its rectilinear design, such change of angle heightens only the depth in the photograph, and not the lines. Because the 15mm f/3.5 can focus so close and has such tremendous depth of field, these techniques can be explored to their fullest while rendering everything tack sharp.

Like many rare lenses, the 15mm f/3.5 can be rented at lens rental houses. Because of its popularity, it is also stocked new by many stores. Before buying this lens, though, rent one to see if its wide coverage suits your style of photography. Make sure that all the hoops you must jump through to get the perfect photograph fit the way you like to take pictures, as well.

Nikkor 16mm f/2.8D AF

Original release: 1993
Angle of coverage: 180°
Physical size: 2.2 x 2.5 inches (5.6 x 6.4 cm)
Weight: 10.1 ounces (286 g)
Filter size: 39mm bayonet
Lens hood: Built in
M.F.D.: 0.85 foot (0.26 m)
Aperture range: f/2.8-f/22
Unique features: Full-frame fisheye

The 16mm f/2.8D AF is basically just an AF update of the traditional 16mm f/2.8 (see "oldies but goodies" chapter for the full description of that lens). One advantage the AF lens has over the manual version are the techniques that can be applied to it because it has AF technology—extending its chameleon capabilities even more from its manual configuration. More than any other lens in photography, changing the technique of using the 16mm f/2.8D AF can radically change its effect on a scene.

Because the camera can focus the 16mm f/2.8D AF without the eye of the photographer, doing remote photography with it gives this "chameleon" one more way to change colors. For a lens that can be in focus at any point at infinity, autofocus will

Nikkor 16mm f/2.8D AF

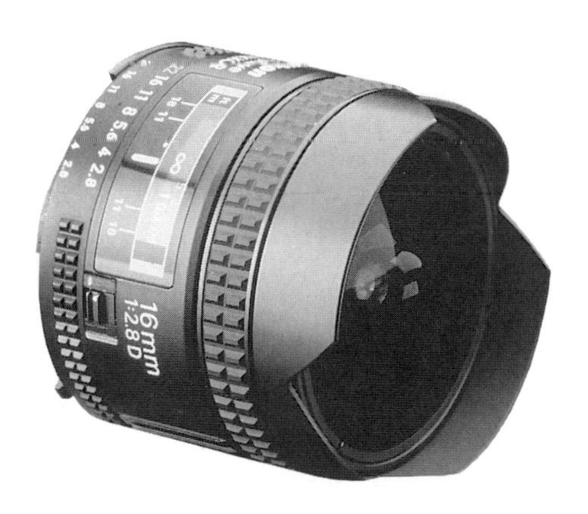

come into play when the lens is used close to the subject. Whether the photographer is holding it above a crowd and shooting down, holding it up on a pole to photograph the side of a building or down a canyon wall, the autofocus will allow close focusing while still capturing the stunning 180° view.

In future years, magnificent photographs will come from this lens, as those with imagination and creativity greater than 180° put it to use. This will bring the popularity of the 16mm f/2.8 and its effect back into the limelight, as new and creative uses are found for its unique perspective.

Filtration on the 16mm f/2.8D AF is the same as on its manual version, as on the 13mm f/5.6 and the 15mm f/3.5: 39mm bayonet filters attached to the rear element. A variety of filters can be used with rear-bayonet filtration by simply taping gels to the rear element. Polarization can even be accomplished in this way, though it is difficult. Using color-correcting filters for this purpose is common; if you do this, just remember to keep the gel small enough to avoid interference with any camera/lens interfacing.

Nikkor 18mm f/3.5

Original release: 1982
Angle of coverage: 100°
Physical size: 2.9 x 3.0 inches (7.4 x 7.6 cm)
Weight: 12.4 ounces (784 g)
Filter size: 72mm
Lens hood: HK-9
M.F.D.: 0.85 foot (0.26 m)
Aperture range: f/3.5-f/22
Unique features: CRC

An amazing lens, the 18mm f/3.5 has to be one of the least known of Nikon's ultra wides. Part of its incredible performance is the inclusion of an aspherical element. With its sexy crinkled-metal finish, large, gorgeous front element, relatively small size, and tack-sharp performance, it's a wonder that more photographers don't own this lens. There are a number of reasons for this, but primarily its price versus its coverage compared to the 20mm f/2.8 AF; this has caused the 18mm f/3.5 to be left, all too often, on the store shelf. Even so, it is commonly stocked by pro camera stores and often found in journalists' camera bags.

Those who use the 18mm f/3.5 are true artists and technicians who know the secret to making this lens work. It has all the benefits of the 13mm f/5.6 and 15mm f/3.5: wide coverage, close focusing, and basic straight-line rendition. Applying the techniques of these ultra wides to the 18mm f/3.5 is the secret of success with it. It is often used, held overhead, by photojournalists to photograph into a crowd; because it does not distort, it is a natural in this application. By using the 18mm on the F5 or F100, where you can select the AF sensor you wish, you can shoot overhead and still capture a sharp image with the composition you require. This makes the 18mm a top choice for getting close to a subject and relating it to its background as well, another common photojournalist communication technique.

The 18mm has the big advantage over the 13mm f/5.6 and 15mm f/3.5 of accepting filtration. It accepts 77mm filters—which are common, coming in many "flavors" to fit almost any situation. But filtration is limited to just one, as stacking of filters is not possible because of vignetting (the second filter cuts into the photograph). This means that warming up the scene and polarizing it can be difficult. Combination warming and polarizing filters can allow you to use two filters at once; attaching a Lee filter gel to a standard polarizer is another option for making two filters into one.

The 18mm's ability to be filtered while providing the benefits of an ultra wide makes it a natural for scenic photographers. Its rear-focusing system permits the lens to focus even faster than previous models; in addition, unlike the 13mm f/5.6 and 15mm f/3.5, it does not flare. With all these attributes, it is not hard to understand why those who own and shoot with the 18mm f/3.5 swear by it.

Nikkor 20mm f/2.8D AF

Original release: 1994
Angle of coverage: 94°
Physical size: 1.7 x 2.6 inches (4.3 x 6.6 cm)
Weight: 9.2 ounces (258 g)
Filter size: 62mm
Lens hood: HB-4
M.F.D.: 0.85 foot (0.26 m)
Aperture range: f/2.8-f/22
Unique features: CRC

The 20mm is probably responsible for getting more photographers into ultra wides than any other lens. Though slightly larger than its predecessors, the f/2.8 version—now with "D" technology—has caught even more photographers' attention. Its extremely compact size, reasonable price, wide angle of view, and incredibly sharp performance make it a great choice for nature photographers.

The 20mm f/2.8D AF combines all of the technological benefits of the 13mm f/5.6, the 15mm f/3.5, and the 18mm f/3.5, with

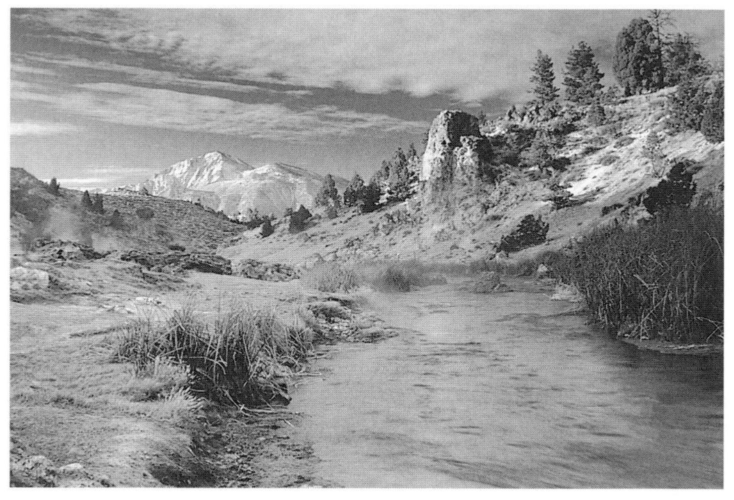

I used the 20mm f/2.8D AF to capture the entire vista—from foreground grasses to rocky cliffs—of this scenic shot of Hot Creek, in California.

the added advantage of more filtration options. Filter systems such as those from Tiffen® can be used with the 20mm without vignetting. Tiffen's 2-stop graduated filter, which is in a rotating mount, can also be used on the 20mm, thus compacting the exposure latitude down within the range of today's film. The 20mm will not work with two stacked filters; the exception to this is using Nikon's A2 with the 62mm polarizer. And, as Nikon's 62mm polarizer has a built-in step-up ring, vignetting is negligible in the corners.

Of all the ultra wides, an application only possible with the 20mm f/2.8D AF is close-up photography. The most common use is reversing the 20mm. The Nikon adapter BR-5 is required, screwing into the 62mm filter thread of the 20mm. It can then bayonet onto a camera body or, more commonly, onto a bellows unit. On a camera body, this setup provides 3x magnification; on the Nikon PB-6 bellows, a maximum of 10x magnification is possible. Focusing is accomplished by moving the camera/lens either physically closer or farther from the subject. Both meter and automatic aperture coupling are lost when a lens is reversed.

Even without reversing, the 20mm is great in close-up. It can focus down to 0.85 foot (1.5 m), and, as it has CRC (close-range correction), its image quality is magnificent. If there is a trick in using this lens, it is in applying it to situations other than scenic shots. Many stunning photographs taken at close range with the 20mm have left photographers viewing the image and wondering how it was done. That's why the 20mm f/2.8 AF is so popular—it captures the imagination!

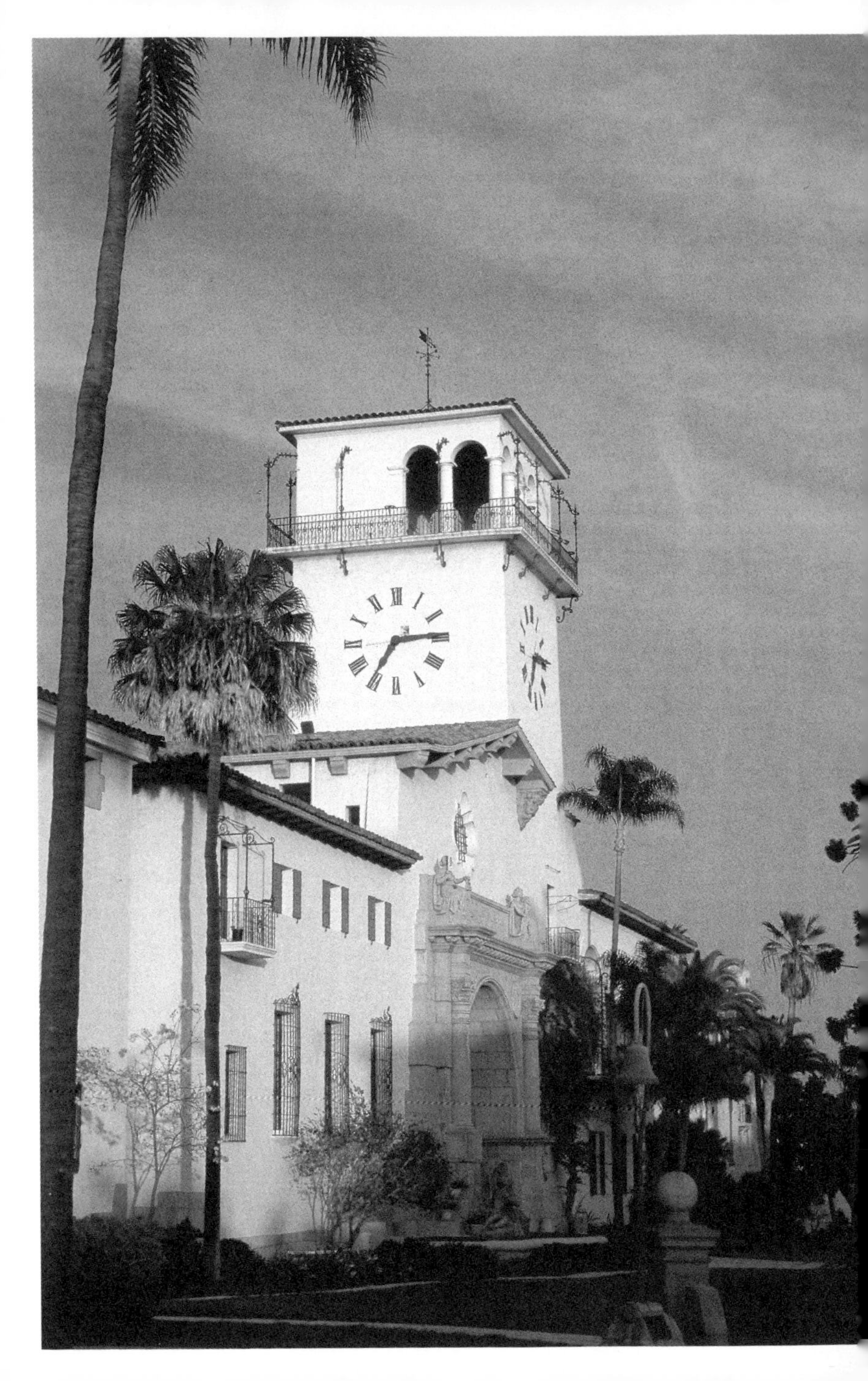

Wide-Angle and Normal Lenses

Using the Tools

The lenses in this range are the most familiar to photographers. For three decades, the "normal," or 50mm, lens was the most common lens, as it came with every camera body ever sold. Because the 50mm has the same perceived perspective as our vision, it became known as the "normal." This focal length also became the most discarded.

The wide angles in this range are the widest most photographers ever explore. There are two reason for this. One is they are the widest lenses most stores stock. The second reason relates to the first—the wide-angle view cannot show off its talents in the confines of a store showroom. The best salespersons for wide angles are the captions in photo magazines, noting that the wonderful shot had been captured with a particular wide angle.

Using these tools to the fullest has to do with the way wide angles are pointed. Walking up to a scene and clicking right at eye level is the least effective way to use a wide angle (or normal lens, for that matter). Getting up close physically to the subject, then angling the lens down to sweep over the scene, is much more effective—and a common technique of the pros as well. This technique can be used whether shooting a macro subject or grand vista; it isolates the subject while relating it to its background, taking advantage of the inherently large depth of field and spacious angle of view of the wide angle.

As with ultra wides, eliminating unwanted elements is critical. This is easier with wide angles, as their angle of view is not as great as ultra wides. With ultra wides, every millimeter of frame must be checked for junk; with wide angles, unwanted elements are found in just one area or another in the frame. This makes using wide angles faster in that less "technical" time is required. Using a camera with 100% view still is an asset with wide angles,

This photo of the Santa Barbara courthouse is a perfect example of why a 50mm lens should not be overlooked.

though. If you're using cameras with less than 100% viewing, then you must make a careful examination to make sure unwanted elements are not inadvertently being captured—the easiest way to do this is just to move the camera slightly to reframe on a slightly larger area.

Getting more out of the wide angle is a common photographic quest. Many photographers want to achieve the grandeur of the ultra wide with their wide angle. This can be visually accomplished by using elements to create depth in the photograph. Including lines such as roads, trails, fallen logs, a coastline, or any element that starts in the foreground and continues to the horizon adds to the feeling of depth and creates the illusion of an ultra wide in the narrower view of the wide angle. Getting low and having large elements in the foreground on one side of dead center can create the same illusion; the trick in either case is creating and depicting depth in the photograph. This is something that can be accomplished by lighting as well—but that is a book in itself.

The slam on normal lenses has always been they do not capture any pizzazz. They are not supposed to! And here lies the trick to using them. If a survey were to be conducted of all the great photographers, it would be found that they started with a normal lens and then began explorations into creativity. The "non-pizzazz" factor of the normal is really a push toward exploring other realms in photography. These explorations are the basis for techniques later applied to wide angles and telephotos. In addition, they are often applied, by those who have yet to add to their lens collection, to the normal to stretch its potential.

More than any other focal length, the 50mm can be manipulated with auxiliary accessories to accomplish other tasks. Teleconverters, extension tubes, and reversing rings are just a few of the auxiliary accessories that can be easily added to this focal length to start exploring other facets of photography. The techniques learned can be carried on with other focal lengths as your photographic skills and pursuits expand.

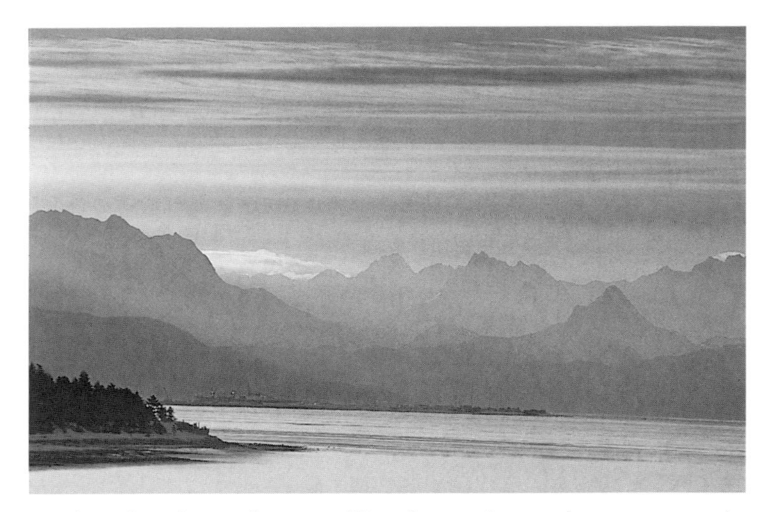

Don't underestimate the versatility of normal-range lenses, as seen in this impression of the yellow and blue layers formed by sky and water in the Kenai Mountains.

Proper Handholding Technique

All of the lenses described in this chapter lend themselves to being shot handheld. This requires using proper handholding technique to capture all the sharpness the lens can deliver. Handholding first requires having the lens rest in the palm of your left hand; grabbing the lens in any other way will force you to fight gravity, which will always be trying to pull the lens from your hands. Use your left fingers to operate both the focusing and aperture rings; use your right hand to operate the camera and grab it so the index finger can reach the shutter release. Next, press the camera body up against your forehead; a rubber eyecup helps by acting as a shock absorber. Then, tuck your elbows in against your stomach to create three points of contact, like the three legs of a tripod.

Handholding with the proper technique is often a better option than using a tripod. First, you don't have to carry a tripod along with all the rest of your gear. Then, maybe even more important, you are not restricted to the rigid placement your tripod demands. You can physically move, with ease and without restraint, to the exact position you desire for the best photograph. This is a much more creative and enjoyable approach to photography, which will help keep your interest at its highest.

With practice, the proper handholding technique can enable *any* photographer to hand hold down to 1/8 second and still capture sharp images. The pros—especially photojournalists, who hardy ever carry a tripod—do this routinely. And practice is not a big deal; it just requires picking up your camera every day and holding it properly. Working the controls and focusing on different subjects and different distances is all it takes. Staying familiar with your camera gear will help you become proficient with proper handholding, so you will be able to capture sharp images at slow shutter speeds.

Nikkor 24mm f/2

Original release: 1978
Angle of coverage: 84°
Physical size: 2.4 x 2.5 inches (6.1 x 6.4 cm)
Weight: 10.6 ounces (297 g)
Filter size: 52mm
Lens hood: HK-2
M.F.D.: 1 foot (0.3 m)
Aperture range: f/2.0-f/22
Unique features: CRC

For the typical photographer, the 24mm f/2 is one of the more esoteric wide angles. Its bright image aids focusing in low light levels, and its fast f/stop assists shooting in available light as well—though this was more important in years past, when quality, faster ISO films were not available. For these reasons, the 24mm f/2 has been very popular with photojournalists since its introduction. Its price and slightly larger size, however, prevent most basic photographers from investing in its speedy optics.

One of the amazing attributes of the 24mm f/2 is its ability to limit depth of field. The inherent tendency of wide angles to have everything in focus can be a drawback at times, especially if isolating the subject is your style of photography. The f/2 aperture on this lens narrows the depth of field enough to make a difference compared to shooting at f/2.8.

Getting physically close is a preferred method of using the 24mm f/2. This limits the depth of field even more, isolating the subject from the background. Photojournalists often do this so the subject is sharp, with other elements in the photograph recognizable but not sharp; this makes the subject pop while still relating it to the background. The technique is rarely seen in scenic shots, though, because so few photographers own the 24mm f/2.

Nikkor 24mm f/2.8D AF

Original release: 1993
Angle of coverage: 84°
Physical size: 1.8 x 2.5 inches (4.6 x 6.4 cm)
Weight: 8.9 ounces (249 g)
Filter size: 52mm
Lens hood: HN-1
M.F.D.: 1 foot (0.3 m)
Aperture range: f/2.8-f/22

Since its original introduction, the 24mm f/2.8 has been incredibly popular; it is the first wide angle more photographers buy. This lens has gone through more cosmetic and optical changes than any other Nikkor lens, and the 24mm f/2.8D AF is the best version to date. Its small size, both physically and monetarily, has made it one of the most commonly owned wide angles.

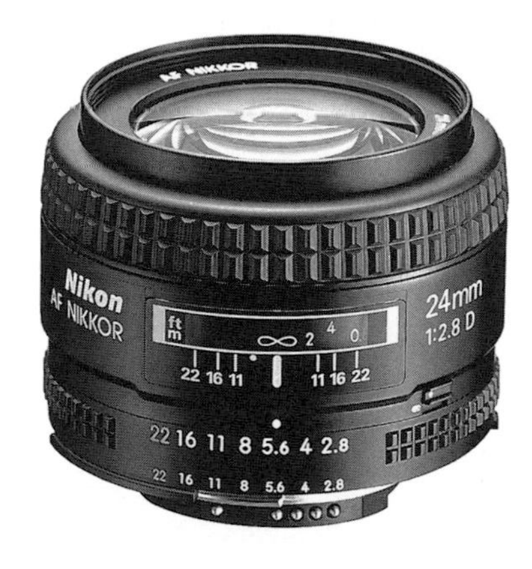

Nikkor 24m f/2.8D AF

The 24mm lens is credited with more scenic shots than any other lens as well. Twice as wide as normal vision, it has a very comfortable feel to its angle of view. It does not have the distortion that many photographers associate with wide angles, which also adds to its appeal. Because of this, its wide coverage is comfortable and not beyond the realm or imagination of most amateur photographers.

Even with all its popularity, though, the 24mm f/2.8 is probably one of the most misunderstood wide angles. Its comfortable feel is partly to blame for photographers not exploring its angle of coverage to the fullest. All of the techniques for ultra-wide-angle lenses can be applied to the 24mm f/2.8 to really make it sing. This includes reversing it for close-up work, as the lens' CRC (close-range correction) delivers incredible edge-to-edge sharpness; it also includes getting close physically and angling the lens down so its coverage sweeps over a scene, or getting down low and sweeping up for dramatic rendering of moody skies.

The 24mm f/2.8 AF has a limited depth-of-field scale on the barrel of the lens. When using the lens and applying the Hyperfocal Distance principle, for example, this scale can be hard to use.

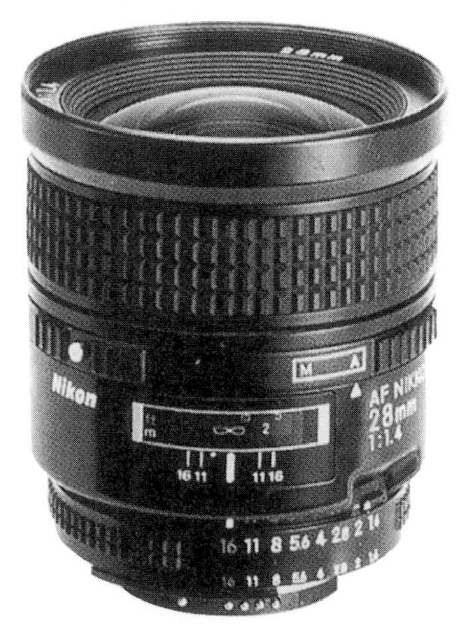

Nikkor 28mm f/1.4D AF

Many photographers conduct their own depth-of-field tests and create their own depth-of-field scale to use with the lens. This scale can be attached to the lens by a stick-on label or by writing the information on a card that is held up to the lens barrel as a guide—an excellent idea when you want to get the same results every time you use this technique.

The 24mm f/2.8 is still wide enough that filtration can be a challenge. Using Nikon's polarizer helps, as it has a built-in step-up ring; this makes stacking filters possible. Off-brand polarizers can be used, but not stacked with other filters. When you're using stacked filters, test by using a camera with 100% viewing if there is a question of vignetting.

Nikkor 28mm f/1.4D AF

Original release: 1993
Angle of coverage: 74°
Physical size: 3.1 x 3 inches (7.9 x 7.6 cm)
Weight: 20 ounces (560 g)
Filter size: 72mm
Lens hood: HK-7
M.F.D.: 1.1 feet (0.4 m)
Aperture range: f/1.4-f/16
Unique features: Fast lens

This is a new f/stop for this traditional wide-angle focal length. For many years, an ultra-fast wide angle has been on the minds of many photojournalists who use the Nikon system. The 28mm f/1.4D AF combines a fast f/stop, AF, and "D" technology, creating a valuable tool for photojournalists. Its use, though, is not limited just to them.

This lens is designed specifically for low-light-level shooting—which, along with its narrow depth of field, is exploited by photojournalists. In photographing an excited crowd on the courthouse steps, being able to use a narrow depth of field to focus in and isolate (differentiate) the defense attorney is critical (the 28mm does not distort the human shape). Remember that photography is the art of communication. The isolating abilities of the 28mm f/1.4D AF are superb, whether it's being used on courthouse steps or in a meadow photographing a deer.

The 28mm f/1.4D AF might have been made with the photojournalist in mind, but it is surely not limited to that use. With it, nature photographers can get close to capture that spectacular wildflower. Sports photographers can apply it to the players, advertising photographers to the product.

A benefit that comes with the fast f/stop—but one photographers often forget—is the ability to use a fast shutter speed; the photojournalist chasing an attorney down courthouse steps, for example, appreciates the fast shutter speed afforded by the 1.4 f/stop. This advantage for the majority of photographers, however, might not justify the price of the lens. And because the majority of scenic shots do not have to be chased down, many nature photographers might pass by the 28mm f/1.4D AF. That could be a mistake, depending on your style of photography.

The 28mm f/1.4D AF incorporates Nikon's automatic CRC (close-range correction) and rear-focusing technology; it also has an aspherical element in the rear assembly. All of this combined makes the 28mm f/1.4D AF an amazingly sharp lens.

Nikkor 28mm f/2

Original release: 1971
Angle of coverage: 74°
Physical size: 2.5 x 2.7 inches (6.4 x 6.9 cm)
Weight: 12.1 ounces (339 g)
Filter size: 52mm
Lens hood: HN-1
M.F.D.: 0.9 foot (0.3 m)
Aperture range: f/2-f/22
Unique features: CRC

The 28mm f/2 is an excellent lens, of the quality that Nikon is famous for producing. But this lens has never been popular, typical for its focal length. The f/2 model was designed with available-light photography in mind. This can be a big asset for photojournalists, but even they have never embraced this lens.

Because of this relative disinterest in the 28mm f/2, there are no particular techniques to recommend, as so few photographers own or use this lens. Nikon's promotional material states that the

28mm f/2 is ideal for "candids, group shots, land- and cityscapes, travel photography, architecture and interiors"—all true, but the same can be accomplished by other lenses that are even more versatile.

Nikkor 28mm f/2.8D AF

Original release: 1994
Angle of coverage: 72°
Physical size: 1.8 x 2.6 inches (4.6 x 6.6 cm)
Weight: 7.2 ounces (202 g)
Filter size: 52mm
Lens hood: HN-2
M.F.D.: 1 foot (0.3 m)
Aperture range: f/2.8-f/22
Unique features: None

The 28mm f/2.8D AF, like all other 28mm lenses (except the 28 mm f/1.4), has never found a place in photographers' camera bags. This compact lens, with really remarkable quality, has the stigma all 28mm lenses have; it's considered "just not very wide." Probably the biggest drawback to selling these lenses is the fact camera stores do not have the Grand Canyon in their showrooms—which would improve the standing of the lens because it could show off its abilities.

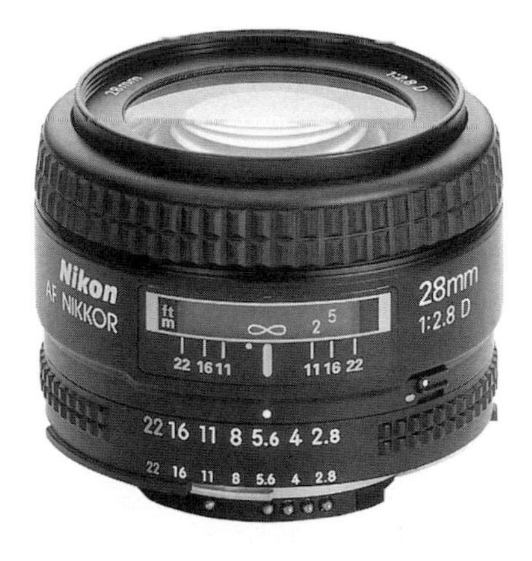

Nikkor 28mm f/2.8D AF

The 28mm f/2.8D AF is considered the "standard wide angle." This is another way of saying not a normal lens and not a wide angle. It is fairly easy to find used, which is an excellent way to add it to your camera bag.

Stretching the 28mm f/2.8's angle of view is possible for scenics. It does require using every technique described with other wide angles, plus a good eye and some imagination. The 28mm does tend to be less effective at a low angle and better at higher angles compared to other wide angles.

The 28mm f/2.8D AF is one of the marvelous lenses that can be reversed (BR-2 ring required). On a bellows, for example, it can deliver 9x magnification with an excellent free working distance; on a body, a magnification of nearly 2x is delivered. Optical quality is not compromised by reversing the lens; it continues to deliver outstanding performance. For those wanting to explore macro photography (especially on a budget), this lens is a great option.

Nikkor 28mm f/3.5 PC

Original release: 1981
Angle of coverage: 74°; 92° when shifted
Physical size: 2.5 x 3.1 inches (6.4 x 7.9 cm)
Weight: 13.4 ounces (375 g)
Filter size: 72mm
Lens hood: HN-9
M.F.D.: 1 foot (0.3 m)
Aperture range: f/3.5-f/22, manual
Unique features: Perspective control (PC)

Unique in the 28mm focal length, the 28mm f/3.5 PC lens is also the most used. As its name says, it can offer perspective control of vertical or horizontal lines because the lens barrel "shifts," which is critical in its application. When the lens is not shifted, it has an angle of view of 74°, increasing to a maximum of 92° when shifted (this is equivalent to the coverage of a 24mm lens).

The key to using the 28mm f/3.5 PC is keeping the camera back parallel with the subject at all times to prevent any lines, either vertical or horizontal, from bending due to distortion. Such position will not be the correct framing of the subject, which will more than likely be cut in half when the camera back is kept parallel. This should not be a problem, though, as the lens shifts to "pull" the subject completely into the frame; the front element section of the lens physically moves, increasing the angle of view and bringing the rest of the subject into the image area.

The amount the lens can be shifted is determined by whether the camera is vertical or horizontal. When horizontal, the lens has only 8mm of shift, compared to 11mm when vertical. The lens is most typically used in a vertical format to maximize shift. And as most buildings, statues, trees, and the like are vertical subjects, this works out to the advantage of the photographer.

Because the lens barrel shifts, there is no automatic aperture linkage. This means the lens has a manual aperture, operated by the photographer. The photographer must take a meter reading prior to any shifting and predetermine the proper exposure. This is accomplished by turning the main aperture ring, which operates the aperture blades. The photographer can then turn a secondary ring (not connected to the aperture blades) to the desired f/stop to lock in the exposure for later reference. The main aperture is then opened back up for bright viewing, shifting, and focusing. Once shift and focus are accomplished, the main aperture ring is turned to close down the aperture to match the preset secondary ring for correct exposure.

The 28mm f/3.5 PC can also be used as a standard 28mm lens, but, because of the manual aperture, it is slow to operate.

Nikkor 35mm f/1.4

Original release: 1970
Angle of coverage: 62°
Physical size: 2.7 x 2.9 inches (6.9 x 7.4 cm)
Weight: 14.1 ounces (395 g)
Filter size: 52mm
Lens hood: HN-3
M.F.D.: 1 foot (0.3 m)
Aperture range: f/1.4-f/16
Unique features: CRC

With 16° wider coverage than a normal lens, the 35mm f/1.4 is for many photographers their normal lens—selected in particular for its extremely fast f/stop, great for low light and/or interior photographs. But the fast f/stop of the 35mm f/1.4 is only a hint of the tremendous quality this lens can deliver.

One of the first lenses to be introduced with multi-coating, the current 35mm f/1.4 delivers incredible clarity. Its slightly higher than normal contrast leads many photographers to think this lens was made with photojournalists in mind. Many photojournalists, in fact, do have this lens in their bag, but a decreasing number are making this their normal lens.

The 35mm f/1.4 is the only 35mm that has CRC (close-range correction). An automatic function, CRC is what partly gives the 35mm f/1.4 its extraordinary resolution, providing edge-to-edge sharpness that is quite remarkable compared to the majority of lenses on the market. In Nikon promotional material for the 35mm f/1.4, it was said to be "ideal indoors or out [for] snapshots, candids, [and] portraits of people in their surroundings." Some of the most famous news portraits taken of prominent figures of our time are testament to this.

The 35mm f/1.4, which is rarely used in close-up photography and almost never reversed, has been pigeonholed probably more than any other Nikkor lens. This is a testament to its quality, but results in a loss of potential images. Because the 35mm f/1.4 can be found on the used-lens shelves with increasing frequency, we will probably see it used more as photographers discover it can do much more than just capture snappy black and whites.

Nikkor 35mm f/2D AF

Original release: 1995
Angle of coverage: 62°
Physical size: 2.5 x 2.1 inches (6.4 x 5.3 cm)
Weight: 7.5 ounces (210 g)
Filter size: 52mm
Lens hood: HN-3
M.F.D.: 0.9 foot (0.3 m)
Aperture range: f/2-f/22
Unique features: None

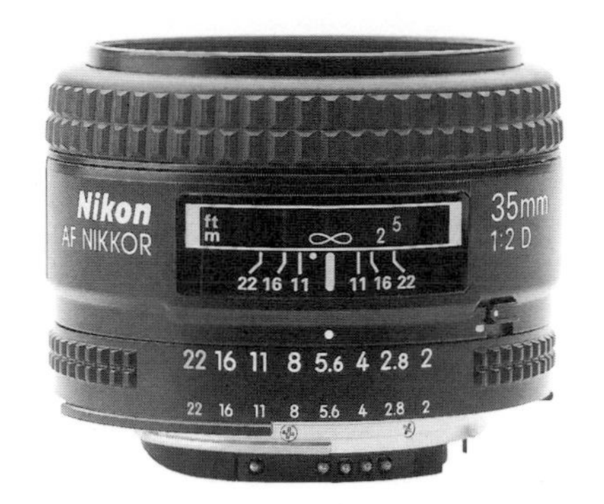

Nikkor 35mm f/2D AF

The 35mm f/2D AF is a cool lens and an excellent choice for a first lens-with-body purchase. Its small size, sharp optics, and reasonable price are just a few of the reasons to buy this lens. It is one of only three AF lenses not to be modified or discontinued since its original release.

This is the closest focusing 35mm lens in the Nikon system. Many nature photographers enjoy using the 35mm f/2D AF in this way, which includes adding a small extension tube such as the PK-11a. Using this lens reversed is also common, as it produces excellent results; reversed on a body, it renders a magnification of approximately 1.5x. Photographers also frequently use it on a bellows, producing a magnification of up to 6x. Because of its remarkable edge-to-edge sharpness, using this lens in any of these ways produces excellent quality.

One of the traits of the 35mm f/2D AF not explored by most photographers is its quick focusing. This reference is not to its AF capability, however, but to how little effort is required to focus the lens from its minimum focusing distance to infinity. The travel distance from these two points is slightly less than 180°. Manual focus is extremely fast because of this, making capturing moving kids, for example, easy. In autofocus, it's extremely quick, making the lens a joy to use.

An old trick of photojournalists is to "shoot from the hip." When photojournalists want to take a photograph inconspicuously, they shoot with the camera hanging from their shoulder, at their hip. This technique is further refined with the AF attributes of the 35mm f/2D. For photographing shy subjects or getting photos in compromising situations, this lens and the tried-and-true technique work marvelously together.

Nikkor 35mm f/2.8 PC

Original release: 1974
Angle of coverage: 62°; 74° when shifted
Physical size: 2.5 x 2.4 inches (6.4 x 6.1 cm)
Weight: 9.8 ounces (274 g)
Filter size: 52mm
Lens hood: HN-1
M.F.D.: 1 foot (0.3 m)
Aperture range: f/2.8-f/32
Unique features: Perspective Control (PC)

The first lens of its type, the current version of the 35mm PC is cosmetically and functionally the best. Though it is physically shorter and smaller than the 28mm f/3.5 PC and has a 52mm filter size, its functions are the same in actual operation.

Metering and focusing should be done prior to shifting. The 35mm f/2.8 PC has a maximum of 11mm of shift with the camera vertical and 8mm of shift with the camera horizontal. When fully shifted, the angle of coverage is 74°, the same as a 28mm lens. The aperture is manual—the photographer must manually open it up to focus, then close it down to take the photograph. (Refer to the 28mm f/2.8 PC for a description of this operation.)

Unlike the 28mm f/2.8 PC, the 35mm f/2.8 PC is not very popular and thus not in general use. The 35mm film format is not like a 4 x 5, so it has very little room for shifting and correction; the 35mm f/2.8 PC can be fully shifted and yet barely correct the image. The 28mm f/2.8 PC provides the greatest amount of coverage in this situation, which is why it overshadows the 35mm f/2.8 PC.

This barrel cactus, standing in the midday sun, was photographed with a 35mm f/2 AF. ⇨

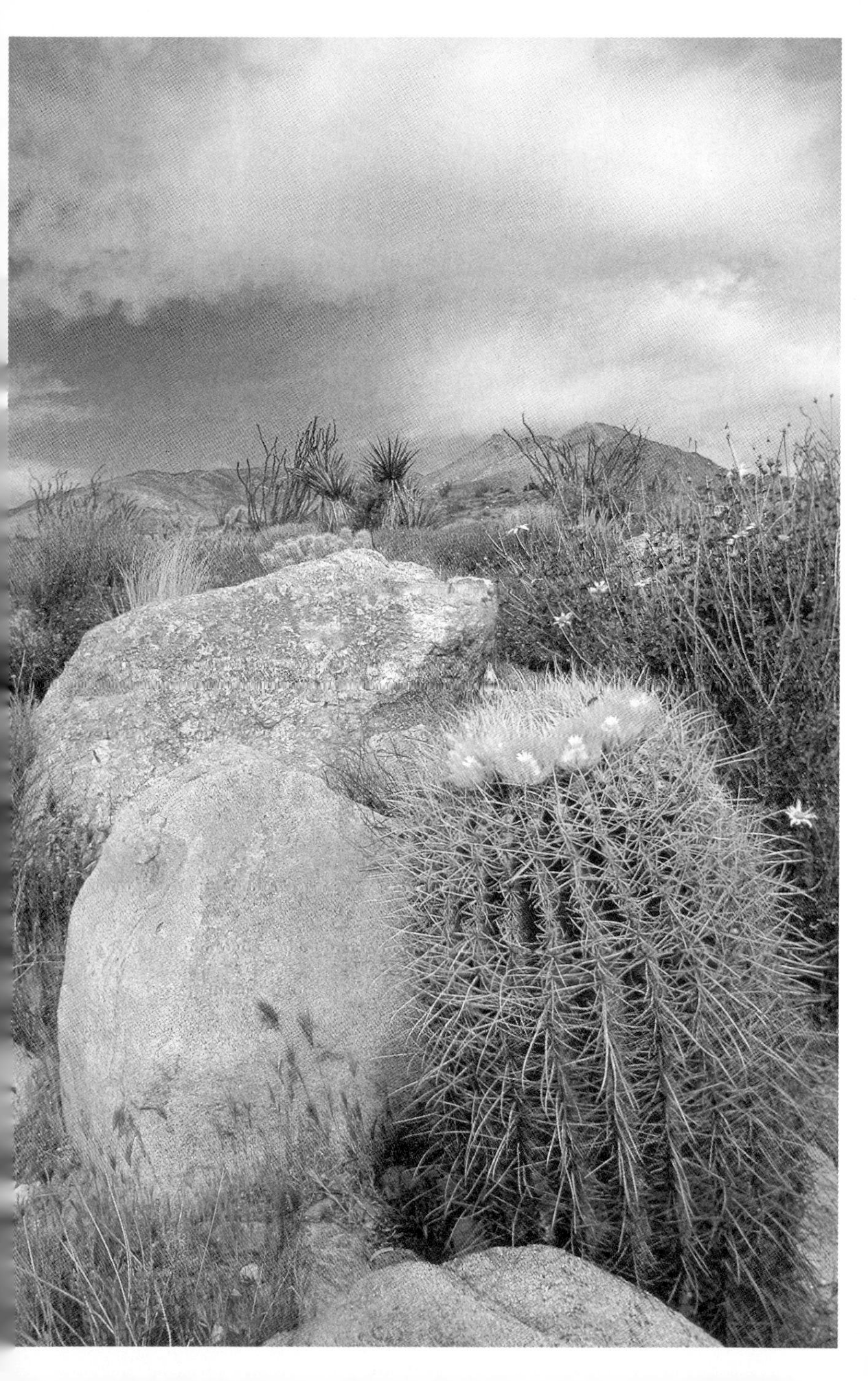

Nikkor 50mm f/1.2

Original release: 1979
Angle of coverage: 46°
Physical size: 2.7 x 2.3 inches (6.9 x 5.8 cm)
Weight: 13.4 ounces (375 g)
Filter size: 52mm
Lens hood: HS-12
M.F.D.: 1.7 feet (0.51 m)
Aperture range: f/1.2-f/16
Unique features: None

Nikon's promotional material says of the 50mm f/1.2, "Tremendously versatile . . . ideal for candids, scenics, and available-light shooting." The "versatile" part is hard to swallow for the majority of photographers, though, because even though the 50mm f/1.2 has a fast f/stop, it is still a 50mm lens.

The 50mm f/1.2 is the fastest f/stop available in the Nikon system. This f/stop is best known in connection with the 58mm f/1.2 Noct, but in the 50mm f/1.2, it costs a lot less. In addition, this lens delivers marvelous sharpness, and is extremely well corrected for coma and spherical aberrations. It flares a tad with a point light source, so it is no 58mm f/1.2, but it still delivers excellent results.

One place this lens has really excelled is in theater photography. This is a situation where its f/1.2 is indispensable, as flash is not allowed. It is also an application where the normal angle of view works well, because live theater is seen this way naturally. Those photographers so using the lens tend to apply it in the same fashion outside the theater.

Agreeing with Nikon's description of the 50mm f/1.2, some photojournalists use it to take candids on the sly. With today's faster films, shooting wide open permits leaving the flash off. The difference between f/1.4 and f/1.2 is not quite 1/2 stop, but in low-light situations it can make all the difference. This is especially true if using a camera with a stepless shutter, where the exposure is not locked in by manual shutter speeds.

Nikkor 50mm f/1.4D AF

Original release: 1995
Angle of coverage: 46°
Physical size: 1.6 x 2.5 inches (4.1 x 6.6 cm)
Weight: 5.5 ounces (154 g)
Filter size: 52mm
Lens hood: HR-2
M.F.D.: 1.5 feet (0.5 cm)
Aperture range: f/1.4-f/16
Unique features: None

Photographers often wonder why normal lenses are still manufactured. With all the bad press about being stuck with a normal, why would anyone buy one? The 50mm f/1.4D AF fits this general consensus; the exception is the young photographer whose first camera comes with a 50mm lens.

The reason for this exception in viewpoint is because these beginning photographers do not know that they shouldn't like the lens. They explore every nook and cranny of their world through the normal perspective, capturing some remarkable images because they don't know they shouldn't. Many seasoned photographers could learn from their young colleagues and attempt photographing their world through a normal perspective.

If a photographer were to take up this challenge, the 50mm f/1.4D AF would be a great lens to do it with. It is physically small and light, making it easy to use. Its image quality is excellent, and the contrast very snappy. It is an excellent lens to manipulate with extension tubes, teleconverters, or reversing rings. In any of these applications, the lens performs with resounding quality.

Nikkor 50mm f/1.8 AF

When a camera store sells a camera body, it is typically with a 50mm f/1.8 lens to keep the package price as low as possible—probably why there are more 50mm f/1.8 lenses lining the shelves of used-lens departments than any other lens. This is really quite criminal, as it is an excellent lens.

The 50mm f/1.8 AF is the best of all versions of this lens. Its very compact size makes it one of the smallest lenses in the

Nikkor 50mm f/1.8 AF

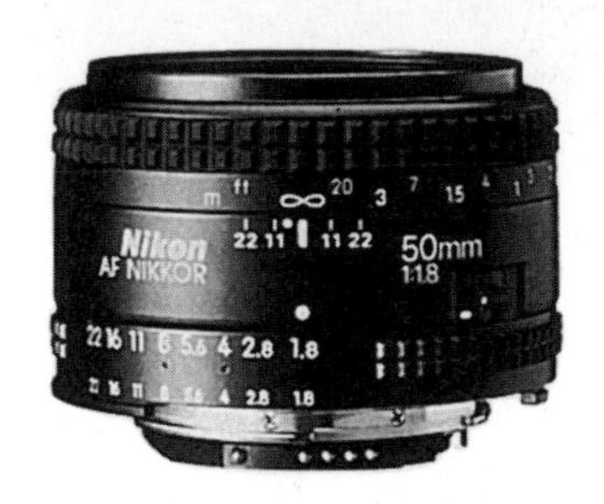

Original release: 1989 **Angle of coverage:** 46° **Physical size:** 1.9 x 2.5 inches (4.8 x 6.4 cm) **Weight:** 5.5 ounces (154 g) **Filter size:** 52mm **Lens hood:** HR-2 **M.F.D.:** 1.5 feet (0.45 m) **Aperture range:** f/1.8-f/22 **Unique features:** None

Nikon system; its ease of focus and bright viewing make it a joy to use. Best of all, its low price makes it easy to own and keep.

Many of today's lenses are of moderate speed. Wide angles, zooms, and macro lenses have apertures starting at f/2.8 or f/3.5, making them hard to use in low-light situations. With its wide availability, excellent image quality, and affordable price, the 50mm f/1.8 AF is an excellent choice for low-light backup. Because the lens is often discarded, picking one up used for basically nothing is relatively easy. If speed needs to be interjected into a lens system, this is a terrific choice. But it's interesting that with Nikon making most lenses these days "D" lenses, the 50mm f/1.8 is the only autofocus not receiving this update. Yet it works just fine on the F5; makes one wonder.

A field of cupped monolopia captured on a breezy day with a 20mm f/2.8 AF. ➪

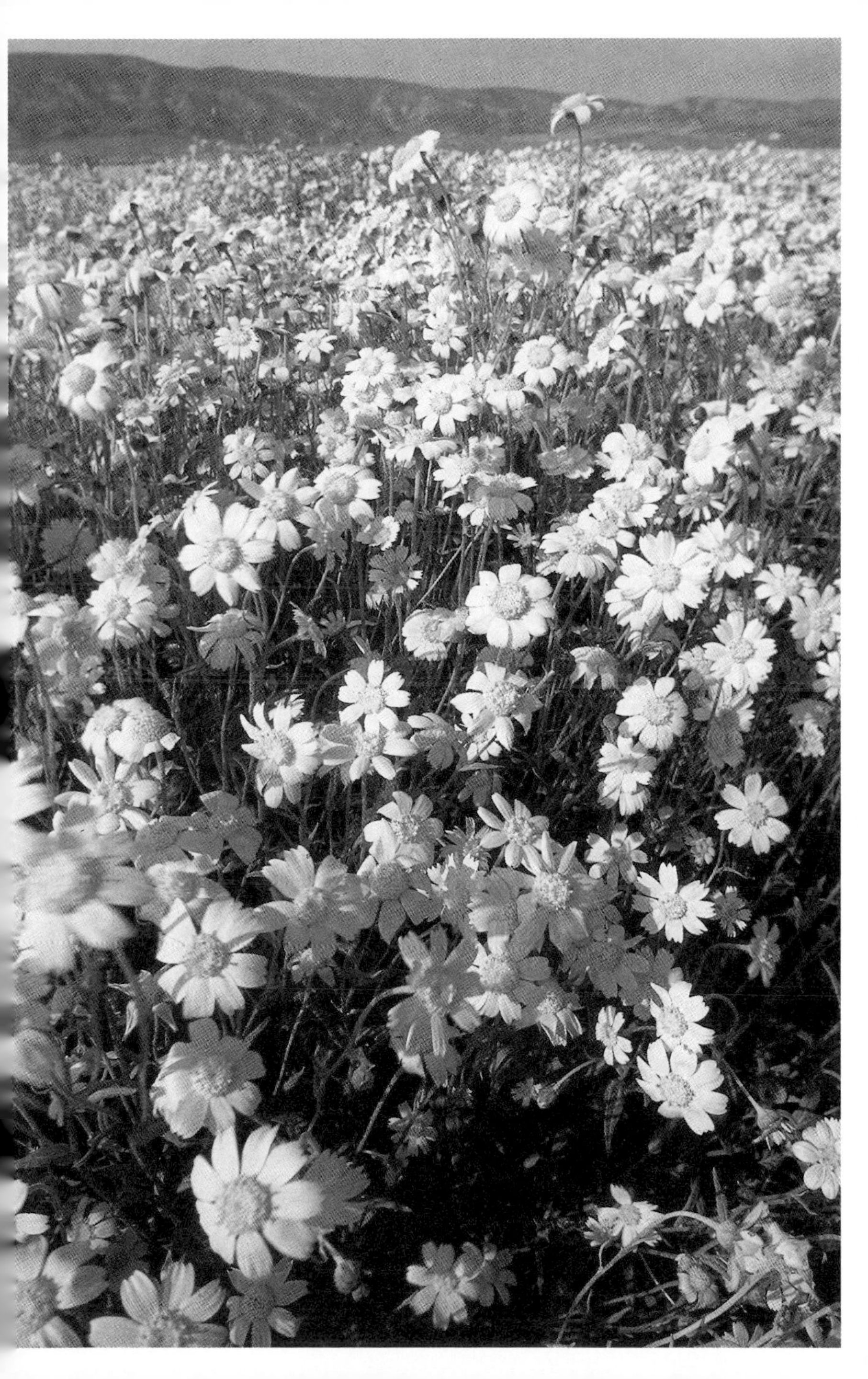

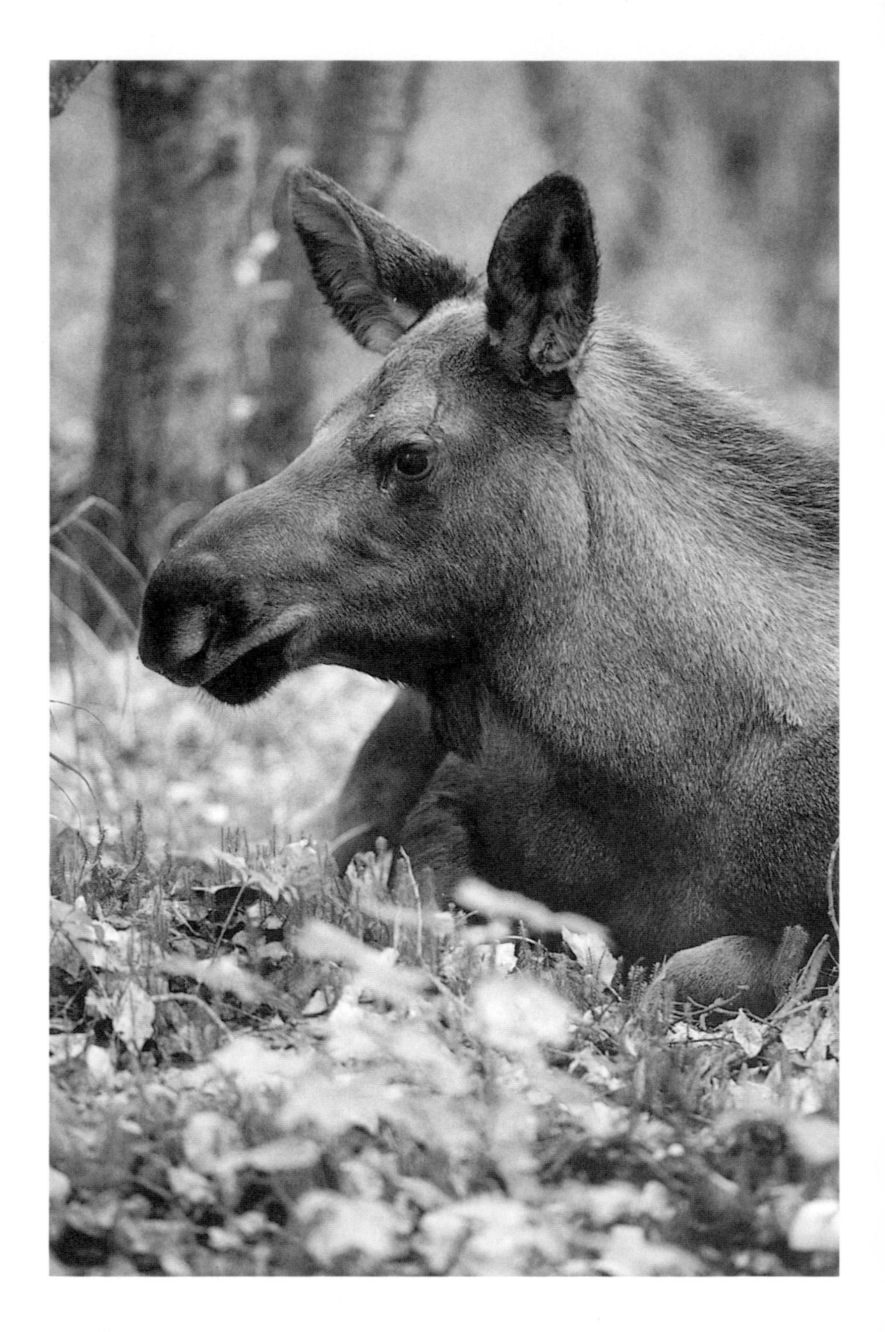

Telephotos

Using the Tools

The lenses in this range were specially designed for taking head-and-shoulder candids. The 85mm, 105mm, and 135mm focal lengths, since their introduction, have always been thought of as portrait lenses. This is because these lenses render a perspective that places the nose in the proper size relationship to the face. At the same time, these focal lengths provide a comfortable working distance between the photographer and subject.

If all these different focal lengths are considered portrait lenses, which is the right one to own? The answer comes from your own personal style. The intimate photographer would like the 135mm, the shy would pick the 85mm, and those in the middle of the road would select the 105mm. Comparing the picture angle of the three focal lengths from the same distance, the 135mm would frame just the head, the 105mm the head and shoulders, and the 85mm the head and upper torso.

The 180mm and 200mm fit into this category as well, because they are prime lenses used by photojournalists for portraits. Most photographers own or have owned at least one of these two focal lengths at some time. Their legendary optics and normal perspective are excellent for portraits, sports, wildlife, and scenic shots. They are also small enough to permit handholding, even in low light.

Isolating the Subject

All current telephotos are fast, something reflected in their higher price. This need for speed relates to the narrow depth of field inherent in their design, making them suitable for many different

Using the Nikkor 80-200mm f/2.8 AF-S, I moved in close and captured this portrait of a moose at rest.

tasks in photography. The combination of their narrow angle of view and shallow depth of field makes them a natural for isolating a subject. For portraiture, this is a must.

The techniques used for isolating a subject with a telephoto differ from that for a wide angle; where a wide angle captures all, a telephoto captures only slices. The principle of isolating with a telephoto is to manipulate the background with the lens' narrow angle of view. By moving the telephoto laterally or up and down—even in small amounts of just inches—different slices of the background can be positioned behind the subject. This permits a light subject to be placed in front of a dark area or a dark subject in front of a light area. In either case, the background isolates and help the subject to pop. Shallow depth of field when these fast lenses are shot wide open can add to isolating the subject.

Compacting the Scene

Telephotos starting at the 180mm range tend to compact a scene—noted, for example, in a scenic in which a farmhouse appears to have far-off mountains in its back yard. This principle is used quite often in the movie industry. Those vehicles in the car chases are not as physically close as depicted, but optically compacted on top of each other by telephoto lenses—one of the great uses of this tool.

Another way to make terrific use of these lenses involves accessories. All of these lenses accept filters—multiple ones if required. The telephotos either come with shades from the factory or have them built in; these need to be in place even if filters are used.

Flare

Flare is the flattening of contrast and color. Telephotos can flare just as any other lens, but the flare is much harder to detect with the inexperienced eye. Telephotos generally do not produce the colored UFOs typical of ultra wides and wide angles; instead, photos have a lackluster appearance to indicate the presence of flare. It takes only a slight ray of light on the front element to create flare. Ridding the front element of this light can be difficult; often, the best option is finding a building or tree to shade the front element.

Handholding Technique

Proper technique for handholding assures capturing all the sharpness these lenses can deliver; refer to page 53.

Nikkor 85mm f/1.4D IF AF

Original release: 1996
Angle of coverage: 28°30′
Physical size: 2.9 x 3.1 inches (7.4 x 7.9 cm)
Weight: 19.8 ounces (554 g)
Filter size: 77mm
Lens hood: HN-31
M.F.D.: 3 feet (0.9 m)
Aperture range: f/1.4-f/16
Unique features: None

"Natural perspective and superlative image sharpness" is the leading phrase Nikon uses to describe the 85mm f/1.4, and photographers who have shot with this lens would probably find it an understatement. It has been one of the lenses all photographers have heard of and many aspire to own—an incredibly sharp lens, absolutely beautiful!

The 85mm f/1.4D IF AF is the latest update of this legend. Its large, 77mm sparkling front element is a big part of its allure, but it is only a hint of the magnificent array of elements making up this lens. The incredible edge-to-edge sharpness of the 85mm f/1.4D IF AF at all focus points tends to make you think that the close-range correction (CRC) incorporated in earlier versions might be in this one as well. But CRC is not part of the 85mm f/1.4D formula. Instead, internal focusing (IF) has been included—a first. While Nikon states it went to IF with this lens to speed up AF performance (and the lens *is* fast), IF also brings element design changes that, in my opinion, make this the finest 85mm f/1.4 ever made by Nikon.

The extremely narrow depth of field of the 85mm f/1.4D IF AF is one of its biggest attributes. Photographers buy this lens initially because of its speed and apparent ability to shoot in low light. They quickly find out that its narrow depth of field isolates a subject so remarkably that it can communicate like few other lenses. It makes incredibly fast shutter speeds available with a small telephoto that's great for many outdoor sports.

The 85mm f/1.4D IF AF is unique in one other way; it is used only as a straight lens. Where most lenses are used with an extension tube, teleconverter, or for doing close-up work, the 85mm f/1.4D IF AF typically is not. This is not to say it does not work well in these different ways; it does. But it is such a superior lens as is, photographers do not use it any other way.

Nikkor 85mm f/1.8D AF

Original release: 1994
Angle of coverage: 28°30′
Physical size: 2.7 x 2.8 inches (6.9 x 7.1 cm)
Weight: 14.6 ounces (409 g)
Filter size: 62mm
Lens hood: HN-23
M.F.D.: 3 feet (0.9 m)
Aperture range: f/1.8-f/16
Unique features: None

The 85mm f/1.8D AF is one of the original AF lenses Nikon released; it is also, until this version, one of three original AF lenses never to be modified or discontinued since its release. Nikon's first 85mm f/1.8, a remarkable lens, was introduced in 1964, to be replaced by the 85mm f/2. The 85mm f/1.8D AF—a prime lens many photographers have in their camera bags—carries on the legend of the original 85mm f/1.8.

Its compact size and light weight make the 85mm f/1.8D AF an outstanding lens to handhold in low-light situations. It is one of a few AF lenses manufactured by Nikon that is truly fast when autofocused by the camera, made even faster with the incorporation of rear-focusing technology. This is partly because of its bright image, which makes it easy for the AF sensor to operate—an operation even further facilitated by the focus throw on the lens, which is so short, the camera's AF motor needs little effort to focus the lens.

The 85mm f/1.8D AF is an excellent lens to use with extension tubes. Its minimum focusing distance is not any less than a standard 85mm lens, which is unusual for AF technology. Its edge-to-edge sharpness, when used with an extension tube, is remarkable—for example, the addition of the PK-11a (8mm tube) brings the minimum focusing distance down to 24 inches (61 cm). This provides nearly a 1:3 magnification, with excellent working distance and image brightness. There is the loss of matrix metering when an extension tube is added, but that is the only drawback to extending this lens.

All this makes the 85mm f/1.8D AF an extremely versatile lens. Whether using it for its designed purpose of portraiture, adding an extension tube for macro work, or capturing tack-sharp scenic shots, it is one of the best all-around lenses in the Nikon system.

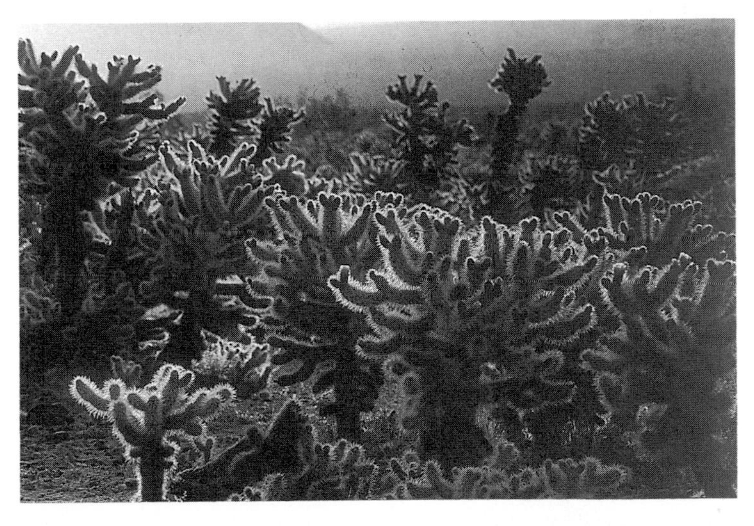

These glowing Bigelow chollas were captured at sunrise with an 85mm f/1.8 AF.

Nikkor 105mm f/2D DC AF

Original release: 1993 **Angle of coverage:** 23°20′ **Physical size:** 4.4 x 3.1 inches (11.2 x 7.9 cm) **Weight:** 21.9 ounces (613 g) **Filter size:** 72mm **Lens hood:** Built in **M.F.D.:** 3.3 feet (1 m) **Aperture range:** f/2-f/16 **Unique features:** DC and RF systems

105mm has been generally thought of as *the* portrait focal length. To reinforce this, Nikon manufactures the 105mm f/2D DC AF (just saying the nomenclature takes an hour), which incorporates Nikon Defocus Image Control (DC) and rear focusing (RF) systems.

The DC system allows the photographer greater creative control on which elements are out of focus and by how much. By turning the DC system ring, you can throw out of focus the elements in front of the focused subject or behind the focused sub-

Nikkor 105mm f/2D DC AF

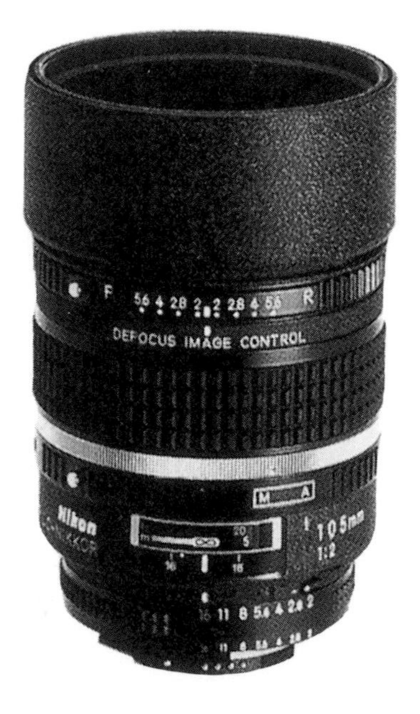

ject; this is in addition to depth of field. To assure an even, soft blur to the image, additional blades are incorporated in the aperture design to create a more rounded opening. Out-of-focus elements at any f/stop are complemented and softened by this design.

The RF system can be thought of as internal focusing. When the lens is focused, the RF system moves the rear lens group internally to focus the image. This both keeps the physical length of the lens constant and makes the autofocusing speed amazingly fast. The optics also have a dustproof rear glass plate to prevent any dust from getting into the internal optics.

The 105mm f/2D DC AF is a pricey lens, but is its only use portraiture? What if you wanted to photograph wildlife behind wire cages at the zoo? The DC system, set to Front, can make that wire disappear. What about photographing racecars on a track? Lots of depth of field could be used, and, with the DC set to Rear, the grandstands disappear! The DC system has many applications. Probably every photographic situation where the photographer wants complete control over all the elements in the photograph could be solved with this lens.

Nikkor 105mm f/2.5

Original release: 1959
Angle of coverage: 23°20′
Physical size: 2.7 x 2.5 inches (6.5 x 6.4 cm)
Weight: 15.4 ounces (431 g)
Filter size: 52mm
Lens hood: Built in
M.F.D.: 3.5 feet (1 m)
Aperture range: f/2.5-f/22
Unique features: None

One of the first lenses ever to be introduced by Nikon, the 105mm f/2.5 has long been a legend. It has gone through more cosmetic changes than any other Nikkor lens through the years, but with virtually no change to the optical formula. Sizing down and the addition of Nikon Integrated Coating (NIC) have made the current 105mm f/2.5 the best of all the versions of this lens.

When photographers think portraiture, they think 105mm f/2.5. This is where this lens has been pigeonholed since its

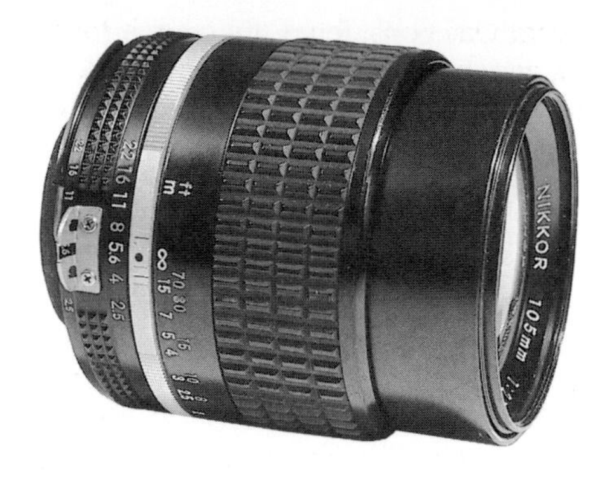

Nikkor 105mm f/2.5

introduction—simply because its angle of view and picture coverage most typifies what photographers want in a portrait lens. In the 1980s, the 105mm f/2.5 was especially popular with fathers photographing their new arrivals. Its small size and very reasonable price made it a natural for just such events.

With the advent of zooms in the 35-105mm range, the popularity of a prime 105mm lens has fallen off. This is also partly because the 105mm f/2.5 has never been applied to other photographic situations, limiting its perceived versatility. Very few photographers combine the lens with an extension tube or teleconverter—probably in large part because the 105mm f/2.8 AF micro focuses down to 1:1 without any tubes.

Use with the TC-14A can lead to "occasional vignetting," according to Nikon's literature, but this is a rare occurrence.

Nikkor 135mm f/2D DC AF

Original release: 1997
Angle of coverage: 18°
Physical size: 4.7 x 3.1 inches (11.9 x 7.9 cm)
Weight: 28.6 ounces (801 g)
Filter size: 72mm
Lens hood: Built in
M.F.D.: 4 feet (1.2 m)
Aperture range: f/2-f/16
Unique features: DC and RF systems

In the early 1960s, the 135mm was considered *the* portrait focal length. It lost that niche long ago, but Nikon is bringing it back in the 135mm f/2D DC AF (a tongue twister in lens descriptions). Like the 105mm f/2D DC AF, the 135mm f/2D DC AF incorporates the Nikon Defocus Image Control (DC) and rear focusing (RF) systems (see the 105mm f/2D DC AF for a description of these two systems).

It wasn't long after its introduction that the 135mm f/2D DC AF was in wide use in the fashion industry. The ability to make elements in the background disappear when photographing models on a runway is a tremendous advantage; for the same reason, this lens has also found a home photographing indoor sporting events. It hasn't been popular with the general photographic market, though, because of its price, a condition not likely to change.

Nikkor 180mm f/2.8D ED IF AF

Original release: 1995
Angle of coverage: 13°40′
Physical size: 5.7 x 3.1 inches (14.5 x 7.9)
Weight: 25.2 ounces (706 g)
Filter size: 72mm
Lens hood: Built in
M.F.D.: 5 feet (1.5 m)
Aperture range: f/2.8-f/22
Unique features: None

One of the original lenses to be released with AF technology, the 180mm f/2.8D ED IF AF is the fourth version of the lens. When first introduced as an AF lens, it had the reputation and legendary status of the manual version to compete with, which was formidable. It wasn't until this latest version that the legend of the manual version has been finally put to rest.

The 180 f/2.8D is a very versatile lens. Its prime use has always been in photojournalism; its fast f/stop, shallow depth of field, and great reach made it a natural for that application. These same attributes have been applied to fashion photography as well. But the sexiness of the manual and AF versions have endeared the lens to all photographers, who put it to many uses.

Nikkor 180mm f/2.8D ED IF AF

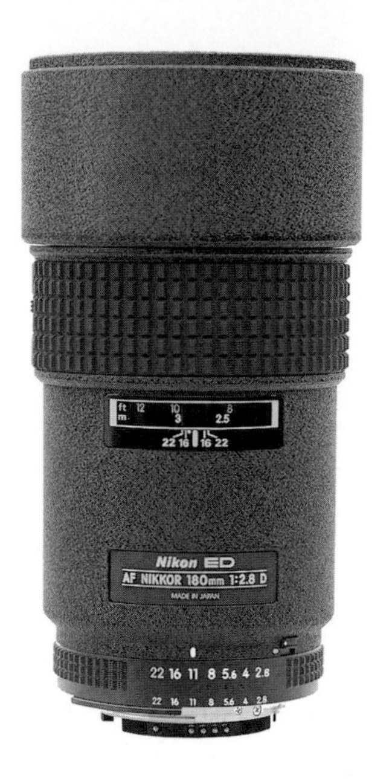

It is a very common lens in macro photography; no surprise there. Quite often coupled with the PN-11 extension tube, rendering almost 1:2 magnification, it is used quite often with the TC-201 to make a 360mm f/5.6, excellent for wildlife photography. Its minimum focusing distance is still five feet, but it has the magnification of 360mm with very limited depth of field—great for isolating the subject. This is especially true when photographing big game, whether or not with a teleconverter.

The 180mm F/2.8D ED IF AF, though slightly on the heavy side, is still quite easily handheld. Its price is not outrageous, being well within the range of most photographers. All of these factors are what make the lens popular. Its extreme flexibility in so many facets of photography makes it an excellent choice for many photographers focusing in on a diverse range of subjects.

Page 81:
Shots like this portrait of a red-faced cormorant are not a dime a dozen. Thanks to Nikon's engineered compatibility between telephoto lenses and converters, I successfully captured this with the 600mm f/2.8 AF-S and the TC-14E.

Page 82-83:
The haunting beauty of a wildfire is heightened by the crystal-sharp rendition of the 58mm f/1.2.

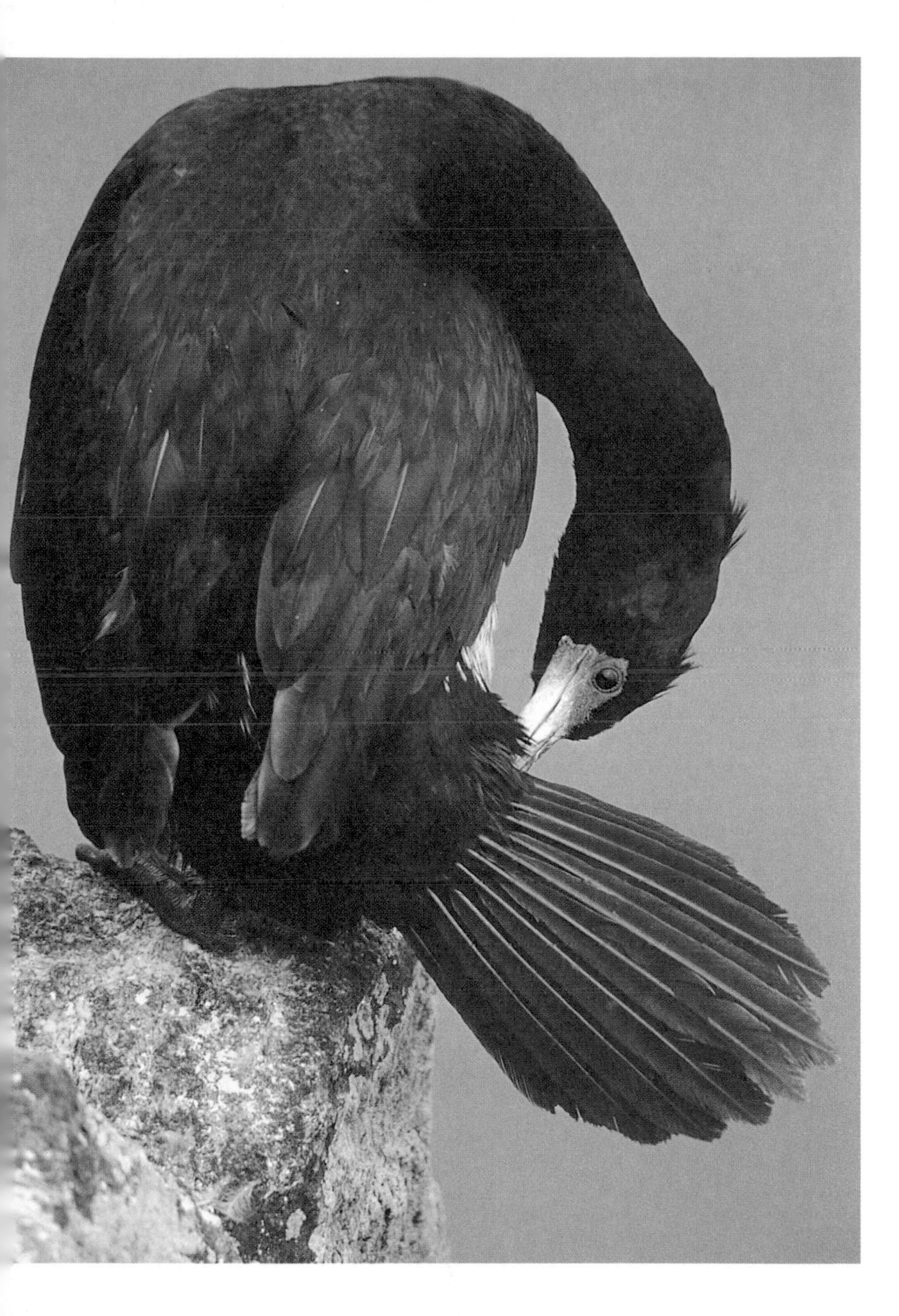

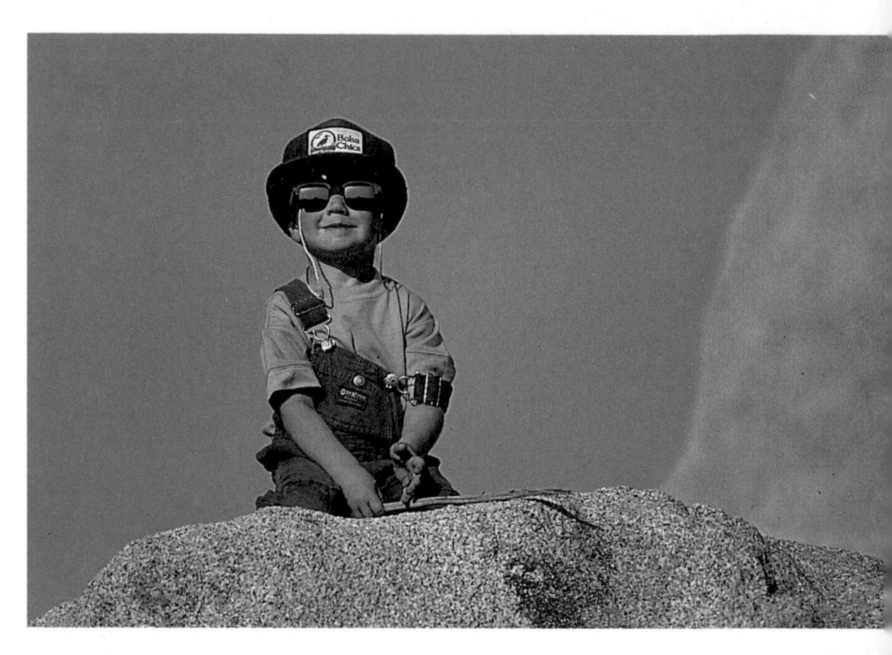
Bolsa
Chica

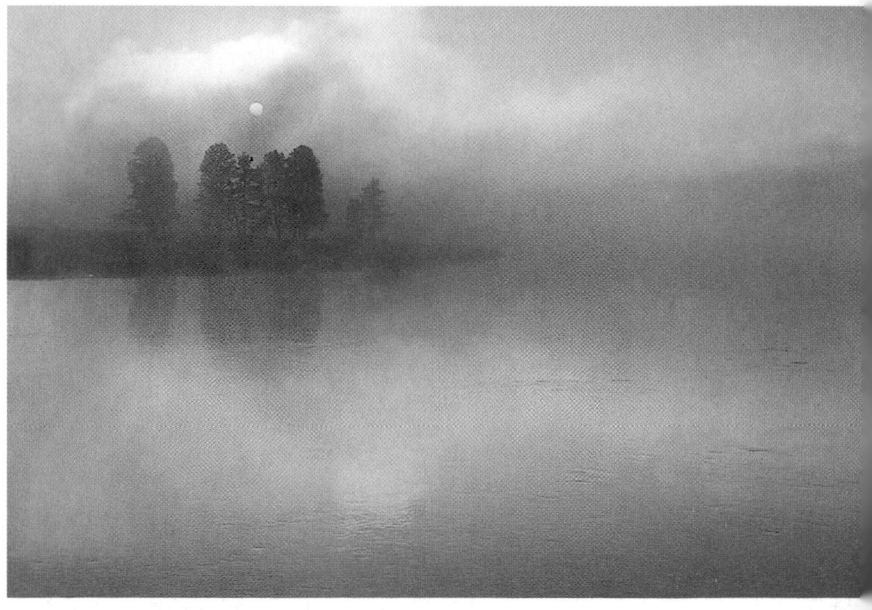

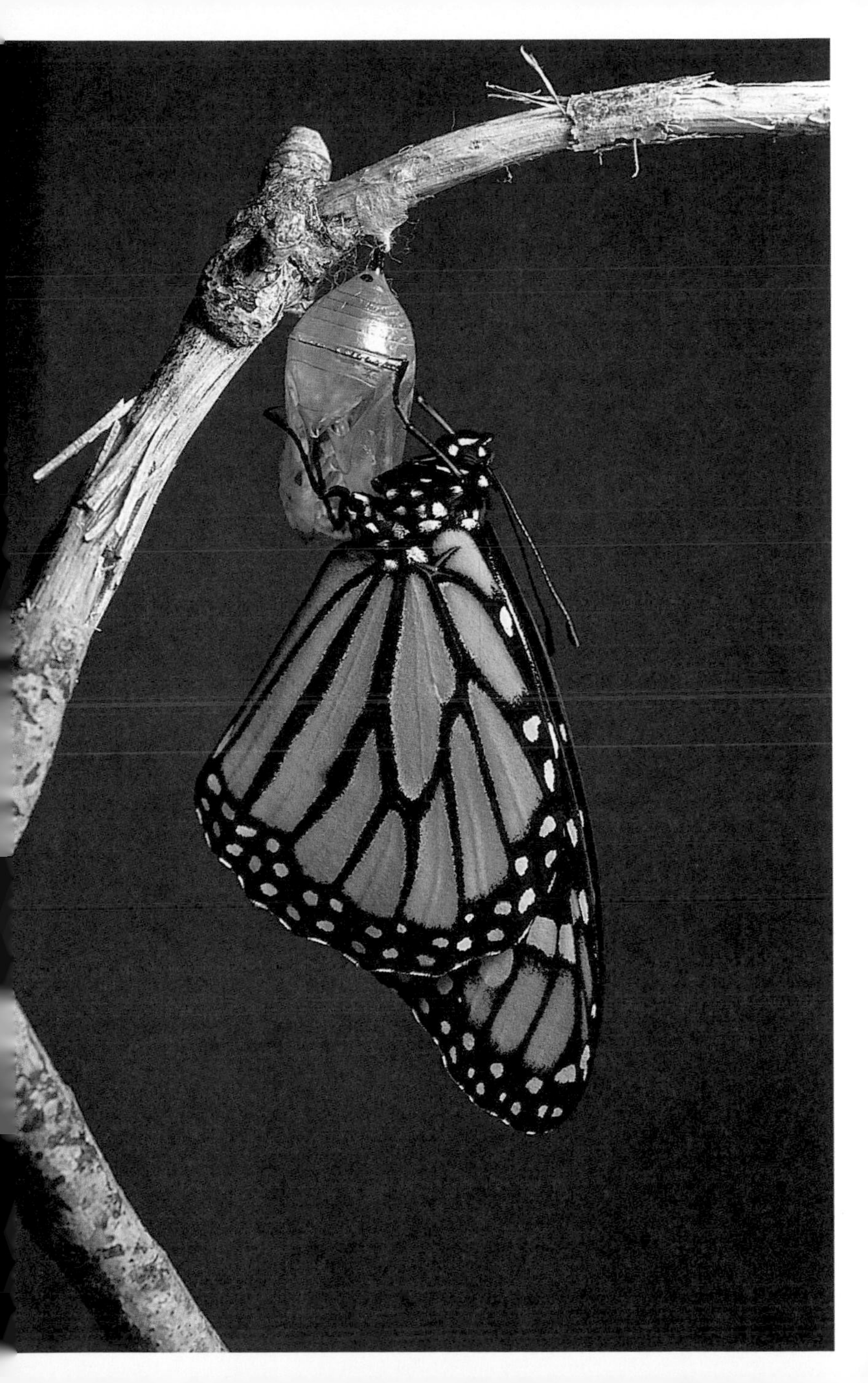

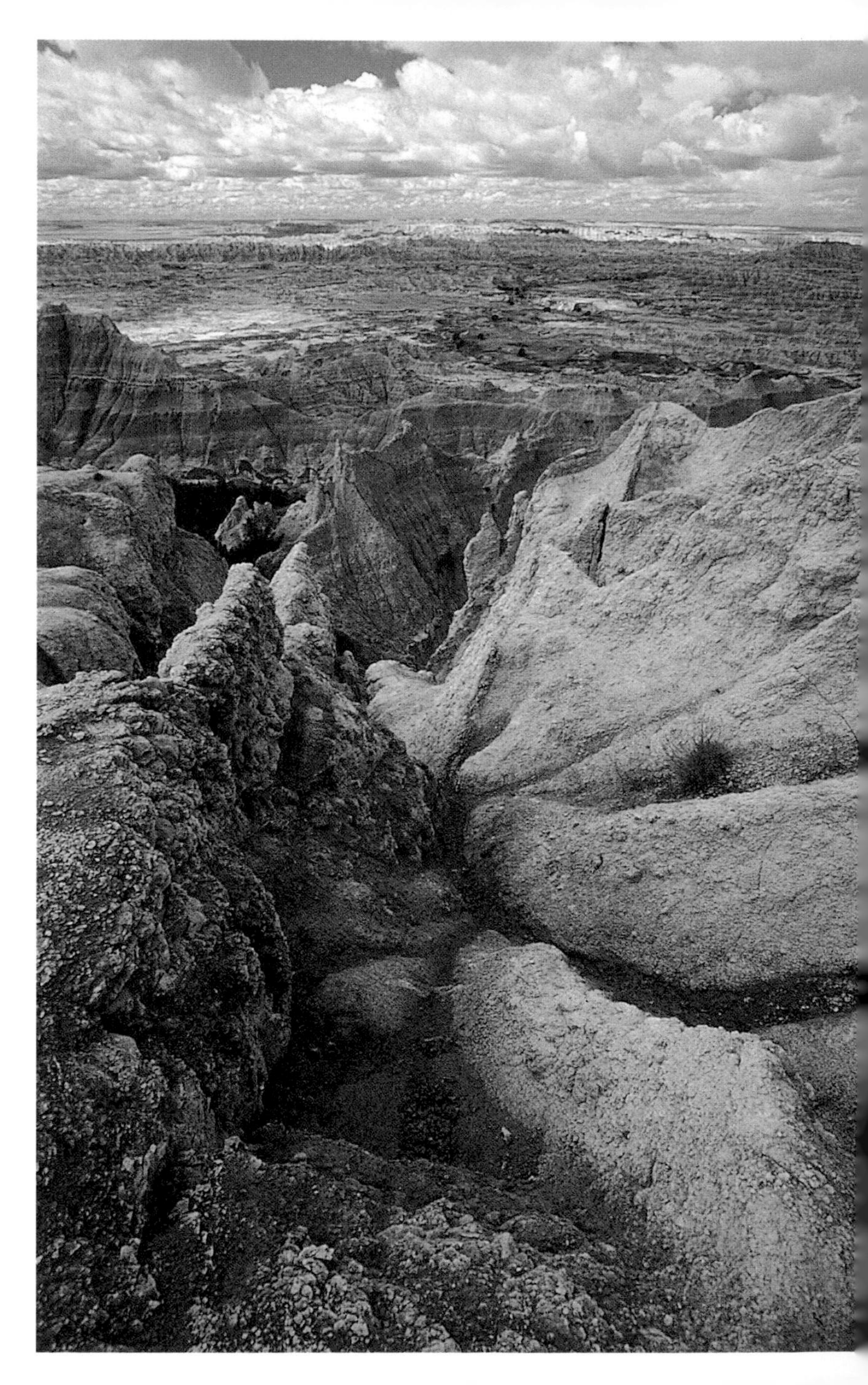

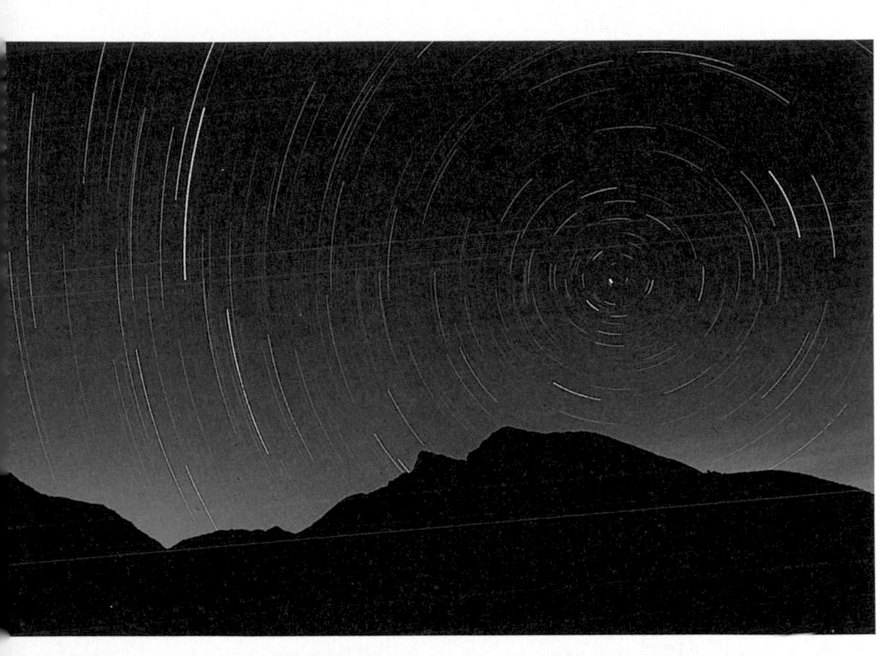

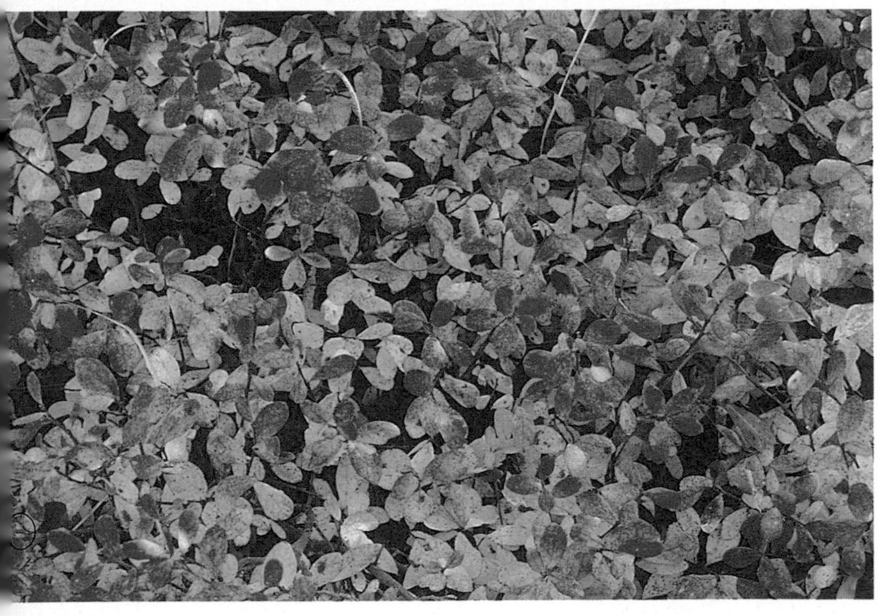

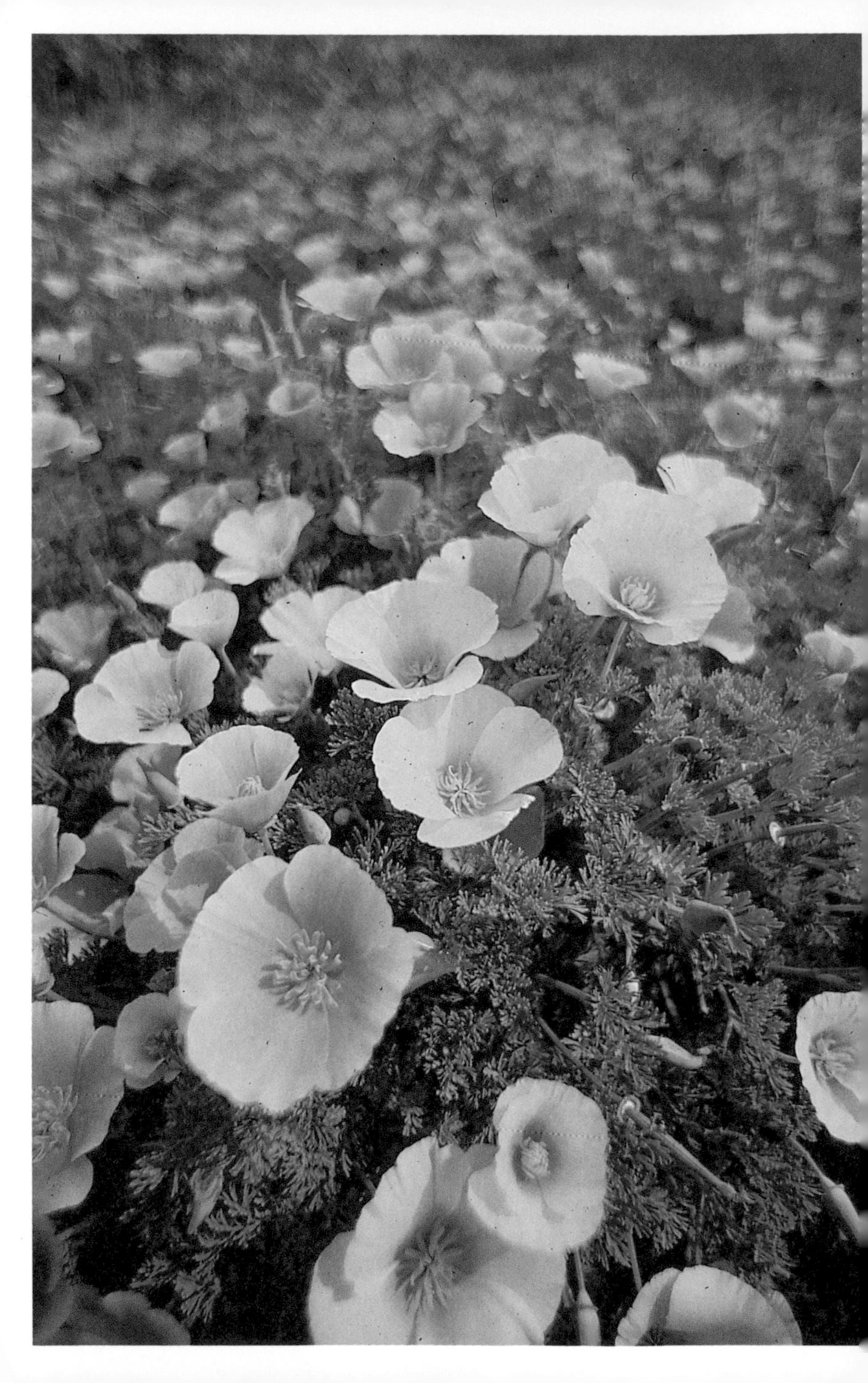

Page 84, top:
The triumph of conquest of the "giant" rock is captured from a distance with the 300mm f/2.8N AF.

Page 84, bottom:
Atmospheric scenics like this are often captured by super wides. I used the 18mm f/2.8 AF and was rewarded with a picture of the Yellowstone River that could have inspired Henry Mancini to write "Moon River."

Page 85:
The simple elegance of an emerging monarch butterfly was captured in the studio with a 60mm f/2.8 AF and flash.

Page 86:
A normal-range zoom is a great travel companion. I zoomed in the versatile 28-70mm f/2.8 AF-S to the 28mm position and stopped down to maximize this focal length's inherent depth of field in this photograph of the Badlands.

Page 87, top:
Bringing home the desert night sky is done with a 20mm f/2.8 AF and a six-hour exposure to the heavenly lights.

Page 87, bottom:
I keep reaching for my 70-180mm AF micro. Here, I used it to capture this colorful study of leaves in autumn.

Page 88:
By adding an extension tube to the 20mm f/2.8 AF, the poppies in the background were blurred to make those in the foreground pop.

Nikkor 200mm f/2 ED IF

Original release: 1986
Angle of coverage: 12°20′
Physical size: 8.9 x 5.2 inches (22.6 x 13.2 cm)
Weight: 5.3 pounds (2.39 kg)
Filter size: 122mm (unusable gel holder)
Lens hood: HE-4
M.F.D.: 9 feet (270 cm)
Aperture range: f/2-f/22
Unique features: None

The 200mm f/2 ED IF is one of Nikon's least known lenses. Short, stubby, and with a 122mm front element, the very profile of the 200mm f/2 is often mistaken for a 300mm f/2.8. When first introduced, the lens was gobbled up, but with the introduction of other fast telephotos—and the 180mm f/2.8 only a stop slower and considerably smaller—the 200mm f/2 ED IF has lost many of its early supporters.

The lens is not so large that it cannot be handheld, but it does require a practiced technique and a little arm strength. The lens is still widely used in sports photography, especially indoor sports. It seems to be losing its hold there, though, with the fast f/stop ED AF zooms now available.

Because of this, there are many 200mm f/2 ED IF lenses on the used-lens market at a fairly low price. Many photographers are now finding out that the lens is a real jewel when used with an extension tube for macro work. It works great with the TC-14B, making it a 280mm f/2.8 lens. It also works with the TC-301, making an excellent 400mm f/4 able to focus down to nine feet (2.7 m). (Do not use with TC-201 or TC-14A; image quality at the corners suffers.)

It is also a great lens for big-game work. The comfortable working distance between the subject and camera and its excellent magnification and isolation ability make it a natural for this type of photography. And because it is so fast, available-light

Nikkor 200mm f/2 ED IF

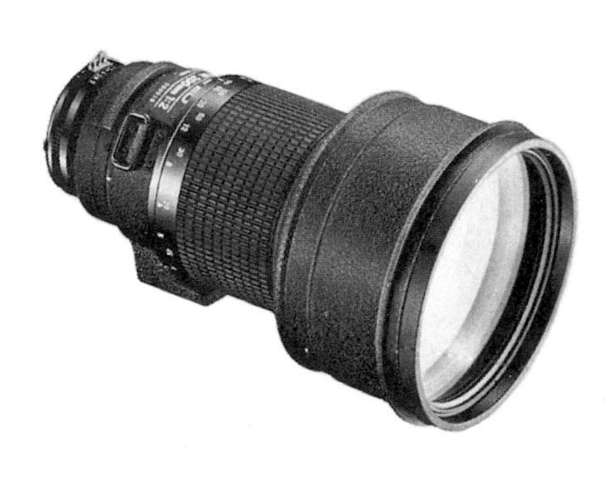

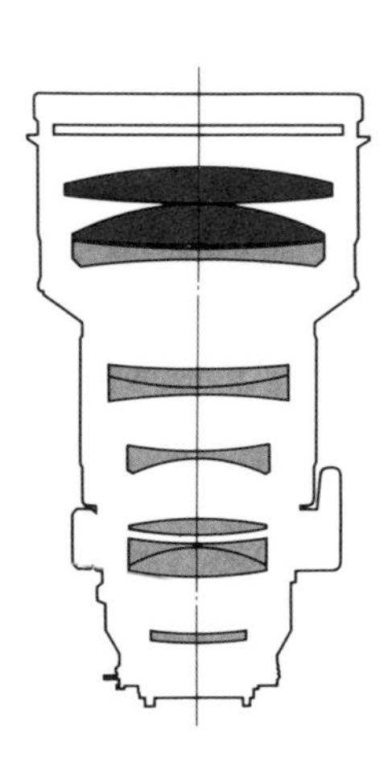

photography can be squeaked out to the very last ray of light. For photographing many big-game mammals, this is ideal.

Because speed is such a big factor in many lens purchases today, the 200mm f/2 ED IF is an excellent choice. With the mainstream, fast prime lenses in great demand, their price is always high and availability low. The 200mm f/2 is an excellent way to break into speed, as this lens is normally lower priced and easier to find. There is no sacrifice, though, in quality, versatility, or function in buying a 200mm f/2. For those wanting to break into fast telephotos without breaking the budget, this is the best buy around.

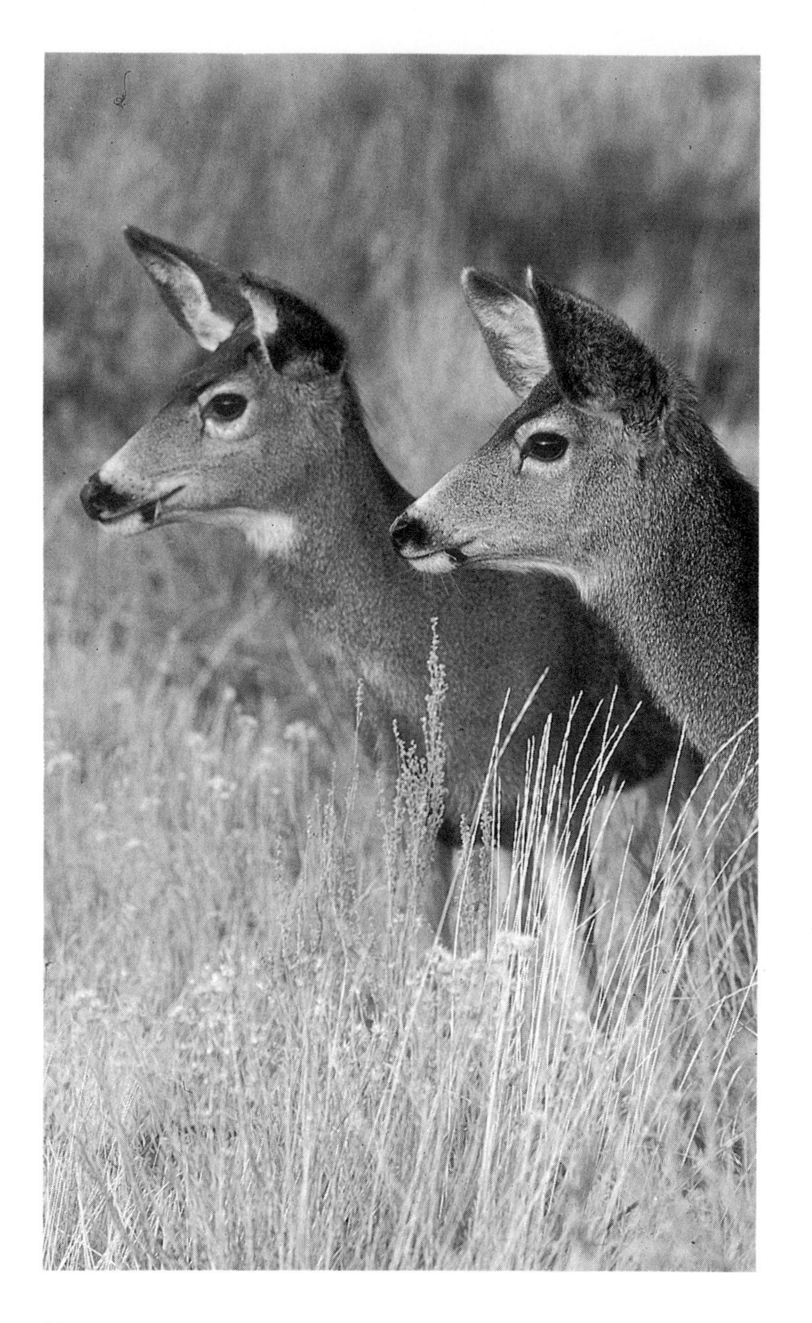

Super Telephotos

Using the Tools

Super telephotos are *the* most glamorous, sought after, and idolized group of lenses in photography. Whether for fashion, sport, wildlife, industrial, or armchair photographers, this group of lenses is universal in its appeal. Seeing the sidelines filled with sports photographers and their long lenses, or the fashion runways lined with huge front elements glistening in the lights, photographers are dazzled by the allure of the super telephoto.

There is no arguing it; the photographs taken with these lenses are some of our most memorable. There is one simple reason for this—angle of view. Telephotos have a very narrow angle of view, providing an incredible amount of control over the background. The photographer, understanding this, manipulates the background to support the subject while at the same time isolating it. This is the cleanest and purest form of communication available in photography.

Where wide angles take in all of the background and telephotos capture slices, super telephotos reveal only slivers. Literally, a lateral movement of only a few inches can radically change the background when using a super telephoto. Mastering the technical side of using these lenses is easy, but manipulating the background takes imagination and talent. Those who excel with telephotos are those who have mastered isolating the subject by selecting the right background.

Lens Speed

Buying your first super telephoto can be a trying situation. After the question of focal length is resolved, the problem of which f/stop arises. Fast telephotos have become the demigods of

⇦ **These mule deer, grazing on rare grasses in winter, happened to wander into the view provided by my 300mm f/2.8 AF.**

photography, with few understanding why. True, some photographers use them in low-light situations, possibly extending shooting time a few minutes. But fast telephotos were not designed with that in mind. Speed was built into these lenses to further enhance their isolating power via depth of field and provide the fastest possible shutter speed when using them.

The predecessors to modern telephotos had f/stops of f/4.5, f/5.6, and slower. They let background detail creep in, were dark to focus, and so physically large that photographers had to sit in the grandstands rather than on the playing field to shoot. Furthermore, they were often shot partially closed down to obtain maximum results, making them even slower and darker (no automatic aperture, either). To solve all these problems, ED glass and internal focusing (IF) were developed. (See the introductory chapter on Nikon technology for a discussion of these terms.)

The question remains, though: Does a photographer buy a fast telephoto or slow one? What does he or she gain by paying three or four times the price for one extra stop? (More isolating power and a lens three times larger.) If a photographer is going after football players, that extra stop means the player on the field pops from the crowd, which has been rendered as a wash of color. That same lens, though, pointed at a bird, would have to be closed down to gain enough depth of field for the eyes and beak to be in focus. If that is the case, spending the extra money for a lens that must always be closed down does not make sense. These are the pros and cons each individual photographer must answer—that and/or a spouse asking, "How much?!"

Filters

Super telephotos either have a 122mm or 160mm front element. Threaded filters this size are not available—which is OK, because Nikon's current super telephotos no longer accept filters in the front. The early ED IF lenses leading up to the current production super telephotos accepted filters; Nikon manufactured them. But they have been replaced with a built-in, permanent front "dust filter." Filtration for any of these lenses, old or new, can be done through a rear filter drawer with either a drop-in 39mm or 52mm filter, depending on the lens.

In the super telephotos, the 122mm lenses accept a 39mm filter via a filter drawer, and the 160mm lenses accept a 52mm filter via a filter drawer. The 52mm drawer accepts any standard 52mm filter, but the 39mm will accept only those in a Nikon 39mm filter mount. That is because, though the diameter of the glass is 39mm, the mount has a lip, reducing the size to 33mm. Using these drawers for color correction or black-and-white filters is not a problem.

Polarizing super telephotos is easy to do as well. Nikon makes four drop-in polarizers for super telephotos. These drop-in filters have a wheel on their exterior so you can rotate the filter, which is in the interior of the lens barrel, to polarize. The following lists which lenses accept one of the four polarizers: **CPL1L**—300mm f/2.8D ED IF AF-S, 400mm f/2.8 ED IF AIS, 400mm f/2.8D ED IF AF-S, 500mm f/4D ED IF AF-S, 600mm f/4D ED IF AF-S, 800mm f/5.6 ED IF AIS; **CPL1S**—300mm f/2.8 ED IF AF, 300mm f/2.8 ED IF AIS, 300mm f/4 ED IF AF, 400mm f/3.5 ED IF AIS, 500mm f/4P ED IF, 600mm f/4 ED IF AIS, 600mm f/5.6 ED IF AIS, 800mm f/8 ED IF, 1200mm f/11 ED IF AIS; **CPL2L**—400mm f/2.8D ED IF AF-I; **CPL2S**—300mm f/2.8D ED IF AF-I, 500mm f/4D ED IF AF-I, 600mm f/4D ED IF AF-I.

Focus Controls

All of the manual focus and a few of the early AF super telephotos have a prefocus click stop. This has caused more confusion for photographers than probably any other feature. The click stop can be set to provide an audible and momentary "click" lock anywhere in the focusing. For example, a photographer shooting a baseball game could prefocus on second base for the eventual steal and set the prefocus click at that point. The lens could then be used to photograph the game and when the steal occurs at second, the lens can quickly be turned to the preset, prefocus click to capture the action.

All of these ED super telephotos can focus beyond their infinity point. The ED elements in the super telephoto can be affected by extreme heat or cold; they expand or contract with temperature, affecting the way they focus. In –12°F (–24°C) temperature, my old 800mm f/5.6 was affected and focused past the infinity

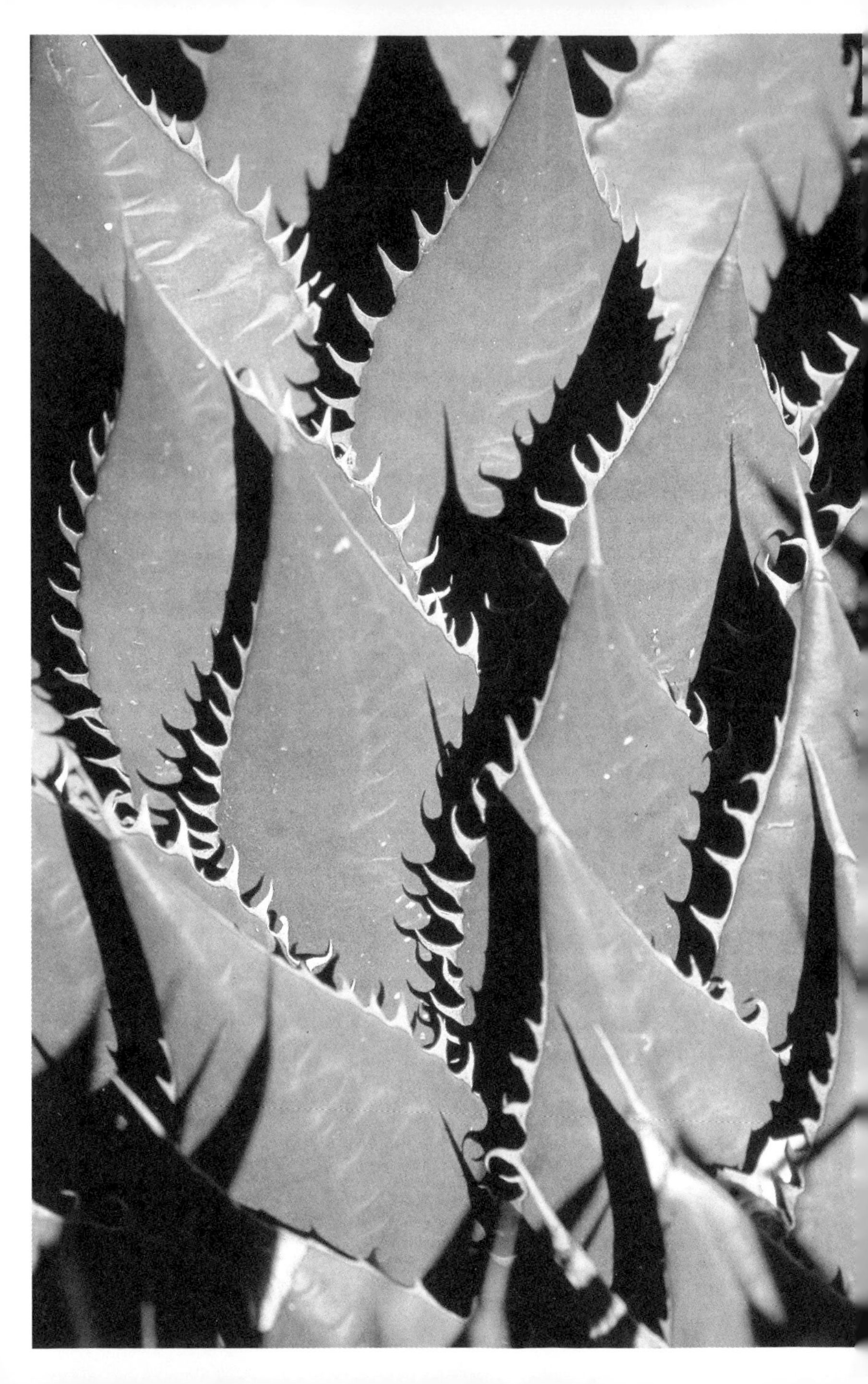

mark, but that is the only time I've had that occur. My 400mm f/2.8D AF-S and 600mm f/4D AF-S have not had that happen to them, even though I've shot in just as cold a temperature.

To help speed up the AF operation, current AF super telephotos have a focus-limiting switch, and older lenses have a ring. If the lens is limited to focusing within a small range and not from infinity to its minimum focusing distance, it can focus much faster; most lenses have three settings to limit the range of focus for this reason. Commonly, though, most photographers have the limit switch set to infinity.

AF lenses also have a very important feature: the M/A switch. When the lens is at this setting, the lens can focus automatically via the camera's autofocus; the lens can also be focused manually when in this mode. With the shutter release is slightly depressed, you can rotate the focusing ring on the lens to manually focus. By depressing the shutter release all the way and taking a picture, or by taking your finger off the shutter release, the focus point obtained manually will be lost and you will have to refocus again manually if required, or you can go back to AF with no other adjustments.

Lens Shades

Super telephotos come with a variety of shades. One type is built into the lens and rotates in and out from storage to being in place. The second type is a one-piece shade that physically comes off and reverses into place. Some lenses have a reversible shade that attaches to the first shade, which rotates out. The 400mm f/2.8D ED IF AF-S and 600mm f/4D ED IF AF-S have two reversible shades, one attaching to the other. While the first one does the job, the second is used often by sports photographers for personal protection more than for flare protection. Many photographers do not realize that they have a two-part shade system. Read the lens' instruction manual carefully to take full advantage of all shades.

Often thought of as a portrait lens, the 105mm f/1.8 turned this image of an agua cactus into a graphic study of angles and shadows.

Super Telephoto Technique

If the subject is not in focus, of course, best results with the super telephoto cannot be achieved. Using telephotos successfully requires the proper technique. Telephoto design places the focusing ring directly above the tripod head (the exceptions are the 800mm f/8 ED IF and 1200mm f/11 ED IF). Draw an imaginary line up the center column of a tripod, through the tripod head and to the top of the lens (normally where the focusing ring is located). Here is where your hand should rest (just as if resting your hand on your lap) to minimize any camera/lens movement. Because the focusing ring is here, there should not be any problem doing this and focusing at the same time. When firing, press your forehead/eye against the camera viewfinder, preferably with an eyecup attached, to eliminate any camera movement.

Transportation

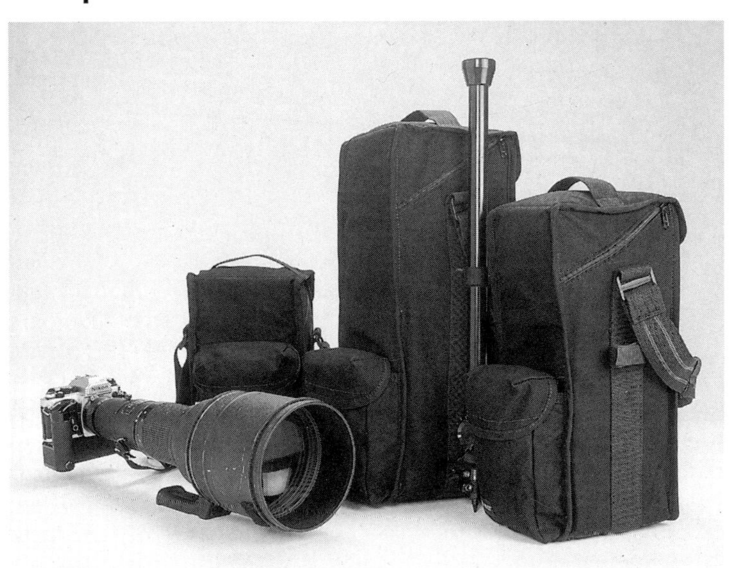

Domke's aptly named "Long Lens Bags" ease the burden of carrying 300mm, 400-500mm, or 600mm telephoto lenses. The well-padded bag keeps a lens safe and accessible, whether mounted on a camera or not.

These super telephotos all have strap lugs on their barrels. This is a hint from Nikon not to carry a big lens by letting it dangle from the camera's lens mount. The strap lugs on the lens are designed to support the weight of the lens and camera when carried. The weakest point of a lens/camera combo is the camera's lens mount (just ask the photographer who was tackled at the football game); this applies to using a tripod as well. Attach the lens—and not the body—to the tripod when using a super telephoto.

My final note concerns the large trunk cases that come with these lenses. Many photographers wonder what the compartments are for in the interior—they hold the TC-301 and TC-14B teleconverters. These trunk cases do provide a lot of protection for the lens, but they are overkill. The Long Lens Bags manufactured by Domke® do a marvelous job, taking a lot less space while providing maximum protection and quick access.

Nikkor 300mm f/2.8D ED IF AF-S

Original release: 1996
Angle of coverage: 8°10′
Physical size: 10.6 x 4.9 inches (27 x 12.4 cm)
Weight: 6.6 pounds (3 kg)
Filter size: 52mm
Lens hood: HK-22
M.F.D.: 10 feet (3 m)
Aperture range: f/2.8-f/22
Unique features: None

It was long thought that Nikon could not incorporate motors into their lenses without changing the size of the lens mount (something Nikon says they will never do). Well, Nikon not only put a motor—the new focus-driving AF-S (Silent Wave)—into the 300mm f/2.8D ED IF AF-S, but also redesigned the optics and cosmetics to produce their best 300mm f/2.8 to date.

Nikon went even further in their design: this lens does not need electricity to operate manually. If something should happen to the motor, the photographer is not left with a non-operational lens; for sports or wildlife photographers in particular, this is very important. These lenses can work on older bodies not capable of

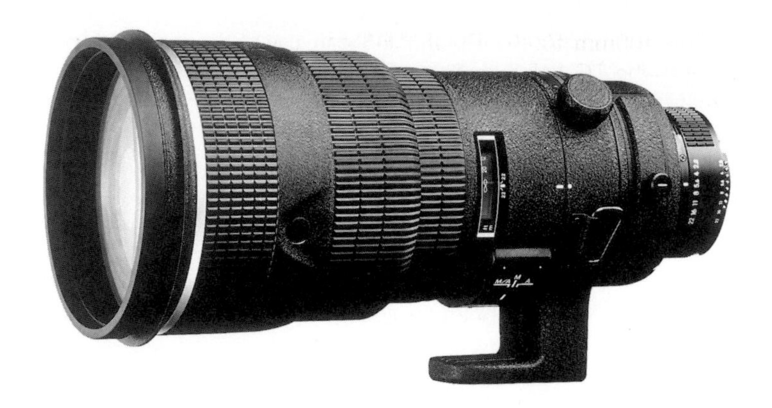

Nikkor 300mm f/2.8D ED IF AF-S

AF operation—maintaining Nikon's credo of "absence of planned obsolescence in models to come."

The lens has microcomputers (CPU), which communicate with the F5 and F100. This includes the "D" technology needed for optimal operation with these models' flash technology; it also has a rotary encoder to assure exact focusing. In addition, as an internal improvement, the AF noise has been eliminated. Unlike its predecessors, this lens is whisper-quiet, whether focused manually or automatically.

The lens also has some other new features. The M/A switch operates in Autofocus mode to provide quick manual override. In M/A mode or when shooting normally in Autofocus mode, the slightest touch of the lens focus ring coverts the lens to manual operation. This can be extremely useful in a situation in which, for example, the lens is being panned and all of a sudden it is looking through a shrub. This might confuse the AF sensor, but with a simple touch of the lens manual focus is operational and the shot possible.

The AF lock on the lens is also redesigned. Four large (thumbnail size) buttons on the lens barrel between the front element and the focusing ring provide instantaneous AF lock. The focus range limiter, incorporated into the barrel and working as other AF limiting switches, provides even faster response time. The filter drawer is still located in the lens barrel; the front element serves as a dustproof plate.

The 300mm f/2.8D ED IF AF-S can use two special teleconverters—the TC-14E, a 1.4x, and the TC-20E, a 2x. Both of these teleconverters are tack sharp, and both maintain complete electrical contact between the camera and lens. This means matrix metering and AF can be accomplished, which wasn't possible prior to their introduction.

Even with all of these improvements, the lens is slightly shorter and easier to handhold. These are probably the main reasons this lens has been difficult to obtain since its release. Almost forgot to mention the optics—outstanding!

Nikkor 300mm f/4 ED IF AF

Original release: 1987
Angle of coverage: 8°10′
Physical size: 10.5 x 4.1 inches (26.7 x 10.4 cm)
Weight: 2.91 pounds (1.3 kg)
Filter size: 82mm front, 39mm screw in
Lens hood: Built in
M.F.D.: 9 feet (2.7 m)
Aperture range: f/4-f/32
Unique features: None

Nikon's AF lenses were not receiving general approval or acceptance at the time the 300mm f/4 ED IF AF was first released, and it made quite an impression; it is quite possible that this lens was

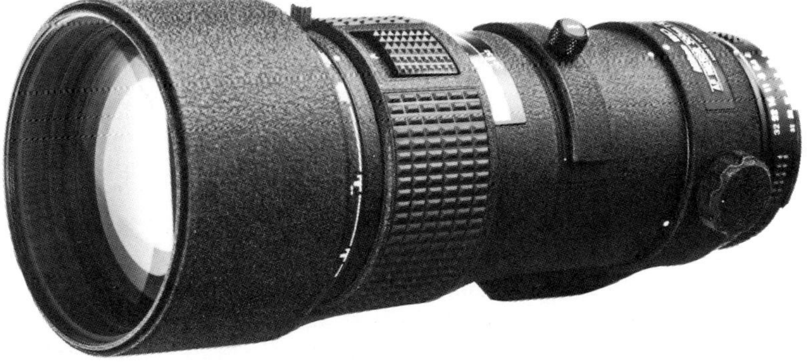

Nikkor 300mm f/4 ED AF IF

most responsible for turning that negative impression around. The quality of this lens can be seen in the fact that its design has never been changed since its introduction. For those photographers wanting this focal length but not able to spend the big bucks on the one stop faster f/2.8, this lens is an excellent choice.

The 300mm f/4 ED IF AF is extremely sharp and handholdable, making it a natural for almost all applications in photography. The placement of the wide-focusing ring is perfect for manual operation. When in AF mode, the switch on the lens barrel can be flipped to lock the focusing ring in place, enhancing its use handheld. (If this is not done, the focusing ring will turn when the lens is focused by the camera body. This can further delay the AF operation, which is already slightly slow.)

The lens is a natural for extension tubes and the TC-14B teleconverter. It is an outstanding 420mm f/5.6 lens, rivaling the 400mm f/5.6 ED IF. With the PK-11a extension tube, the minimum focusing distance is a little more than seven feet (2.1 m). With its built-in, 360° rotating tripod collar, the lens is marvelous for close-up work on a tripod. A teleconverter and extension tube can be used at the same time, providing even greater magnification and versatility.

Another excellent application of this lens is with a combination of extension tubes. For example, by adding a PN-11 and PK-13 (80mm of extension) to the lens, it gains the magnification of 1:2 with a three-foot (0.9 m) free working distance. Depth of field is a slight battle, because the extension tubes have moved the lens away from the film plane, but the image quality is outstanding. One application for this would be photographing wildflowers.

The front filter size is 82mm, which precludes using filters; as with other super telephotos, the 300mm f/4 ED IF AF has a 39mm filter drawer. A Nikon polarizer can be used with the lens, though, via the drop-in filter drawer. If you want to use more than one filter, you could place a warming filter on the front element in combination with one in the filter drawer.

This is a marvelous focal length for photographing big game. It compacts the animal enough to show off its size and strength, but not enough to distort it. It also provides a marvelous working distance with even the largest big game—for both the photographer's and subject's safety.

Nikkor 400mm f/2.8 ED IF

Original release: 1985
Angle of coverage: 6°10′
Physical size: 15.2 x 6.4 inches (38.6 x 16.3 cm)
Weight: 11.3 pounds (5.1 kg)
Filter size: 52mm, screw in
Lens hood: HE-3
M.F.D.: 15 feet (4.5 m)
Aperture range: f/2.8-f/22
Unique features: None

The 400mm f/2.8 has remarkable optics, rendering incredible sharpness, color, and contrast. It has also had a hard time finding a niche in the photography market. This is due to its physical size, price, and similarity to the lower priced 400mm f/3.5. Such relative insensitivity is probably fine with those who own the lens, as it is one of Nikon's best kept secrets. This lens is sharp!

It is physically big, only inches shorter than the 600mm f/4. It has a 160mm dustproof front plate (accepting 52mm drop-in filters), and tends to be slightly front heavy because of the large front-element array. This weight problem might be why it is not as widely used in sport photography. It is awkward to use on a monopod.

The 400mm f/2.8 is one of the best lenses for isolating a subject—still one of its biggest draws for many photographers. The narrow angle of view of 400mm, coupled with its f/2.8 aperture, creates an unbeatable package. This gives the photographer control over the background as well as the specific area around the subject. On larger subjects, the slim depth of field can isolate the subject from itself. This combination is what produces many of the great print images we enjoy.

This lens is a killer when used with a teleconverter. Many wildlife photographers use this lens either as a 560mm f/4 (TC-14B) or 800mm f/5.6 (TC-301). The results are magnificent with either, which is why these combos are so commonly used; many photographers use extension tubes with the lens as well. This versatility in the field is what attracts wildlife photographers, as they have a lens for low-light situations, or one with long reach, all in one package.

It is the 400mm f/2.8's narrow angle of view, depth of field, and extreme flexibility and versatility that make it such a marvelous lens to own. This is also why it is seldom available for purchase and why few rental houses stock it. There is also an automatic version of this lens.

Nikkor 400mm f/2.8D ED IF AF-S

Original release: 1998
Angle of coverage: 6°10′
Physical size: 13.9 x 6.3 inches (35.3 x 16 cm)
Weight: 10.6 pounds (4.7 kg)
Filter size: 52mm
Lens hood: HK-25
M.F.D.: 12.5 feet (3.8 m)
Aperture range: f/2.8-f/22
Unique features: None

One of my favorite manual lenses has been made a whole lot sweeter with the addition of AF-S technology. While I loved and once shot all the time with the manual version of the 400mm f/2.8, I never took the plunge to buy the AF-I version—too front heavy and just overall big. Well, Nikon went and pried some more money out of my already thin wallet when they came out with this latest, and to me best, version of the 400mm f/2.8.

The first thing you'll notice on the 400mm f/2.8D ED IF AF-S is its size and weight reduction. Nikon actually has in one of its press releases "used hand-held," giving you an idea of what we've got here; the lightweight design was achieved through the creation of a lighter optical system (less glass). The 400mm f/2.8D ED IF AF-S also uses advanced engineering resin and carbon fiber material for the lens' chassis (the parts that hold and move the glass). This construction design and material deliver the lightweight feature we all like, while maintaining the durable construction we demand from Nikon optics.

The AF-S (Single Wave) motor design is still proprietary, but we now have a measurement of speed for this motor, going from infinity to 12.4 feet (3.7 m)—minimum focusing distance—in a mere 0.27 second. And if you plug an F5 onto this lens, it flies!

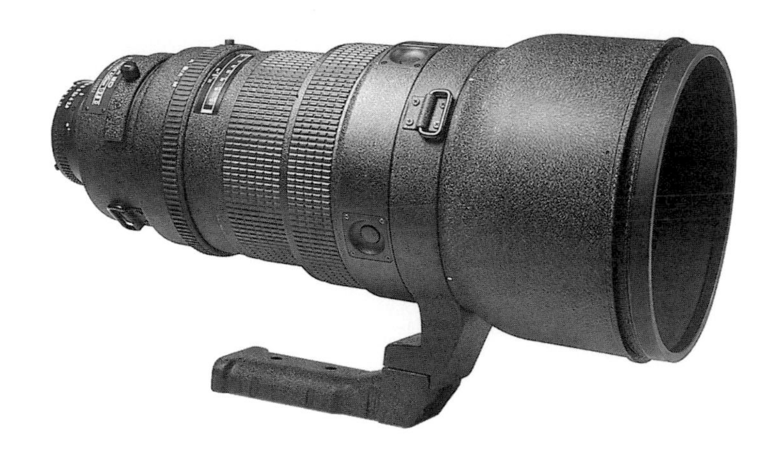

Nikkor 400mm f/2.8D ED IF AF-S

I was fortunate to have both the AF-I and AF-S 400mm f/2.8 at the same time to compare performance, but this is Nikon's slant on the subject: "The new lens incorporates a totally new optical design and upgraded construction. In brief, compared to the AF-I lens, the new AF-S lens has improved performance for correction of chromatic aberrations, improved flat characteristics at the image-forming surface, improved picture blue characteristics by adopting a rounder shaped 9-blade diaphragm, and improvements for multi-layer Nikon Integrated Coating."

Many wildlife photographers are now considering the 400mm f/2.8D ED IF AF-S as their primary lens, because they can add the 1.4x or 2x and get a 560mm f/4 or 800mm f/5.6 lens or incredible quality. While the optical quality of these combos is outstanding, however, the usable depth of field is not the same as the effective f/stop. This misunderstanding leads many photographers to think the 400mm f/2.8 AF-S and teleconverter pairing isn't as sharp as it should be—when in reality, it's just the shallow depth of field. This is truly a dynamite lens!

Nikkor 400mm f/3.5 ED IF

Original release: 1977
Angle of coverage: 6°10′
Physical size: 12 x 5.3 inches (30.5 x 13.5 cm)
Weight: 6.2 pounds (2.8 kg)
Filter size: 39mm screw in
Lens hood: Built in
M.F.D.: 15 feet (4.8 m)
Aperture range: f/3.5-f/32
Unique features: None

The 400mm f/3.5 ED IF is a super telephoto whose popularity comes and goes. This is partly because of its 400mm focal length, which is a tad too long for sports and a tad too short for wildlife. At least that is the general conception—which hasn't stopped some of the top photographers from using it. The 400mm f/3.5 ED IF has all the attributes of a typical super telephoto: a 122mm dustproof front plate (accepts 39mm drop-in filters), 360° rotatable tripod collar, preset focus click, ED glass, and IF focusing. In addition, unlike most super telephotos, it does have minimal shading. This is a lens that can be found used at a low price relatively easily and is a great way to get into fast super telephotos. It works extremely well with the TC-14B and TC-301, but vignetting can occur with TC-14A and TC-201.

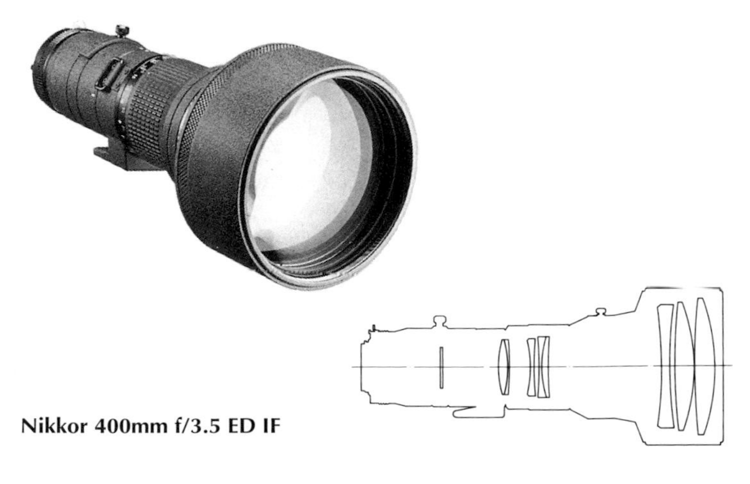

Nikkor 400mm f/3.5 ED IF

Nikkor 400mm f/5.6 ED IF

Original release: 1978
Angle of coverage: 6°10′
Physical size: 10.3 x 3.3 inches (26.2 x 8.4 cm)
Weight: 2.7 pounds (1.2 kg)
Filter size: 72mm screw in
Lens hood: Built in
M.F.D.: 15 feet (4.8 m)
Aperture range: f/5.6-f/32
Unique features: None

At one time *the* lens to own, the 400mm f/5.6 has been left in the dust in terms of speed. It remains, however, an extremely sharp, lightweight lens suitable to almost any application in photography.

This lens can easily be handheld with the assistance of a gunstock, creating a completely portable system to use in any situation. The addition of the gunstock also makes it excellent to use with flash, because altogether it is a small, portable package. Whether the photographer is working in a crowd at a race track or in the midst of trees, this portability is a big asset.

Ever need a handholdable 600mm lens? How about one that can focus down to just 15 feet? Well, you can come pretty close by adding a TC-14B to the 400mm, creating a 560mm f/8. In these days of speed, this combination might not excite many

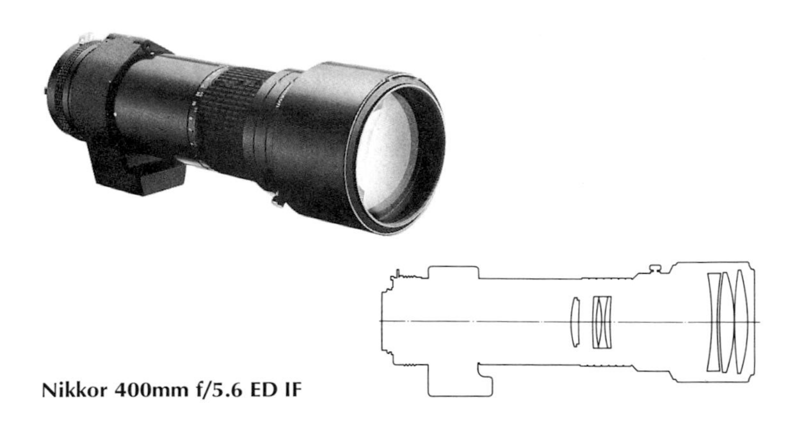

Nikkor 400mm f/5.6 ED IF

photographers, but those who photograph wildlife will quickly see its advantage—in combination, for example, with a flash when chasing small birds in a forest. And when working from a canoe in a marsh, photographers will find this lightweight, close-focusing system invaluable.

The 400mm f/5.6 ED IF is an excellent lens for close-up work. Its light weight allows it to be easily used low to the ground on a tripod. It works well with large amounts of extension, such as Nikon's PN-11, cutting the minimum focusing distance down from 15 feet (4.8 m) to just over seven feet (2.1 m). This extreme amount of extension makes the background a mere wash of color—which, in combination with the narrow angle of view of the lens, isolates the subject like nothing else.

One interesting note: the tripod collar on the AI version is narrower than that of AIS version; this makes the aperture ring on the AI version wider than the AIS version. Those with big hands or fingers might find this difference significant.

Nikkor 600mm f/4 ED IF

Original release: 1979
Angle of coverage: 4°10'
Physical size: 18.1 x 7 inches (46 x 17.8 cm)
Weight: 13.9 pounds (6.3 kg)
Filter size: 39mm screw in
Lens hood: Built in and HE-5
M.F.D.: 25 feet (7.5 m)
Aperture range: f/4-f/22
Unique features: None

This lens captured the imagination of photographers the moment it was introduced. Stores were swamped by those wanting to get a look at it, especially its size. It is still a demigod that many photographers aspire to own. Its allure has to do with its amazing sharpness and incredible f/4 speed.

This is a big lens. Its 160mm front element—how the lens can gather so much light to be an f/4—was the first to be that large; it also makes the 600mm f/4 ED IF a very bright viewing lens to use, especially in low-light situations. This is where the 600mm f/4's reputation was first established, in fact, as many photographers pushed the limit of available light (in the day of slow ISO films).

The size of this lens started the speed frenzy and overshadowed its ability to isolate the subject. Its staggering 4° angle of view translates to 12x magnification of normal vision, allowing it to isolate a subject with very little effort or expertise; combined with this is its narrow depth of field at f/4. Because of this, the 600mm f/4 ED IF was instantly used for photographing sports, such as track and field. The lens compacted the action on the field while isolating the subject, making the background a blur.

The lens originally came from Nikon with a TC-14 teleconverter (today it's known as the TC-14B, available as an accessory). This makes the lens an 840mm f/5.6, which enhances its isolating ability; the angle of view is narrower and the depth of field is reduced by 40%. Nikon's original decision to include the teleconverter is further indication that this super-fast telephoto was designed for its isolation powers, not its abilities in low light. The automatic version of this lens is discussed next.

Nikkor 600mm f/4D ED IF AF-S

Original release: 1996
Angle of coverage: 4°10′
Physical size: 17.5 x 6.5 inches (44.4 x 16.5 cm)
Weight: 12.8 pounds (5.8 kg)
Filter size: 52mm
Lens hood: HK-23
M.F.D.: 20 feet (6 m)
Aperture range: f/4-f/22
Unique features: None

This is a remarkable lens. Some photographers were never swept up in the original 600mm f/4 fever, a few were by the AF-I AF version, but the AF-S version has the photographers going wild! I have to admit it; I'm one of those converts, proudly owning the AF-S version where I never owned any previous incarnation.

One of the more exciting aspects of the lens is it focuses down to a remarkable 20 feet. The manual version focuses down to 25 feet (7.5 m), the 500mm f/4 focuses down to 20 feet, but the AF-S focuses as close and is 600mm in magnification. Even

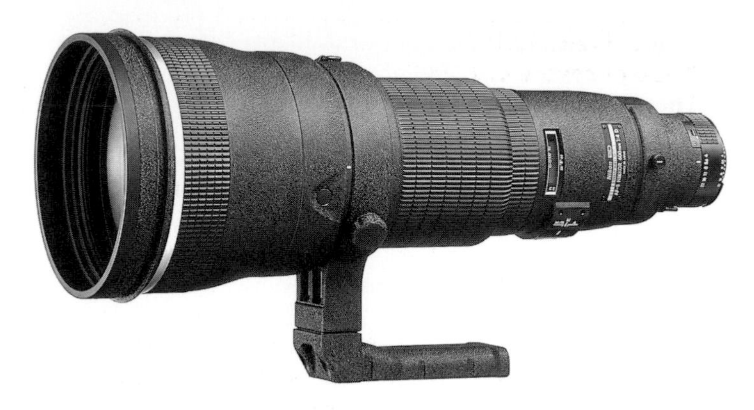

Nikkor 600mm f/4D ED IF AF-S

more exciting is that the 600mm f/4D ED IF AF-S matches up with the 1.4x (TC-14E) and 2x (TC-20E) teleconverters. This means a photographer can have a 840mm f/5.6 AF or 1200mm f/8 lens that autofocuses down to 20 feet. Awesome!

In operation, the 600mm f/4D ED IF AF-S is the same as the 300mm and 400mm AF-S lenses (refer to the 300 f/2.8D ED IF AF-S for complete description), including having AF lock buttons near the end of the lens. This can be a drawback for photographers with short arms, as the buttons might be hard to reach and operate. The focusing ring, though slightly smaller, is still quite easy to use.

The 600mm f/4D ED IF AF-S is probably the quintessential super telephoto of the Nikkor line. Its lightning-fast focusing, combination of narrow angle of view and depth of field, minimum focusing distance, and flexibility with the teleconverters make it one of the essential lenses to own—that is, if it fits your style of photography.

Nikkor 600mm f/5.6 ED IF

In the race for speed, the 600mm f/5.6 was left in the dust—at least that's the general perception, which could not be more unfounded. True, it is a f/5.6, but this small, lightweight lens can be extremely fast to use in the field.

It is smaller than the 600mm f/4D ED IF AF-S . . . lots! It has a 122mm front element and weighs nearly eight pounds less. With

Original release: 1986
Angle of coverage: 4°10′
Physical size: 15 x 5.3 inches (38.1 x 13.5 cm)
Weight: 5.9 pounds (2.7 kg)
Filter size: 39mm screw in
Lens hood: HE-4 and built in
M.F.D.: 20 feet (6 m)
Aperture range: f/5.6-f/32
Unique features: None

the same angle of view as the 600 f/4, it has one stop greater depth of field. It does focus down to just 20 feet, though, unlike the 600 f/4 ED IF, which is at 25 feet. Even with these side-by-side benefits between the two, the 600mm f/5.6 has never had the same following as the 600mm f/4.

The 600mm f/5.6N ED IF works marvelously with teleconverters, making it very flexible. It also is one of the best super telephotos for use with extension tubes, because its minimum focusing distance is already quite short; many photographers, for instance, use this combination to photograph wildflowers. Altering the background is a snap and isolating the subject could not be easier. As the extension tube eliminates any detail in the background, the lens can be closed down to provide the subject maximum depth of field.

This is another super telephoto that can be found used at a reasonable price fairly easily. Do not hesitate to invest in its optics just because it is an f/5.6 lens. Many of the world's top pros use this lens to capture some of our most memorable images—a recommendation not every lens can boast.

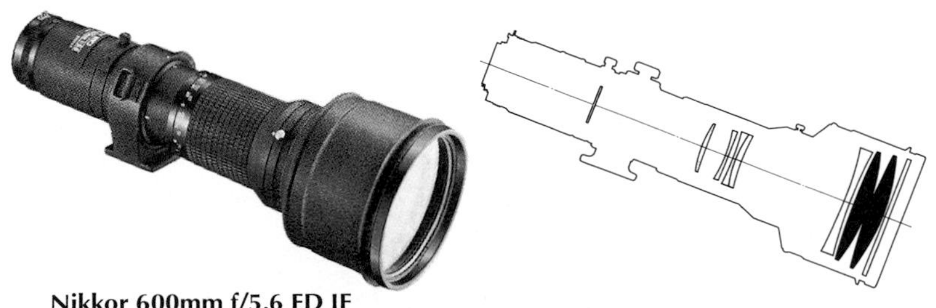

Nikkor 600mm f/5.6 ED IF

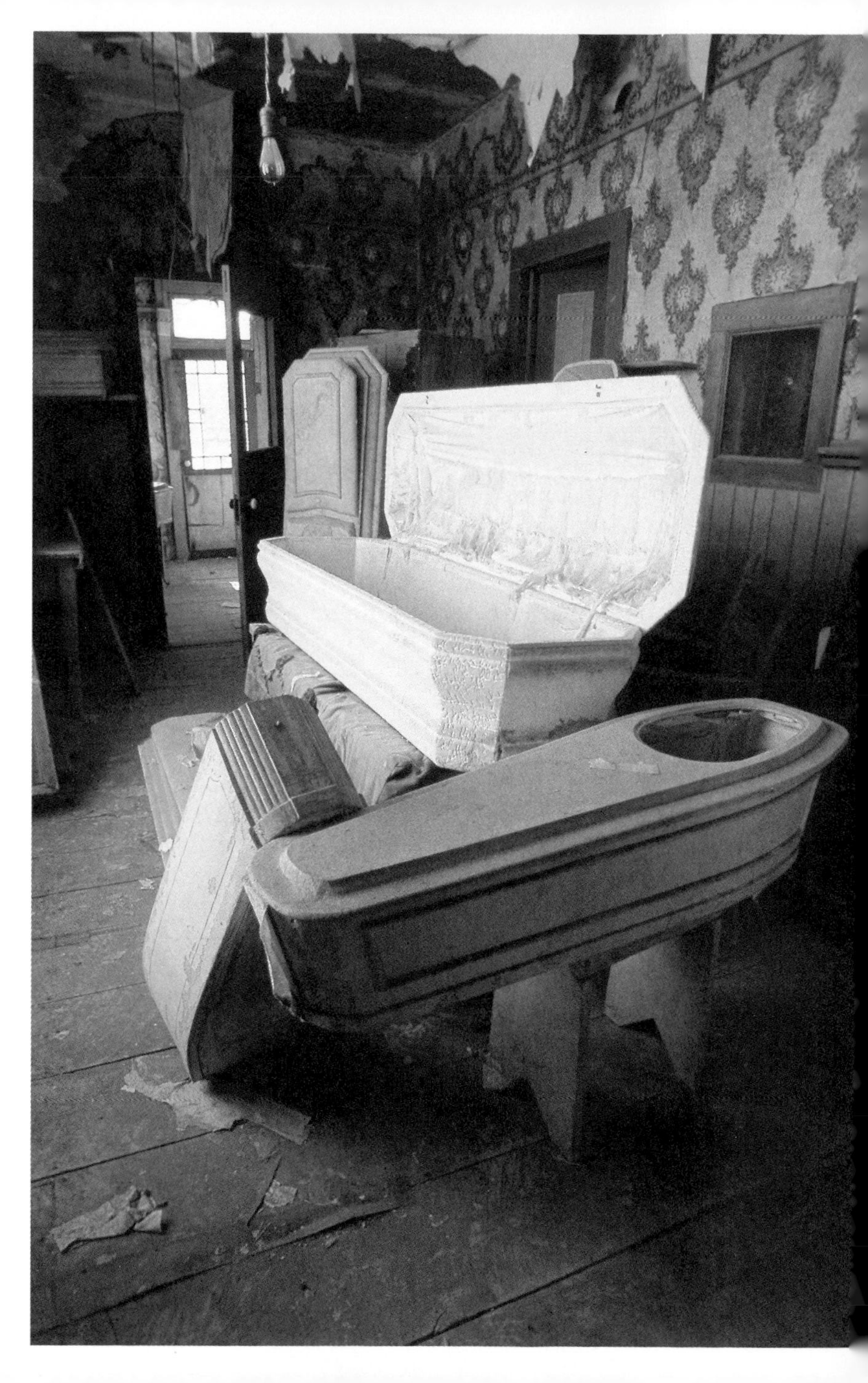

Zooms

Using the Tools

No group of lenses has been more misunderstood or maligned than zooms. The original zooms of the early 1960s and the noise of the original AF zooms gave them all a bad reputation that has only gradually been disappearing with the recent addition of zooms to the Nikon line. If these zooms do not finally convince photographers of the quality and creativity these lenses offer, nothing will.

A zoom lens can replace a number of prime focal length lenses within its single range. For example, the 75-300mm f/4.5-5.6 AF incorporates the prime focal lengths of 85mm, 105mm, 135mm, 180mm, 200mm, and 300mm. This extreme versatility and flexibility is what makes the zoom such a powerful, creative tool for the photographer. It makes zooms very economical to own as well, eliminating the need to purchase all of those prime lenses separately.

Using a zoom requires an observant photographer. Like ultra wides, zooms can capture unwanted elements. But unlike ultra wides, the zoom can simply be zoomed in or out to eliminate the unwanted objects. When using a zoom on a body that provides only 92% viewing, however, this is easier said than done, as not all of the image that is captured on film is seen. With these cameras, zooming wider to see and discover any unwanted elements, then zooming back to eliminate them, is the way to maximize their flexibility.

The ghostly morgue of Bodie State Park, shot with a 35-70mm f/2.8 AF, a perfect lens for the vacationing photographer.

Variable F/Stop Design

One of the biggest complaints about many of the zooms is their variable f/stop design. This comes from old-school photographers still demanding complete control over shutter speed and f/stop. Because the lens changes its effective f/stop when zoomed (where this occurs in the zoom range is provided in the tech sheet that accompanies the lens), photographers have a hard time being in control of the exact f/stop. Those photographers, however, who take advantage of any of the camera's Program modes (and their stepless shutter speeds) don't have to be concerned, because they know they are taking advantage of both photographic realms while maintaining complete control.

That variable f/stop design is very important in today's zoom lens configuration—allowing the small, compact design that so many photographers enjoy. A good example of this is the 35-70mm. The variable f/stop version is only two inches (5.1 cm) long and has a 52mm front element; the constant f/stop version is four inches (10.2 cm) long and has a 62mm front element. The constant f/stop version also has a nearly 300% higher price tag.

Zooms naturally lend themselves to being handheld. This requires proper technique to maximize image sharpness. Some zooms, though, add a twist to this by having two rings rather than one. The focusing and zooming action can still be controlled by the left hand, but care must be taken to prevent knocking the zoom from its desired setting. This simply requires practice.

Macro Plus Versatility

Almost every zoom has a macro feature. Some of these are at a particular focal length, and others are available throughout the entire zoom range. This provides an added degree of flexibility to an already extremely versatile lens. Such flexibility can be enhanced by extension tubes or auxiliary close-up attachments, such as Nikon's 3T, 4T, 5T, or 6T. None of these options affect image quality, nor will the zoom function differently with their addition.

Zooms allow photographers to carry all the focal lengths they might require in just a couple of lenses; an excellent combination

I highly recommend is the 24-50mm f/3.5-4.5 AF and 75-300mm f/4.5-5.6 AF. Both lenses have the same front element size, so only one set of filters is needed. Both lenses have AF technology and will interface with any body with matrix metering. In addition, both lenses offer optical quality that is hard to match. These two lenses in a vest pocket, along with a super telephoto, could support any nature photographer's habit for a lifetime.

AF-S Zooms

Nikon has included into its line a number of outstanding zooms that incorporate the AF-S (Silent Wave) motor (for a full discussion of AF-S, see the chapter on Nikon terminology). These are highly specialized zooms, probably some of the finest optics Nikon has to offer; they also are heavier than other zooms of the same focal range and are more money—so consider that while AF-S zooms do offer the finest lenses, they are not for every photographer, and that you won't necessarily suffer poorer optics by not buying them.

One cool thing you *would* appreciate with these AF-S zooms is that they all have the same 77mm filter size; another big plus is that they can take advantage of the TC-14E and TC-20E teleconverters. For more information on this feature, refer to the chapter on teleconverters.

Nikkor 17-35mm f/2.8D ED IF AF-S

Original release: 1999
Angle of coverage: 104°-62°
Physical size: 4.2 x 3.3 inches (7.5 x 8.4 cm)
Weight: 26.5 ounces (750 g)
Filter size: 77mm
Lens hood: HB-23
M.F.D.: 0.9 foot (0.3 m)
Aperture range: f/2.8-f/22
Unique features: None

I've long awaited this lens! What has to be one of the best focal lengths to combine in one lens for the scenic, location, or travel

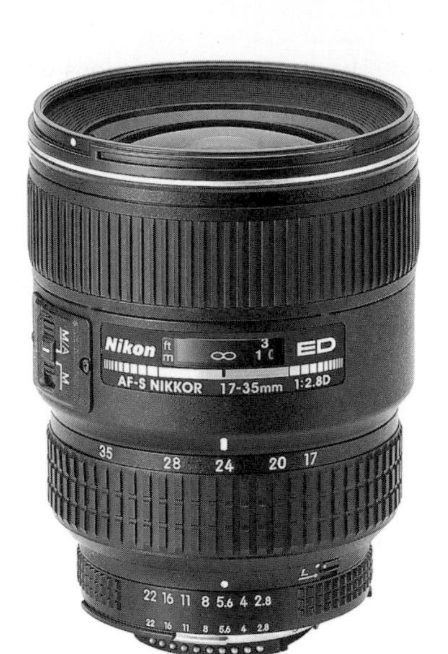

Nikkor 17-35mm f/2.8 ED IF AF-S

photographer has finally come to the Nikon mount. This is a beautiful lens, delivering outstanding quality throughout its entire zoom range. You could easily replace all your lenses in the 17mm to 35mm range with this one lens, and honestly get the best optical quality Nikon has to offer.

The 17-35mm f/2.8 has to be an interesting optical construction; it includes two glass-mold aspherical, one compound aspherical, and two ED lens elements in its 13-element construction. I understand why the aspherical elements are part of the optical formula, but it's the ED glass that's puzzling. Whatever the reason, the lens does perform!

It is an AF-S lens with the M/A feature, making it very easy to use. Its IF focusing and zooming keep it a small package however you use it. But, unlike other AF-S lenses, the 17-35mm f/2.8 cannot be used with the TC-14E or TC-20E teleconverters. The rear element of the zoom, when zoomed to 17mm, is flush at the rear, so would smack into the element of the teleconverter.

While it isn't technically a rectilinear lens, the 17-35mm does deliver straight line rendition throughout its entire zoom range. But the lens does tend to flare like the 15mm f/3.5 when there is any direct light source in the frame. Those who own this lens will capture beautiful images, but will have to learn how to master flare control. In any case, this was a lens that instantly found a home in my camera bag!

Nikkor 20-35mm f/2.8D AF

Original release: 1993
Angle of coverage: 94°-62°
Physical size: 3.7 x 3.2 inches (9.4 x 8.1 cm)
Weight: 20.6 ounces (577 g)
Filter size: 77mm
Lens hood: HB-8
M.F.D.: 1.7 feet (0.51 m)
Aperture range: f/2.8-f/22
Unique features: None

What a marvelous, versatile range! This zoom has become one of Nikon's most popular ultra-wide zooms since its introduction—which, considering the price, makes that an amazing feat. Incorporating what is probably a photojournalist's most used set of focal lengths, this lens is definitely geared toward their style of photography.

The 20-35mm incorporates "D" technology, which will interface completely with the flash technology of the N90/F90. This allows the photojournalist to have the flexibility to use the 20-35mm f/2.8D AF in combination with the N90/F90 for "over the head" shots—the photojournalist simply holds the camera aloft and fires away. The camera will take care of focus and flash exposure, increasing the odds of obtaining the shot.

The quality of the optics is apparent even when just viewing through the lens. Its bright image is magnificent, making working in low light levels easier. It also has less barrel distortion than the 35-70mm f/2.8 (which is minimal already). Of course, it is on the light table that its real brilliance shines, revealing remarkably sharp images.

Scenic photographers are probably a little disappointed in the 20-35mm because of its 77mm filter size—but this size is now shared with the new line of AF-S zooms, so it is less of an

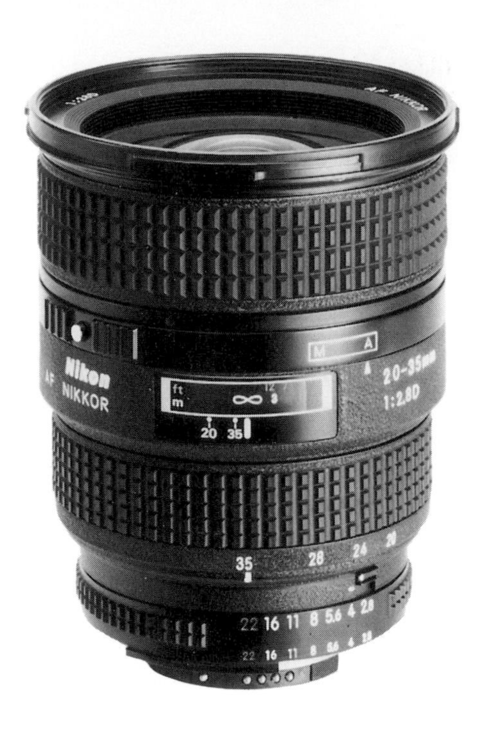

Nikkor 20-35mm f/2.8D AF

oddball. The large angle of view at 20mm also means that stacking filters is out of the question. This is one lens that is a perfect candidate for having color correction filters attached at the rear. The large filter size also eliminates the option of using Nikon's auxiliary close-up filters.

The 20-35mm is physically large and heavy compared to other zooms. Its price is also 300% higher than other zooms. These factors, in combination with some of its limitations for general photographers, might limit its appeal. It is also a two-ring lens—one ring zooms and the other focuses. As with many of Nikon's lenses, this means a small group will own this lens and create the images—while the rest wonder how they were taken.

Nikkor 24-50mm f/3.3-4.5 AF

Original release: 1988
Angle of coverage: 84°-46°
Physical size: 3.2 x 2.8 inches (8.1 x 7.1 cm)
Weight: 13.2 ounces (370 g)
Filter size: 62mm
Lens hood: HB-3
M.F.D.: 1.6 feet (0.5 m)
Aperture range: f/3.3-f/22
Unique features: Macro mode

The 24-50mm f/3.3-4.5 AF was released at a time when faith in Nikon's AF system was wavering. Its variable f/stop design was instantly pooh-poohed, but its optics quickly turned everything around. This is probably why the 24-50mm is still produced—now in a version with "D" technology—has never been changed, and is a favorite worldwide.

The lens covers a choice, comfortable range of 24-50mm, which is what attracts most photographers to it. It is also physically small and light, making it a natural for travel photography. It accepts the Nikon 62mm polarizer with no vignetting. These attributes make this lens a real standout.

Because so many photographers own the 24-50mm f/3.3-4.5 AF, it has been applied to every aspect of photography. It is a good lens for general photography and is often used on remote cameras. And, it is often used in its Macro mode, which produces

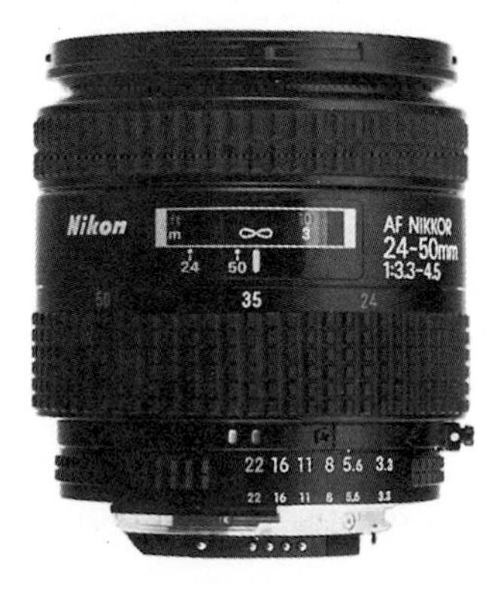

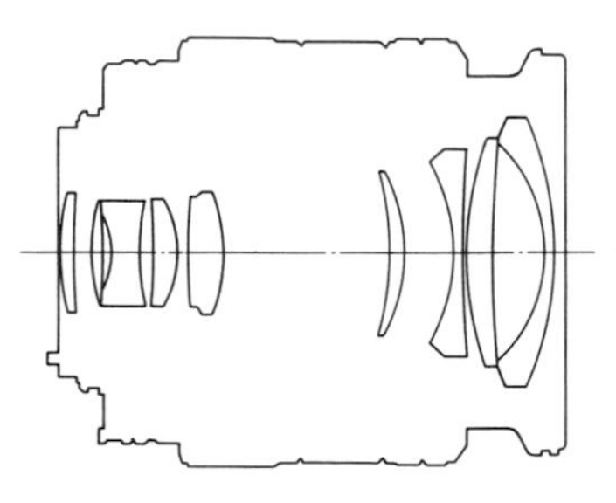

Nikkor 24-50mm f/3.3-4.5 AF

a 1:4 magnification. Extension tubes are frequently added to the lens; a PK-11a makes possible a magnification of 1:2. Its most popular feature, though, is created through the addition of Nikon's auxiliary close-up lenses, 5T and 6T.

This zoom is not a "flat field" lens by design, yet in all these altered versions, the image quality is remarkable. Its zooming and focusing are performed by two separate rings, the "two-touch" lens. This tremendous range of flexibility will keep the 24-50mm f/3.3-4.5 AF one of the most popular lenses in the Nikon zoom system.

Page 121:
A 400mm telephoto lens allows you to bring the subject in closer, narrow the view, and isolate the subject against a blurred background, to tell the story of the animal and its habitat.

Page 122:
The magnificent vista of Bryce's main amphitheater is given air to breathe in the frame by using a 20mm f/2.8 AF.

Page 124, top:
The low angle and wide vista of the 20mm f/2.8 AF captures a part of the main street in the old ghost town of Bodie.

Page 124, bottom:
Capturing the romance of the ghost town of Bodie required a 75-300mm f/4.5-5.6, along with 81a graduated and polarizing filters.

Page 125, top:
This headlight of a junkyard truck takes on new light when highlighted by the 60mm f/2.8 AF micro.

Page 125, bottom:
The sun setting on an old barn in the ghost town of Bodie is captured by the 35-70mm f/2.8 AF. The barn itself has stood for years in this same condition.

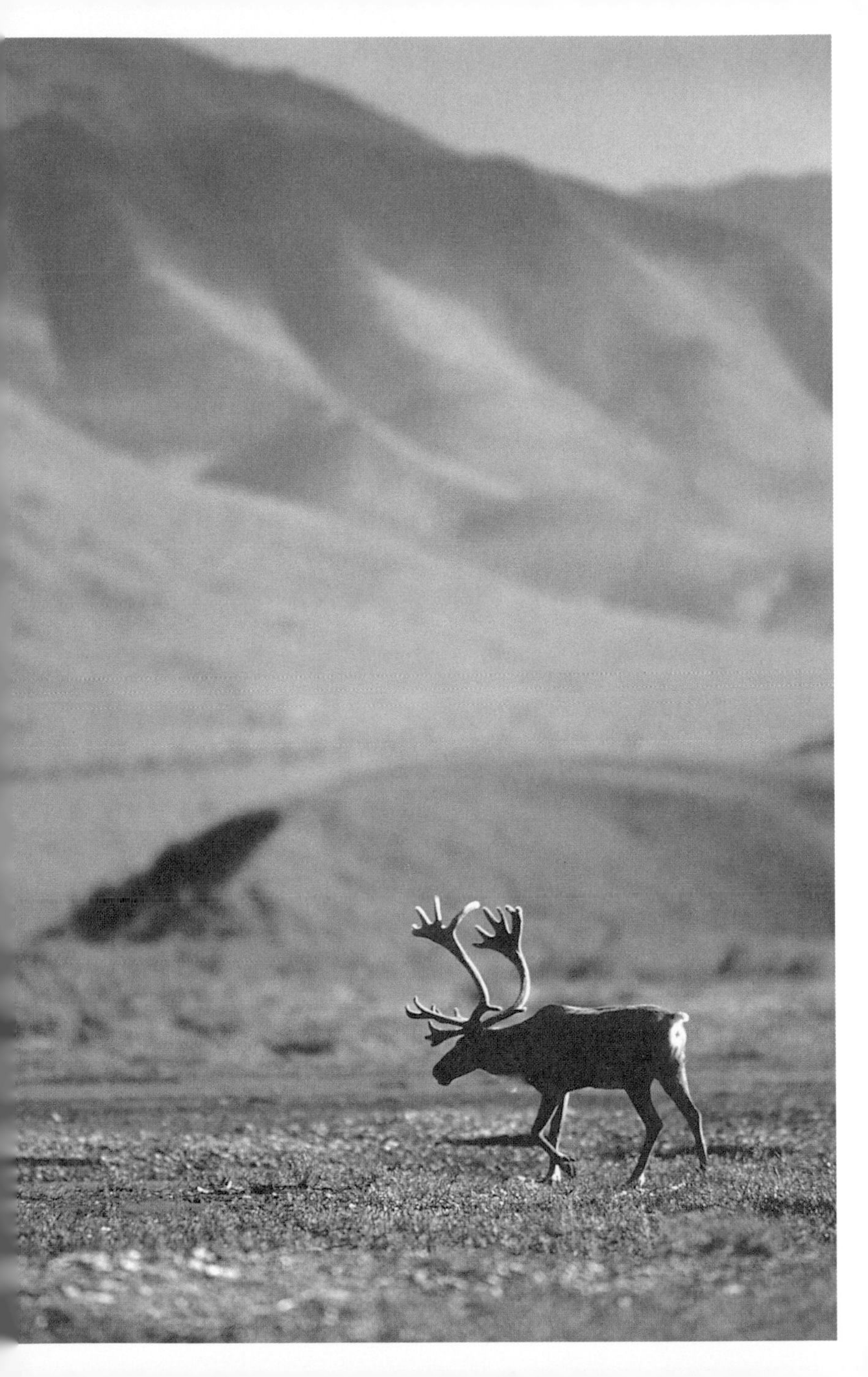

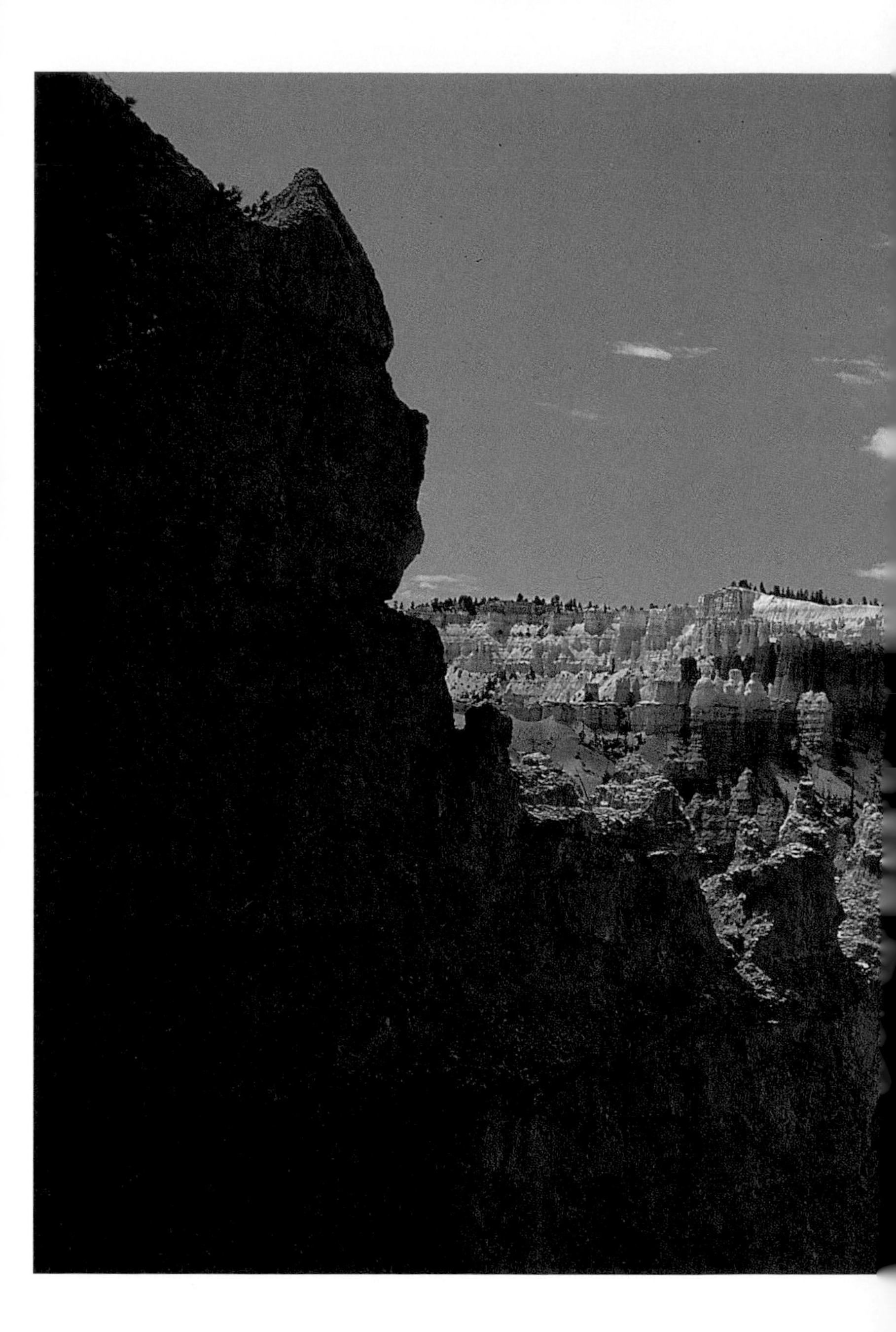

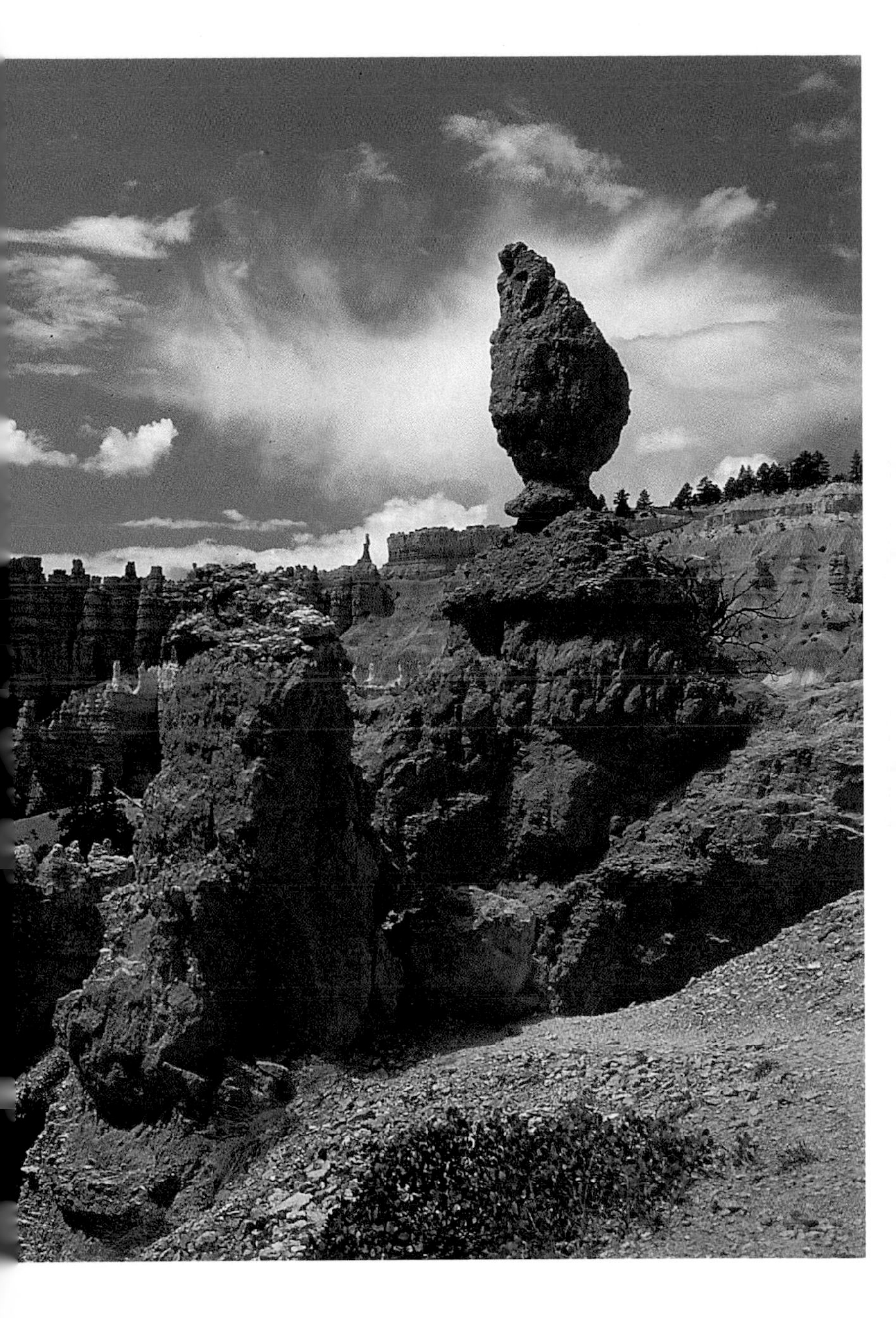

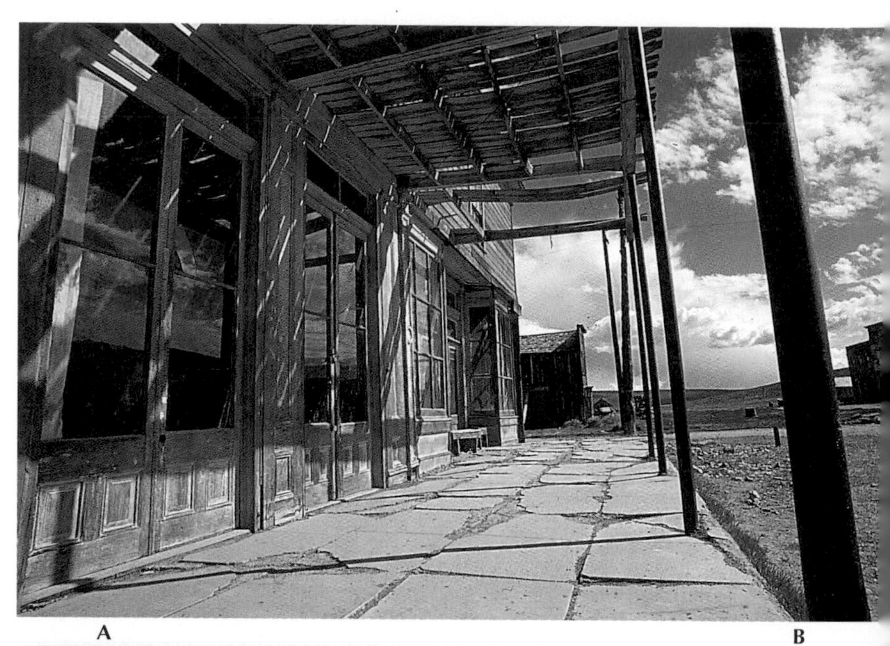

A B

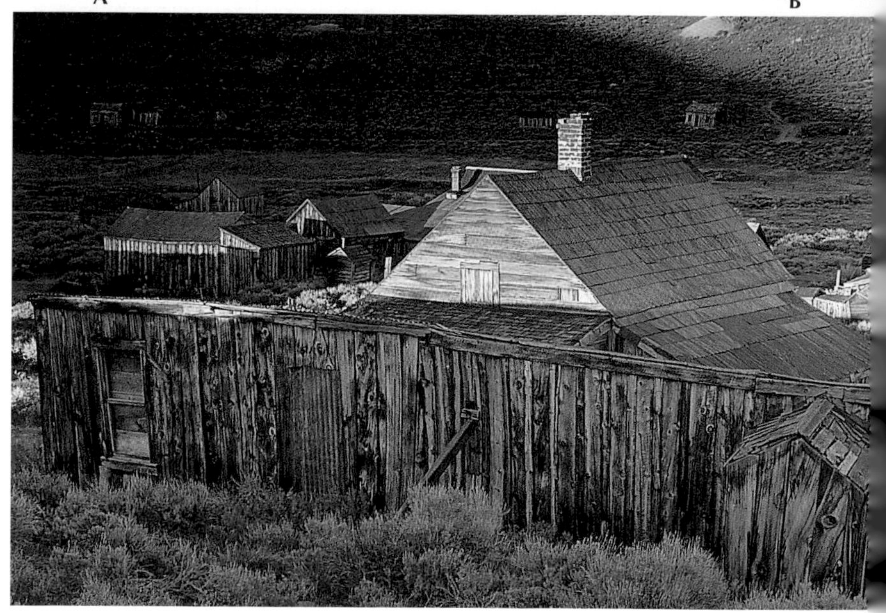

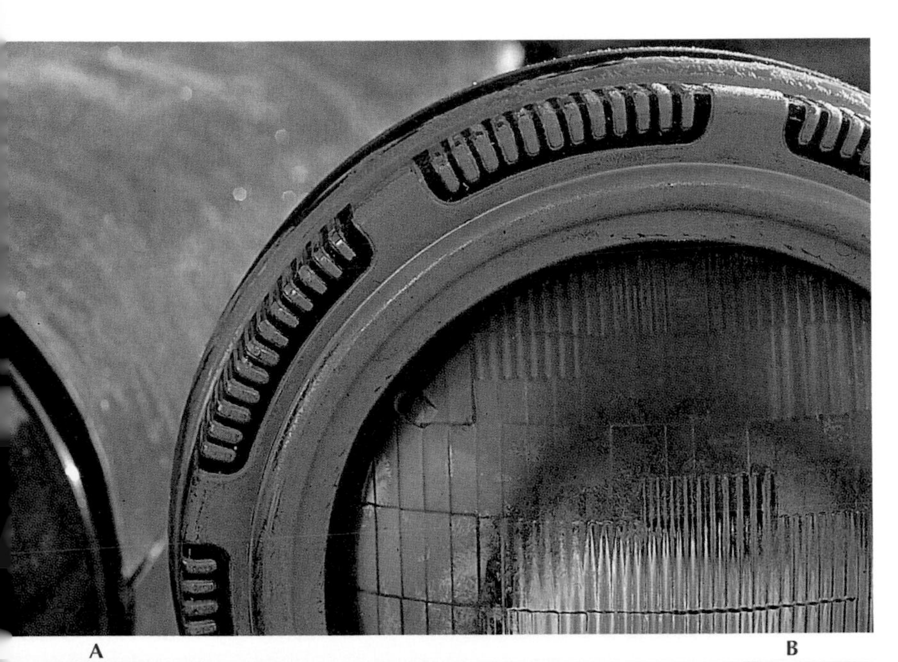

A

B

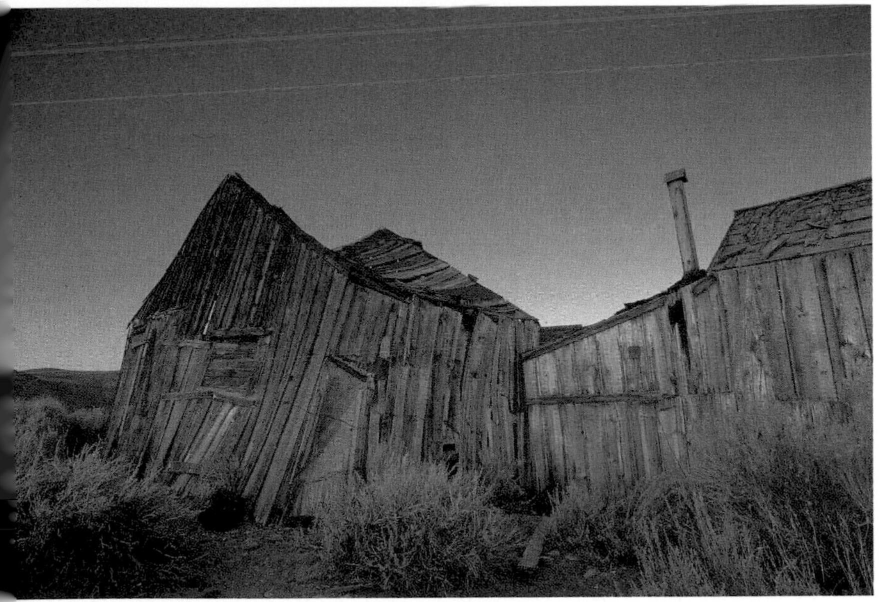

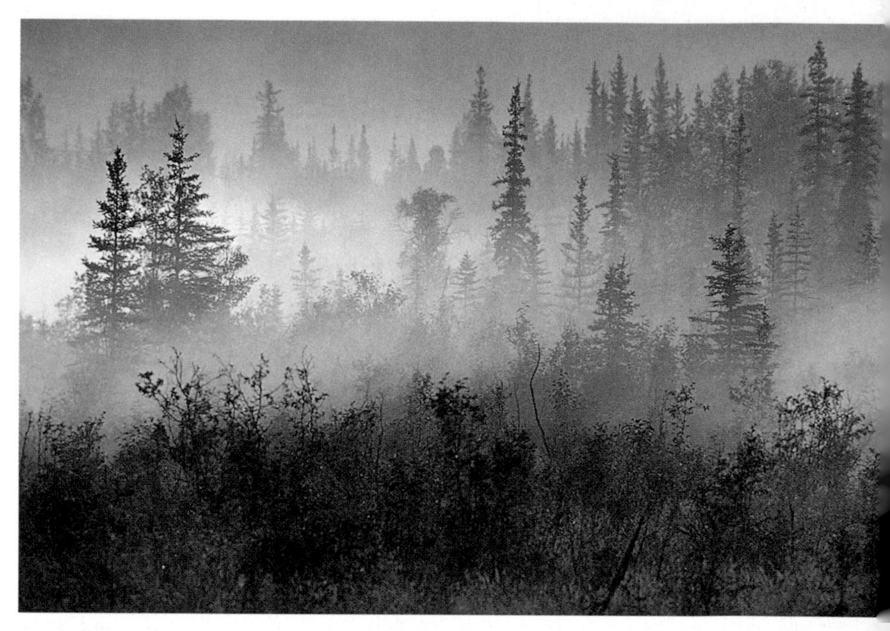

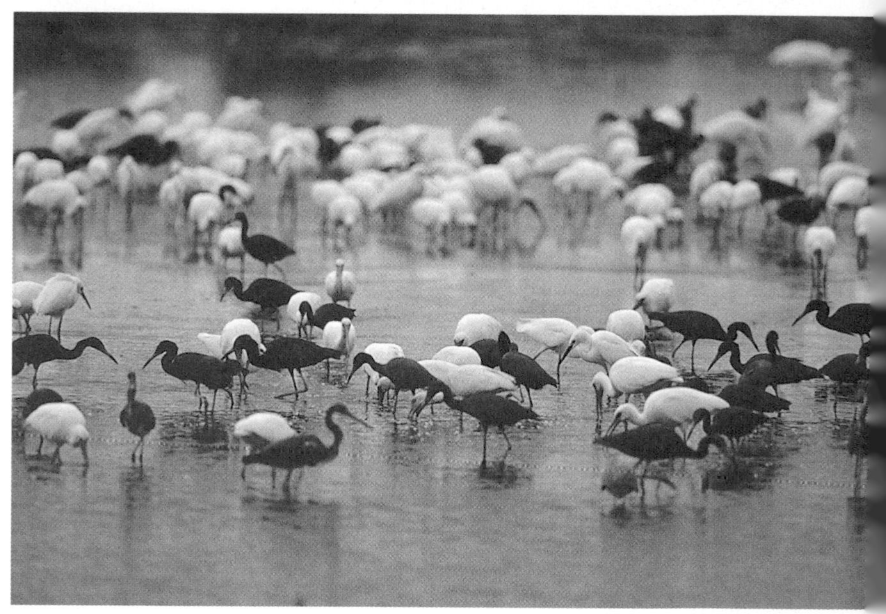

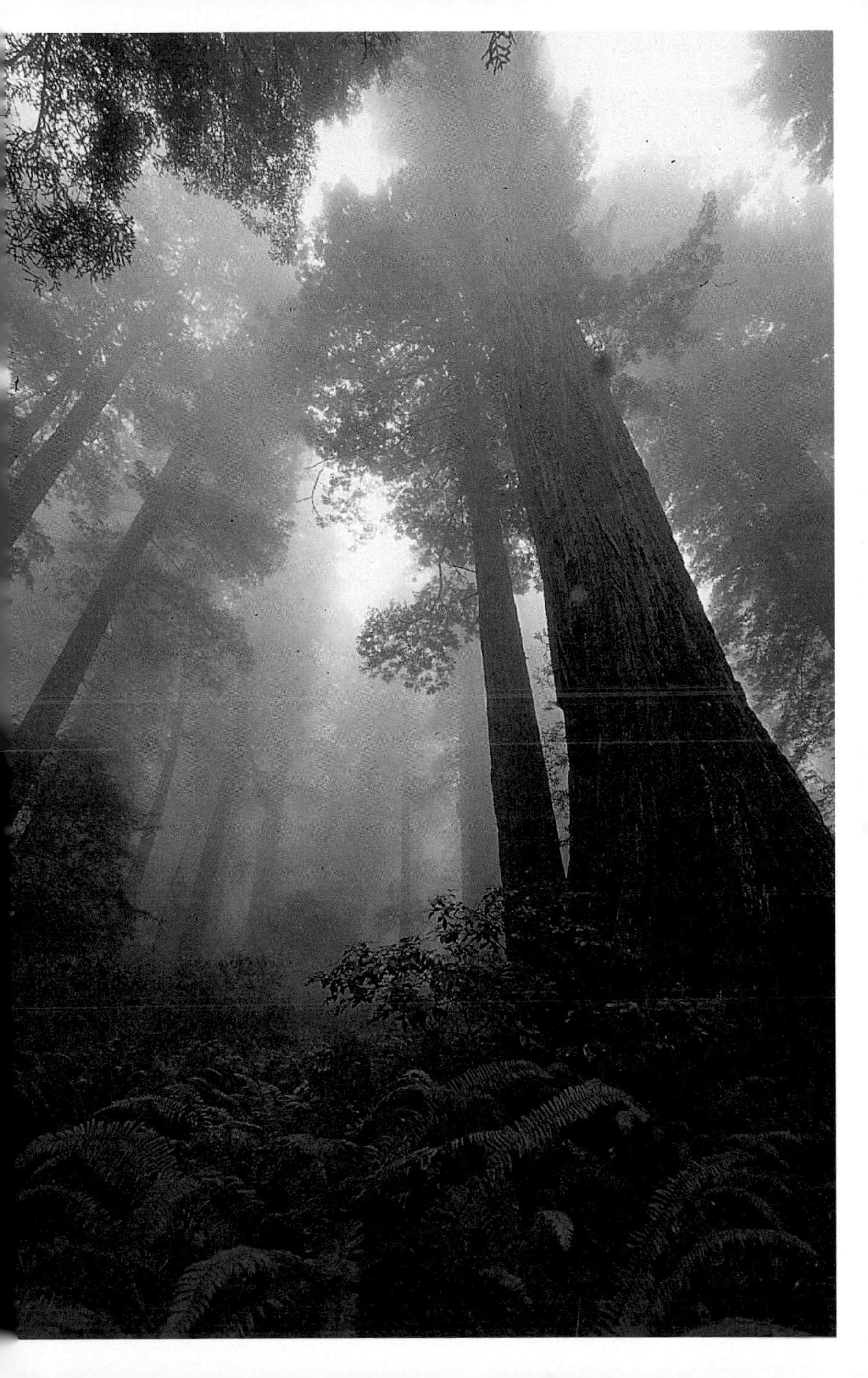

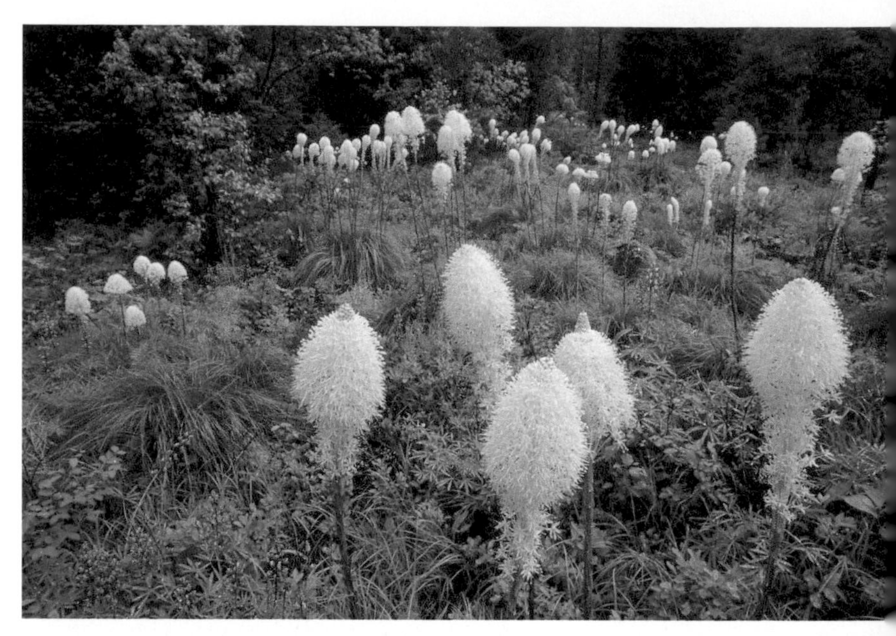

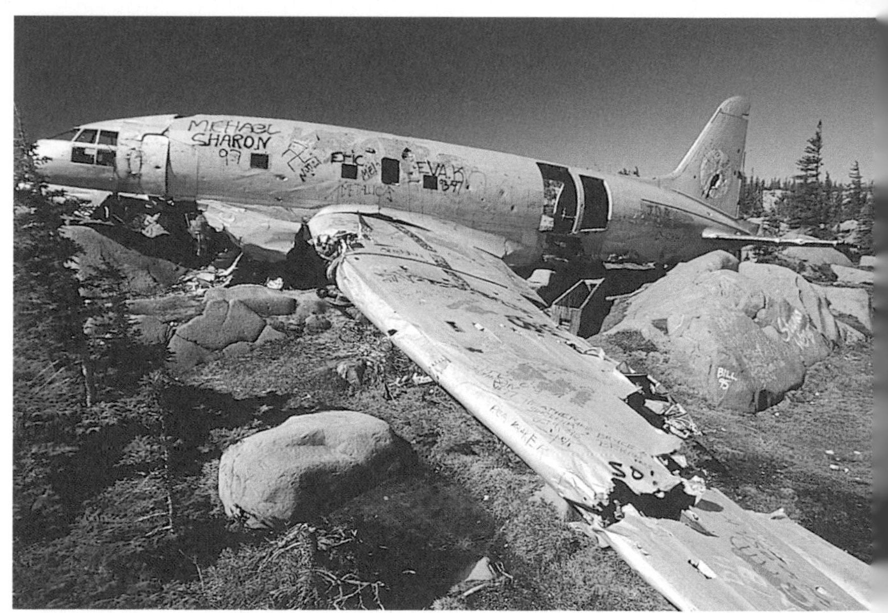
MICHAEL
SHARON
97
BILL
95

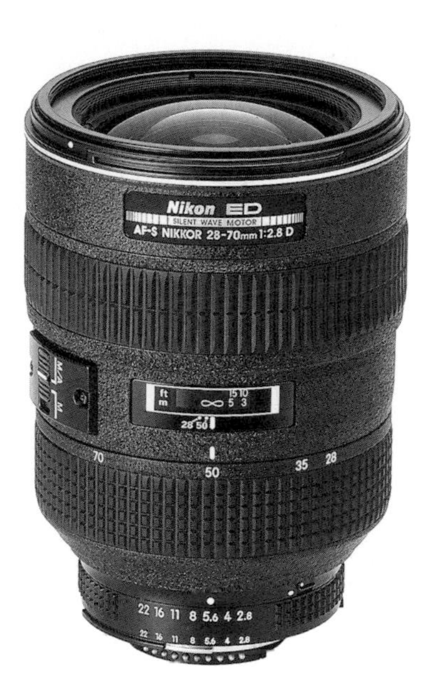

Nikkor 28-70mm f/2.8D
ED IF AF-S

Page 126, top:
Take advantage of early-morning or late-afternoon lighting, and you will be rewarded with results like this soft scenic taken with the versatile 28-70mm f/2.8 AF-S.

Page 126, bottom:
Telephoto lenses are known for their ability to compress the subject spatially from front to back. This characteristic can be used to add impact to a scene where distinct picture elements are scattered throughout the view— whether they are cars, signs, or (as in this case) a flock of wading birds.

Page 127:
The wide world of the 15mm f/3.5 isn't even wide enough for the towering coastal redwoods.

Page 128, top:
What appears to be popcorn on a stick is really bear grass in the Montana Rockies, captured by a 20mm f/2.8 AF.

Page 128, bottom:
I used my 20mm f/2.8 AF to document the detail in this eerie picture of a wrecked plane.

Nikkor 28-70mm f/2.8D ED IF AF-S

Original release: 1998
Angle of coverage: 74°-34°
Physical size: 5 x 3.5 inches (12.7 x 8.9 cm)
Weight: 31.7 ounces (890 g)
Filter size: 77mm
Lens hood: HB-19 (supplied with lens)
M.F.D.: 2.5 feet (0.7 m)
Aperture range: f/2.8-f/22
Unique features: None

The 28-70mm f/2.8D ED IF AF-S is one of my favorite lenses—and probably one of Nikon's sharpest lenses of all time. A zoom of really an unconventional range, it took the lens market by storm and was instantly a much-sought-after lens, rapidly becoming one of the legends that are hard to keep in stock.

This is a physically stout lens. Basically 77mm in diameter from the filter threads to the lens mount, this lens has the muscle to match its weight. It incorporates the AF-S (Silent Wave) motor, which provides it with lightning-fast focusing. The ED glass, IF, and AF-S design all combine to make this heavy lens incredibly sharp.

Being an AF-S lens, the 28-70mm f/2.8D incorporates a M/A switch, which up until now was a feature found only on long telephotos. This added flexibility and versatility only make this lens even more attractive to the photographer. If you own this lens, I highly recommend you have it in the M/A mode all the time; it's like eating your cake and having it too!

The 28-70mm f/2.8D also incorporates a nine-blade aperture. While this doesn't sound special, it makes out-of-focus elements in the background softer, more natural appearing. Combined with the fast f/2.8 maximum aperture, this lens can isolate and make a subject pop like few others.

While I can't write enough glowing things about this lens, I don't recommend it to every photographer. Its size, weight, and price don't make it the perfect lens for everybody; the design and specs of this lens make it clear it was made for the photojournalist. That's not to say only a few can own it, but in all honesty you could buy the new 28-105mm f/2.8D zoom—and still have beautiful optics and a few dollars left in your pocket to buy film. If you want the sexiest lens in this focal length, though, this is the one.

Nikkor 28-70mm f/3.5-4.5D AF

Original release: 1992
Angle of coverage: 74°-34°20′
Physical size: 2.8 x 2.7 inches (7.1 x 6.9 cm)
Weight: 12.4 ounces (347 g)
Filter size: 52mm
Lens hood: HB-6
M.F.D.: 1.3 feet (0.39 m)
Aperture range: f/3.5-f/22
Unique features: Aspherical element

Ever wonder why, with 35-70mms and 28-85mms already in existence, Nikon would introduce a small 28-70mm f/3.5-4.5? The lens is intended for the casual photographer who shoots with a camera with built-in flash. Larger lenses tend to cause cutoff of the camera's in-board flash, creating a dark line in the photograph; this is especially the case with any type of close-up work. The small size of the 28-70mm eliminates this problem, which is why it was added to the Nikon system.

Wonder how they made the lens so small? The 28-70mm has an aspherical element that is not usually found in zoom designs. This enables the lens to be physically small, yet render tremen-

Nikkor 28-70mm f/3.5-4.5D AF

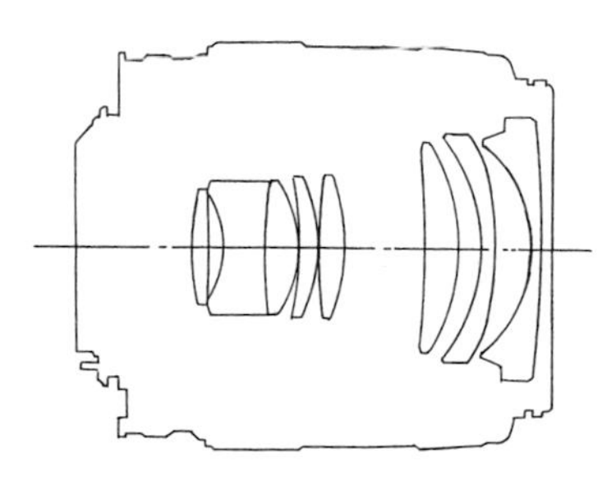

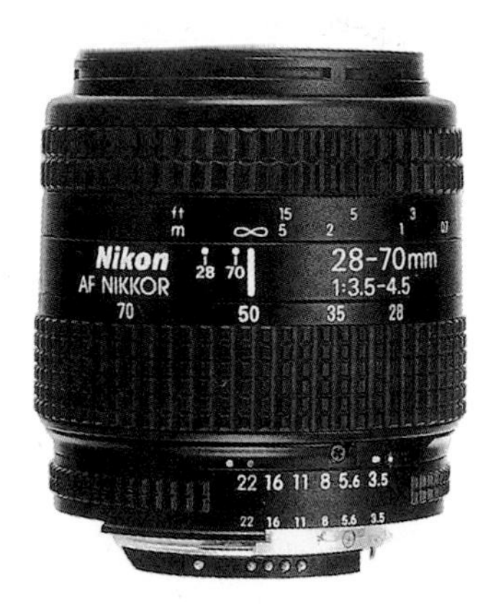

dous sharpness. It also makes the lens very bright and clear to focus even in low light levels.

One drawback to the 28-70mm f/3.5-4.5D AF is that its focal length is generally not popular with "serious amateurs" or pros; another is that it is a "two-touch" lens—a two-ring zoom-and-focus operation. This is what keeps the lens from being widely used, but it certainly was not designed with that goal in mind. It is instead an excellent example of Nikon's commitment to produce optics that fit a specific requirement, filling every photographer's needs.

Nikkor 28-105mm f/3.5-4.5D IF

Original release: 1999
Angle of coverage: 74°-23°
Physical size: 3.2 x 2.9 inches (8.1 x 7.3 cm)
Weight: 17.1 ounces (480 g)
Filter size: 62mm
Lens hood: HB-18
M.F.D.: 0.7 foot (.22 m)
Aperture range: f/3.5-f/22
Unique features: 1/2 life size macro

The 28-105mm f/3.5-4.5D IF is a sweet little lens that is receiving very little fanfare. Its variable f/stop formula is the first thing photographers seem to notice, but don't judge a book by its cover; this small lens delivers big results.

The 28-105mm is a very compact lens, probably because it was designed especially for the traveling or vacationing photographer. But the 28-105mm incorporates a hybrid aspherical element that aids in the small lens size while delivering great results.

If you're a photographer on the go, traveling the world, or the family photographer in charge of recording all the events, this is the lens for you. The very versatile focal length covers everything from the landscape or family gathering to the intimate details or individual portrait. And it does this while providing you with image quality that is really hard to beat.

Nikkor 28-200mm f/3.5-5.6D IF AF

Original release: 1998
Angle of coverage: 74°-12°20′
Physical size: 3.4 x 3.1 inches (8.6 x 7.9 cm)
Weight: 19.6 ounces (556 g)
Filter size: 72mm
Lens hood: HB-12 (supplied with lens)
M.F.D.: 7 feet (2 m)
Aperture range: f/3.5-f/22
Unique features: None

The size and price of the 28-200mm f/3.5-5.6D IF AF led many potential users to think it's not that great—but nothing could be further from the truth. Following on the 24-120mm, this lens delivers the same quality, in the same compact design.

This lens was purposely designed for the not-so-advanced photographer who wants a sharp, small, wide-range lens for little money. While that might have been the modest intent, the final package is a hot little number that incorporates a hybrid-aspherical element and IF design, elements normally reserved for the more pricey lenses. But it's these little extras that make this a marvelous lens for the "one lens" photographer. Match the 28-200mm f/3.5-5.6D IF AF up with the N60 or F100, grab some film—and you could be out shooting for months and never need another lens. That's the idea behind this lens, and it delivers.

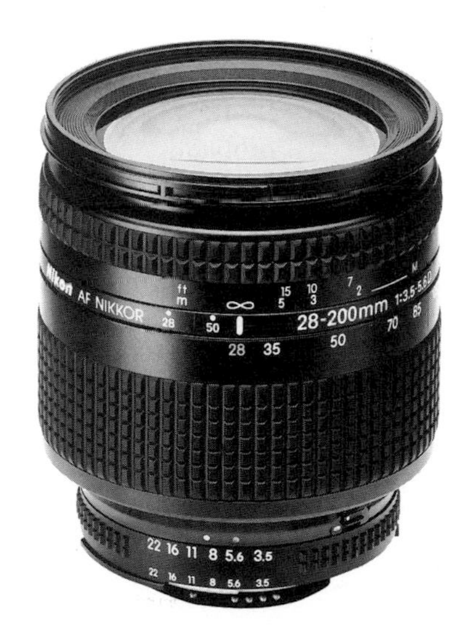

Nikkor 28-200mm f/3.5-5.6D IF AF

Nikkor 35-70mm f/2.8D AF

> **Original release:** 1992
> **Angle of coverage:** 62°-34°20′
> **Physical size:** 3.7 x 2.8 inches (9.4 x 7.1 cm)
> **Weight:** 23.5 ounces (658 g)
> **Filter size:** 62mm
> **Lens hood:** HB-1
> **M.F.D.:** 0.9 foot (0.3 m)
> **Aperture range:** f/2.8-f/22
> **Unique features:** Macro mode

The 35-70mm f/2.8 D AF was one of the original AF lenses to be released. It is one of the few that was instantly accepted and has never been modified since its introduction (except for "D" conversion). Although for many this is a dull and limited range, the 35-70mm is extremely popular with those in the press. Its constant f/stop is what has caught the attention of other photographers—and from this, word of mouth has made it one of the more popular AF lenses.

The 35-70mm f/2.8D's sharpness from corner to corner adds to the versatility of this zoom. It is a push-pull operation, with 35mm at the end of the push. This is where the lens must be set to use Macro mode (35mm focal length only). It has the ability to

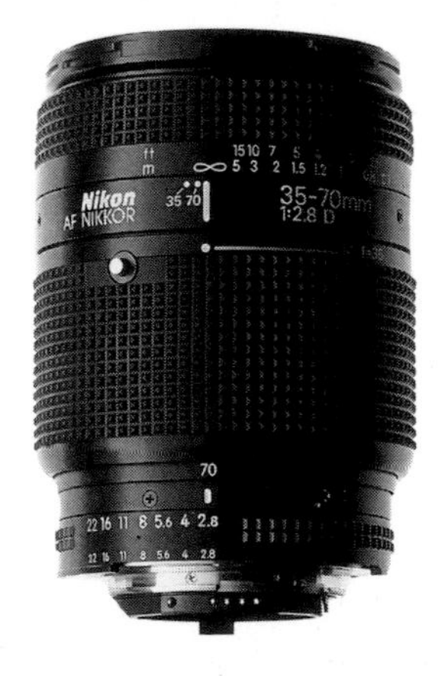

Nikkor 35-70mm f/2.8D AF

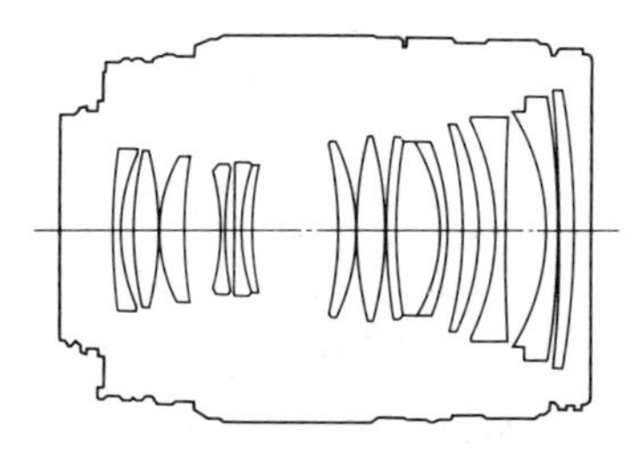

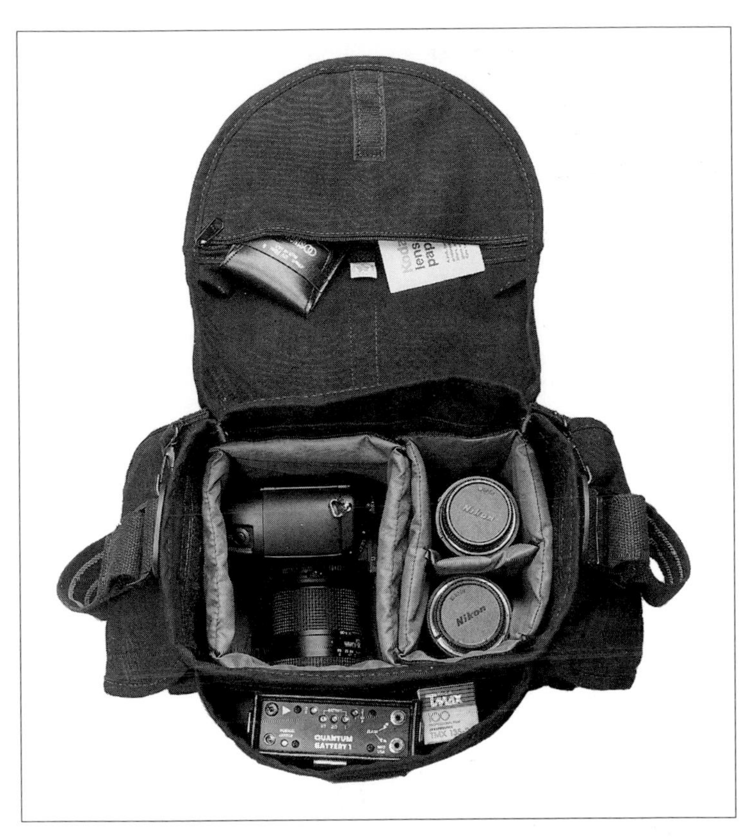

Domke's F-4AF "Pro System" bag is designed to accommodate a variety of autofocus systems.

achieve 1:4 magnification at this setting; with the addition of a PK-11a extension tube or 6T filter, the lens can reach nearly 1:1 magnification. It provides a free working distance of approximately seven inches (17.8 cm) in Macro mode. Even in this application, the lens still performs magnificently.

Physically, the 35-70mm is big, as much as 300% larger than other versions. Its price tag is just as inflated, but even so, the lens is extremely popular. This is due in part because it is a push-pull zoom rather than a two-ring affair. It is also due to its fitting into a basic system of 20mm f/2.8D AF, 35-70mm f/2.8D AF, and

75-300mm f/4.5-5.6 AF lenses. These three lenses, all with the same filter size, provide coverage of a tremendous range with the best lens quality available.

Nikkor 35-80mm f/4-5.6D AF

Original release: 1993
Angle of coverage: 62°-30°10′
Physical size: 2.7 x 2.6 inches (6.9 x 6.6 cm)
Weight: 6.3 ounces (176.4 g)
Filter size: 52mm
Lens hood: HN-3
M.F.D.: 1.2 feet (0.3 m)
Aperture range: f/4-f/22
Unique features: Macro mode

The 35-80mm f/4-5.6D AF is an interesting little lens, made to go up against the inexpensive off-brand lens for the first-time camera buyer; it delivers nice results and is a good little lens for such a buyer. If you're serious about photography, though, this is probably not your best investment.

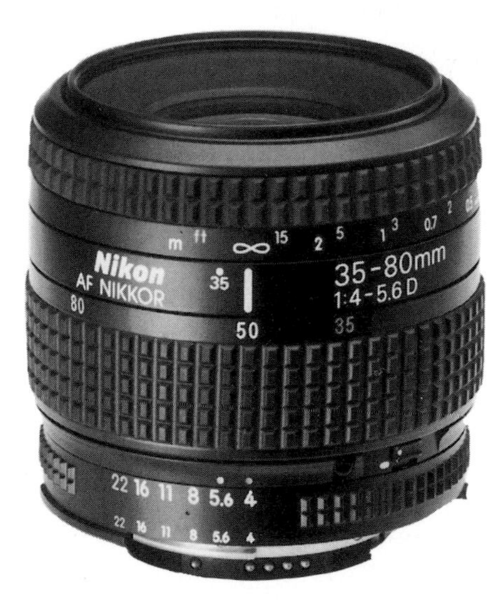

Nikkor 35-80mm f/4-5.6D AF

Nikkor 35-105mm f/3.5-4.5D AF

Original release: 1991
Angle of coverage: 62°-23°20′
Physical size: 3.4 x 2.7 inches (8.5 x 6.9 cm)
Weight: 16.1 ounces (451 g)
Filter size: 52mm
Lens hood: HB-7
M.F.D.: 1.3 feet (0.4 m)
Aperture range: f/3.5-f/22
Unique features: Macro mode

The 35-105mm f/3.5-4.5 has always been a popular focal length with general shooters; its small size and price have only enhanced its popularity. Family photographers especially like this focal length, which is great for group shots as well as individual portraits. The redesign of the cosmetics version placed many of the original design on the used lens shelf, making them an excellent first zoom purchase.

This version's biggest improvement is in its response. The zoom has a push-pull action, while the original version had a two-ring operation. At the end of the zoom collar is the focusing ring, which travels with the collar when zooming. This makes for fast reaction time.

The lens has a Macro mode with a maximum of 1:3.5 magnification (105mm focal length only); its excellent free working distance lends itself to macro work. The addition of Nikon's three extension tubes, PK-11a, PK-12, and PK-13, achieves a little better than 1:1 magnification, and the lens delivers marvelous quality—probably why this is a lens commonly found in the nature photographer's bag.

Nikkor 50-300mm f/4.5 ED

A throwback to the beginnings of Nikon, the 50-300mm f/4.5 had the greatest zoom range of its day. A big lens, its zoom is a two-ring affair—one ring zooms, the second focuses. Its moderate f/stop and great range create a large package that few photographers can handhold. Its optical design and ED glass make it an amazingly sharp lens at any focal length.

The only limitation to this lens' versatility is that because fil-

Original release: 1978
Angle of coverage: 46°-8°10′
Physical size: 9.7 x 3.9 inches (24.6 x 9.9 cm)
Weight: 4.3 pounds (1.9 kg)
Filter size: 95mm
Lens hood: HK-5
M.F.D.: 8.5 feet (2.6 m)
Aperture range: f/4.5-f/32
Unique features: ED glass

tration is restricted at the front, many photographers tape filters to the rear. The lens is probably is owned by very few, though, despite its quality and versatility. It is used mostly by nature and wildlife photographers, who enjoy its zoom range and very bright image. It is particularly well suited for working from a blind, where its zoom range becomes quite handy.

The earlier versions of the 50-300mm f/4.5 ED can be found used with little effort. This is probably the best version, but you should not hesitate to buy an older one. As it is relatively low priced, this lens is a great help in determining which focal length fits your style of photography. It is also great for remote work if there is any concern over the lens' welfare. Because of its size and weight, wind has very little effect on it, another bonus when using it remotely. The 50-300mm f/4.5 ED is a lens you'll probably see in use only rarely. Those who do own it, though, are very loyal and have remarkable images to substantiate its performance—perhaps why, in this age of speed and autofocus, the lens is still available from Nikon.

Nikkor 70-210mm f/4-5.6D AF

Original release: 1993
Angle of coverage: 34°20′-11°50′
Physical size: 4.5 x 2.8 inches (11.4 x 7.1 cm)
Weight: 20.6 ounces (577 g)
Filter size: 62mm
Lens hood: HN-24
M.F.D.: 4 feet (1.2 m)
Aperture range: f/4-f/32
Unique features: Macro mode

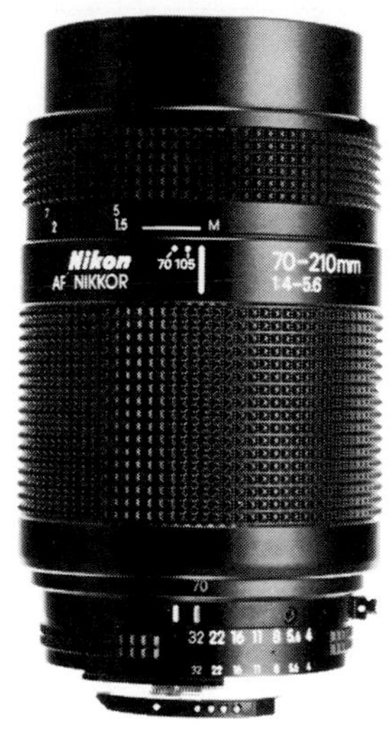

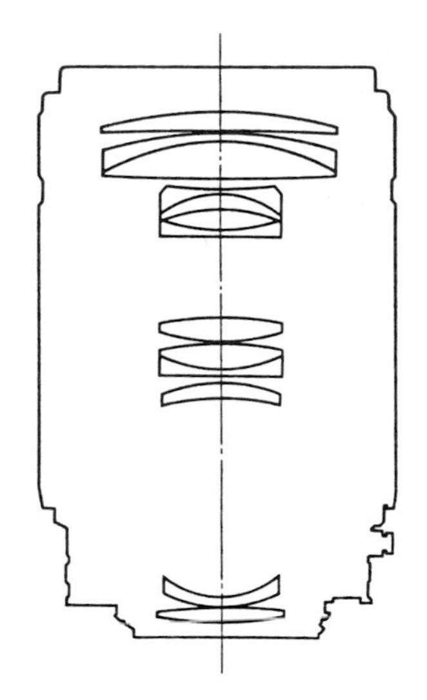

Nikkor 70-210mm f/4-5.6D AF

One of the first AF lenses to be introduced, the 70-210mm f/4-5.6D AF has gone through a number of changes. An "N" version represented cosmetic, operational (push-pull) and optical changes that improved its overall performance. The "D" is an identical lens to the 70-210N, with the addition of the "D" technology; the change from a fixed f/4 to a variable f/stop is what made it smaller. Its compact size, ease of use, and economical price make this lens extremely popular.

All versions of the 70-210mm have excellent sharpness. This is also true for corners, which is not typical for zooms. It has a Macro mode providing a 1:4.5 magnification—not earth shattering. Trying to use extension tubes to extend this range has minimal results as far as increasing magnification, but there is no optical loss. Nikon's close-up attachments, 5T and 6T, work great, though.

If there is a drawback to the 70-210mm f/4-5.6D AF, it is its zoom range. Other lenses now incorporate this range and speed in their design, somewhat bypassing the 70-210mm. This is by no means an indication of the quality of this lens—just a natural state in photography as more versatile optics are introduced.

Nikkor 70-300mm f/4-5.6D ED AF

Original release: 1998 **Angle of coverage:** 39°20′-8°10′ **Physical size:** 4.6 x 2.9 inches (11.7 x 7.4 cm) **Weight:** 18.2 ounces (510 g) **Filter size:** 62mm **Lens hood:** HB-15 **M.F.D.:** 5 feet (1.5 m) **Aperture range:** f/4-f/32 **Unique features:** Macro mode

Like so many of Nikon's lower priced lenses, the 70-300mm f/4-5.6D ED AF came in under a cloud of controversy. This marvelous little lens can be considered as the unofficial replacement for the 75-300mm f/4.5-5.6 AF. In a smaller package, with the addition of ED glass and the polycarbonate construction, it's a lens for the millennium year.

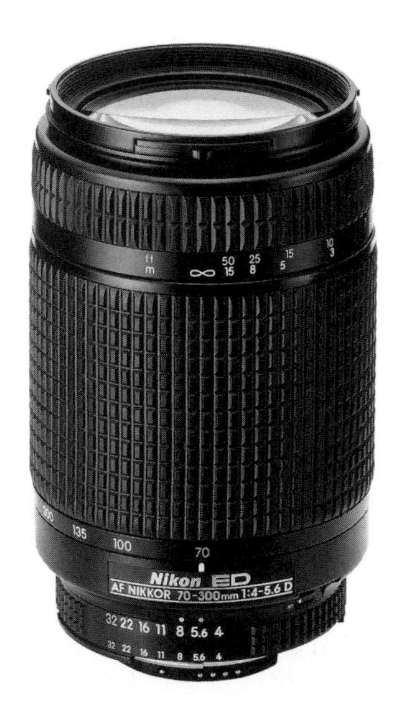

Nikkor 70-300mm f/4-5.6D ED AF

This is a small lens, with the traditional 62mm filter size. Its 18.2-ounce weight, though, makes it a marvelous lens for anybody desiring a sharp 300mm lens in a lightweight package. Whether for traveling or hiking, this one lens delivers beautiful images throughout its entire range. Part of its lighter weight is the lack of a tripod collar, which was on the 75-300mm. This might make it a little more difficult to use on a tripod shooting vertically, but it shouldn't really be a problem.

The close focusing ability of the 70-300mm is slightly better than the 75-300mm. By having a 62mm filter size, the Nikon close-up attachments 5T and 6T can be used on the 70-300mm, making it a marvelous macro lens. It has an excellent working distance doing this, so flash or other light modifiers can be used easily with the lens.

The last thing you should do is to underrate this lens because of its price or weight—it delivers the quality Nikon is well known for. I can't think of a better lens, in fact, for the new wildlife or sports photographer.

Nikkor 80-200mm f/2.8D ED IF AF-S

Original release: 1992
Angle of coverage: 30°10'-12°20'
Physical size: 7.3 x 3.4 inches (18.5 x 8.6 cm)
Weight: 2.64 pounds (1.19 kg)
Filter size: 77mm
Lens hood: HB-7
M.F.D.: 4.9 feet (1.47 m)
Aperture range: f/2.8-f/22
Unique features: Macro mode

The 80-200mm f/2.8D ED IF AF-S is one of Nikon's finest lenses—totally new optical design, incorporating an AF-S (Silent Wave) motor, ED glass, and IF focusing, all wrapped up to produce a truly beautiful lens. After shooting side by side with other photographers using the previous AF 80-200mm f/2.8, I know personally that the AF-S version is the fastest in the land.

Its speedy f/stop provides it a shallow depth of field. Many indoor sports photographers prefer this lens just for that reason;

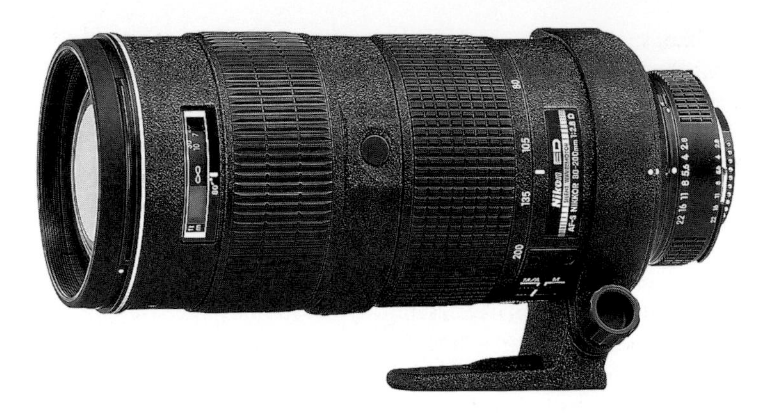

Nikkor 80-200mm f/2.8D ED IF AF-S

this holds true as well for fashion-runway and wildlife photographers. Its extreme clarity while wide open makes it a marvelous tool for isolating subjects.

The one controversy or complaint about the 80-200mm f/2.8D ED IF AF-S has been its tripod mount. If the tripod collar lock has been slightly loosened when rotating the lens, there is a "chatter." Now I personally don't think this is a big deal, because I never shoot when rotating a lens from vertical or horizontal. It's after seeing the final image that I judge a lens, and I know this is one of the sharpest lenses Nikon has come out with. To me, this small operational "announce" is not a big deal. The tripod collar is removable, which I think is a marvelous feature and one I use all the time; I shoot with it handheld continually.

The 80-200mm f/2.8D ED IF AF-S has the same-style deep bayoneting lens shade as the 28-70mm f/2.8D ED IF AF-S. The HB-15 is one of the biggest lens hoods I've seen for a short lens, ever! It does provide great flare protection, even when shooting in the direction of the sun. You could shoot in the rain and not worry about the front element getting wet. But if you're using a polarizer and want to turn it, you'd best have a chopstick with you!

The 80-200mm accepts the TC-14E and TC-20E teleconverters. The optical quality of these combos is mind-boggling, and the images are beautiful. The AF speed is just as fast with the teleconverters attached; just remember that there is a loss of depth of field between the effective f/stop and actual f/stop.

Finally, I must mention the amazingly low price of this lens—truly making this version of the legendary 80-200mm one of the best ever.

Nikkor 80-200mm f/4.5-5.6D AF

Original release: 1995
Angle of coverage: 30°10′-12°20′
Physical size: 7.4 x 3.4 inches (18.8 x 8.6 cm)
Weight: 11.6 ounces (324.8 g)
Filter size: 52mm
Lens hood: HR-1
M.F.D.: 5 feet (1.5 m)
Aperture range: f/4.5-f/32
Unique features: None

The 80-200mm f/4.5-5.6D AF is really a simple little lens with a simple price for those photographers wanting to simply have fun. It was announced and released with no great fanfare. It's not talked about much on the Internet chat rooms or forums, either. But this low-priced lens is hard to find in camera stores because those wanting Nikon quality at a low price and are not fixed on speed have snapped up this fine lens.

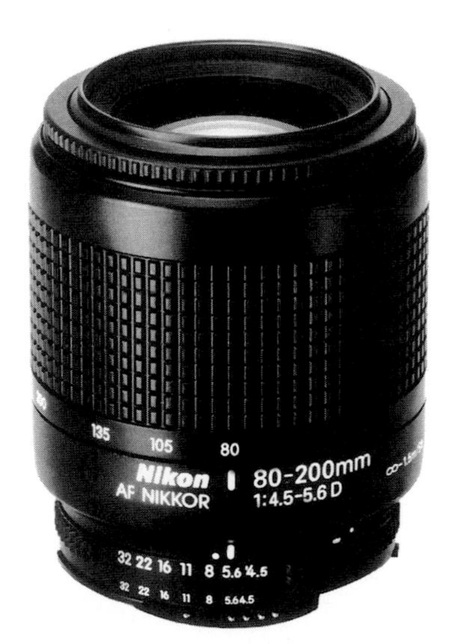

Nikkor 80-200mm f/4.5-5.6D AF

Nikkor 80-400mm f/4.5-5.6D ED VR AF

Original release: 2000
Angle of coverage: 30°10′-6°10′
Physical size: 10.4 x 5.5 inches (26.4 x 14 cm)
Weight: 2.5 pounds (1.1 kg)
Filter size: 77mm
Lens hood: HB-24 (supplied with lens)
M.F.D.: 7.5 feet (2.2 m)
Aperture range: f/4.5-f/32
Unique features: VR

A superb introduction to the new century from Nikon! I know, folks want to know about the Vibration Reduction (VR) technology, but there's a lot more to this lens—for example, it's smaller than the 80-200mm f/2.8 AF-S by inches and it focuses down to just 7.5 feet. Its optical design, with three ED glass elements and a nine-bladed diaphragm, delivers amazing results from this lens at all focal lengths.

The VR technology in this lens does work, but the difference you'll see depends on your abilities; if you know how to properly handhold a lens and pan the camera, for instance, you may not benefit much from it. Nikon claims the system is equivalent to using a shutter speed that is three stops faster, so you have a better chance for making those slow-shutter-speed and low-light photos really sharp. If you're shooting from a car, boat, or other moving vehicle, the VR technology might give you a hand as well. The lens would be outstanding without the VR, but the VR does make it sweeter.

Nikkor 180-600mm f/8 ED

Original release: 1974
Angle of coverage: 13°40'-4°10'
Physical size: 16 x 14.1 inches (40.6 x 10.4 cm)
Weight: 7.9 pounds (3.6 kg)
Filter size: 95mm
Lens hood: HN-16
M.F.D.: 8.5 feet (2.6 m)
Aperture range: f/8-f/32
Unique features: None

The 180-600mm f/8 ED is the super telephoto of the zoom world (there was a 360-1200mm, but it has been discontinued). Physically long, it is surprisingly easy to use because of its narrow profile. It is basically 95mm or smaller in diameter throughout the entire length of the lens, lending itself to many applications where larger lenses would be inappropriate.

The 180-600mm f/8 ED has never caught on in popularity because of its speed and price. It is an old design, which is reflected in its size and speed. While it seems like a perfect lens for wildlife photography, few are in the field because focusing it is slow. Four handles can be attached to the massive zoom collar (it is a push-pull zoom), which is also the focusing ring. These handles are attached to facilitate speed in focusing. A substantial degree of turning must be done to focus on a subject at varying distances. Because this is a slow procedure, many images are lost in the process. The incredible zoom range and tack-sharp images are hard to argue with once you've become fully comfortable manipulating it. For 99% of the photographers, the 180-600mm is forever tripod bound; one photographer I know, though, is very proficient in using it on a gunstock.

One of the very surprising attributes that has always attracted me to this lens is its minimum focusing distance. At 600mm, it is 8.5 feet. No other 600mm lens can do the same; a photographer working in a blind, for example, could get photographs with this lens that no other lens could produce.

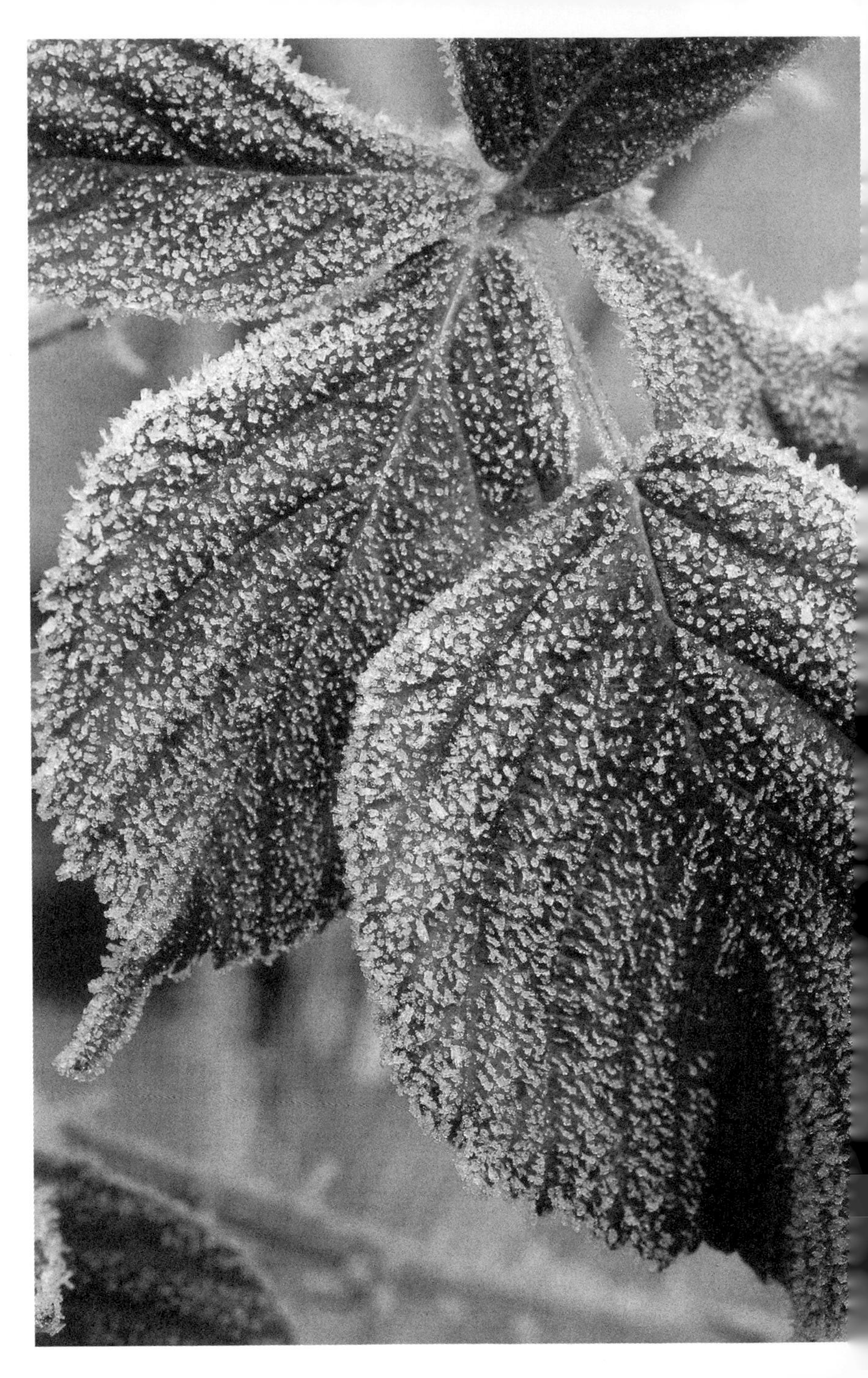

Specialty Lenses

Using the Tools

This very specialized group of lenses has only one thing in common: each is designed to fill a particular and unique niche in photography. Where other groups of focal lengths might have been linked by more general techniques common to each group, that is not the case with these lenses.

Because some of the features and design attributes of other lenses of the same focal length may apply to these specialized lenses, reading about similar lenses in the other chapters will be helpful. But most of these features and attributes are specific to the particular lens—which is why they are specialty lenses.

Nikkor 58mm f/1.2 Noct

Original release: 1978
Angle of coverage: 40°15′
Physical size: 2.5 x 2.9 inches (6.4 x 7.4 cm)
Weight: 16.4 ounces (459 g)
Filter size: 52mm
Lens hood: HS-7
M.F.D.: 1.7 feet (0.5 m)
Aperture range: f/1.2-f/16
Unique features: Aspherical lens

"[The 58mm f/1.2 Noct] was specially designed for photography at night and in poor light." This quote, from Nikon's dealer catalog, cuts right to the heart of the 58mm f/1.2 Noct. This lens was never intended for the general photographic public, and it has never been widely owned because of its price. All this adds up to making the 58mm one of the demigods of the Nikon system.

Fall leaves, tinged with frost, are a treasure-trove of photographs waiting to be taken with the 60mm f/2.8 micro.

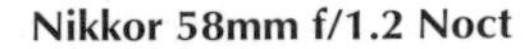

Nikkor 58mm f/1.2 Noct

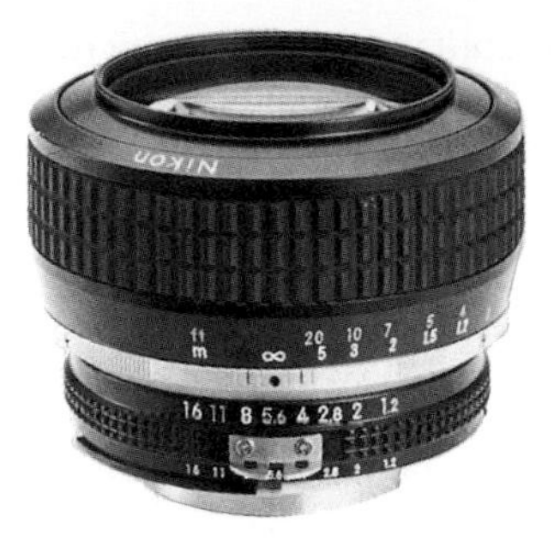

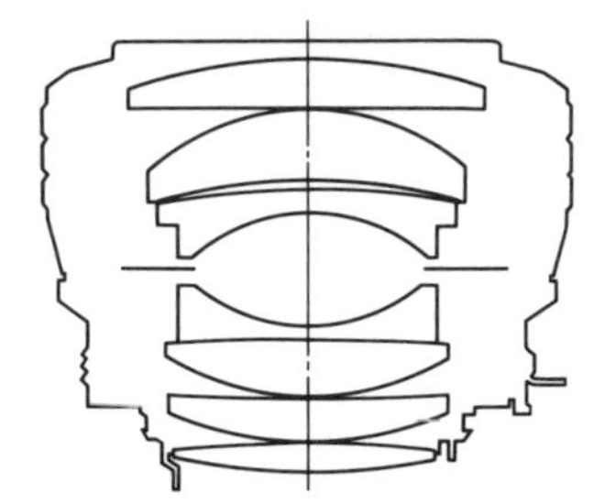

This lens is *sharp!* Its "improved optical system provides virtually distortion-free performance down to the closest focusing distance of 1.7 feet [0.5 m] as well as high-contrast images," notes the dealer catalog. The higher contrast of the lens enhances the perceived sharpness of the "Noct." Though the lens is already sharp, this increase in contrast over the normal Nikkor lens makes its images really pop.

What really makes the Noct a unique special-application lens is its aspherical front element—unlike the majority of speedy lenses, which have a large front element. This feature, states the dealer catalog, "assures optimum correction for coma, particularly at maximum aperture, thus making bright point sources of light near the edges of the picture frame appear as dots rather than comet-shaped blurs." Folks such as astronomers hook this lens to their telescopes for photography; because the stars (point sources) will be recorded accurately, any comet-shaped light might be just that—a comet.

Nikkor 60mm f/2.8D AF Micro

Original release: 1993
Angle of coverage: 39°40′
Physical size: 2.9 x 2.8 inches (7.4 x 7.1 cm)
Weight: 16 ounces (448 g)
Filter size: 62mm
Lens hood: HN-22, HN-23
M.F.D.: 8.8 inches (22.6 cm)
Aperture range: f/2.8-f/32
Unique features: Focuses 1:1

One of the first lenses Nikon ever manufactured was a micro. The 60mm f/2.8D AF micro—now with "D" technology—carries on Nikon's commitment to this specialized lens and its mission to outperform itself. Prior to the 60mm micro, this meant that all previous micros in this range have had a focal length of 55mm; they could reach the magnification of 1:1 only with the addition of an extension tube (matched PK-13). The 60mm micro departs from tradition in that it is able to go 1:1 without any tubes, but It carries on the high standards of previous Nikkor micros in sharpness and performance.

The 1:1 magnification is accomplished by an internal rearrangement of the element array. The elements physically move and change their relationship to each other with the addition of air gaps. In this way, the lens does not require adding an extension to the rear of the lens to get this magnification, as it is accomplished internally. This translates into only losing 1-2/3 stops when at 1:1, rather than the expected 2 stops. The free working distance at 1:1 is approximately 3.8 inches (9.5 cm).

The lens' autofocus isn't quick. The AF operation involves not only engaging it at the body, but on the lens as well. There is a ring with a lock button, which must be depressed before turning to engage the autofocus. To improve on the lens' AF ability, Nikon has included a limit switch to prevent it from searching for focus from infinity to its minimum focusing distance. The switch can be set to limit focusing within two zones—one foot (30.5 cm) to infinity and 8.8 inches (22.2 cm) to one foot. When the switch

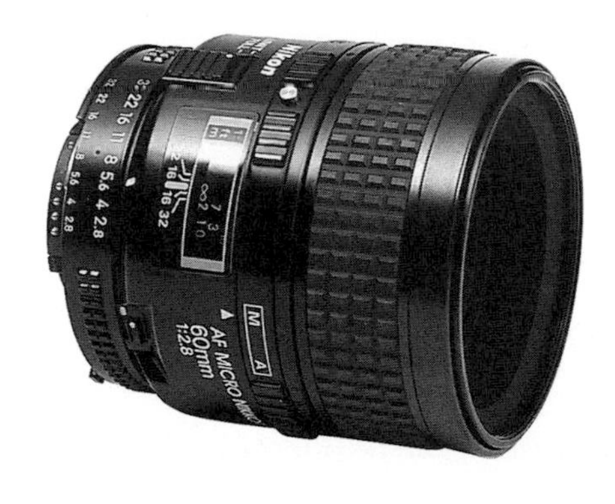

Nikkor 60mm f/2.8D Micro

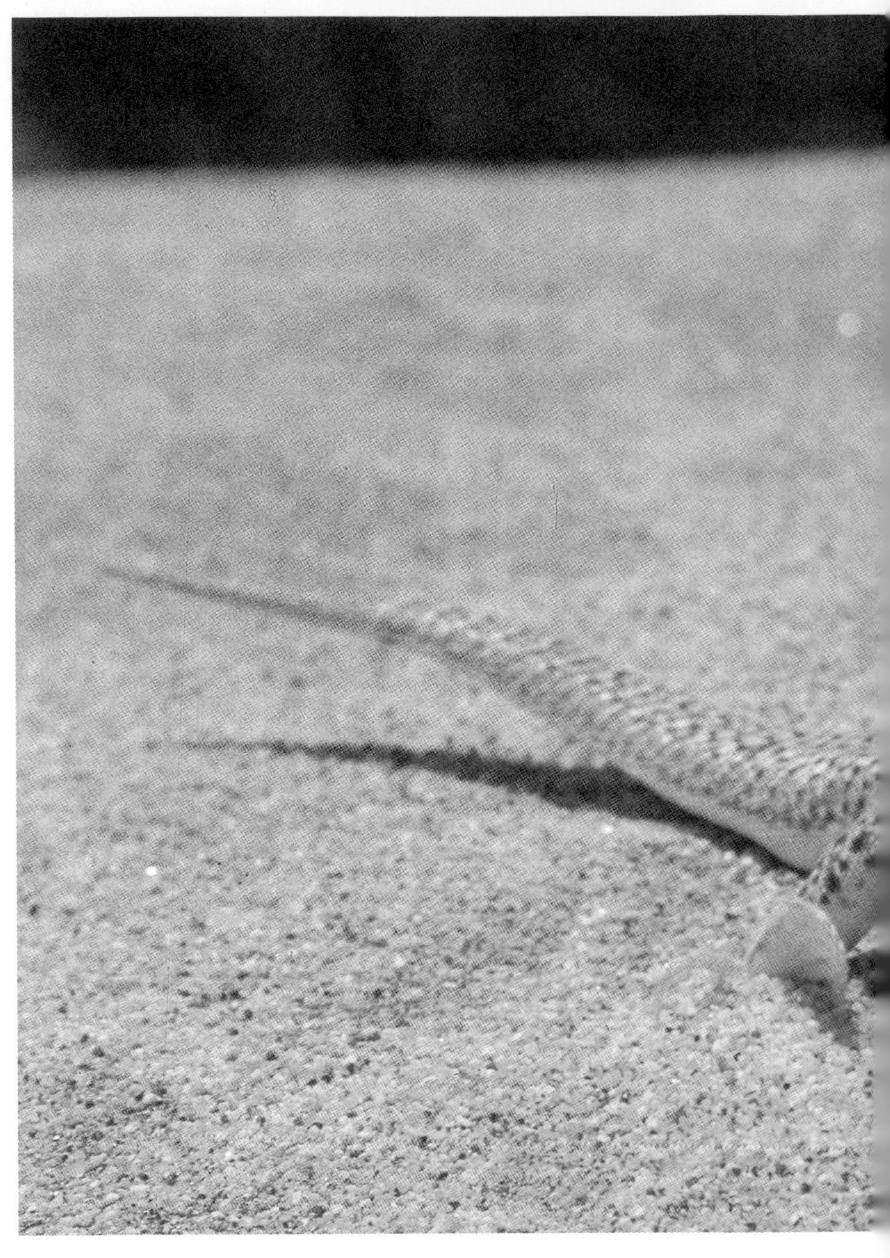

This close portrait of the endangered Coachella fringe-toed lizard was taken with a 60mm f/2.8 micro.

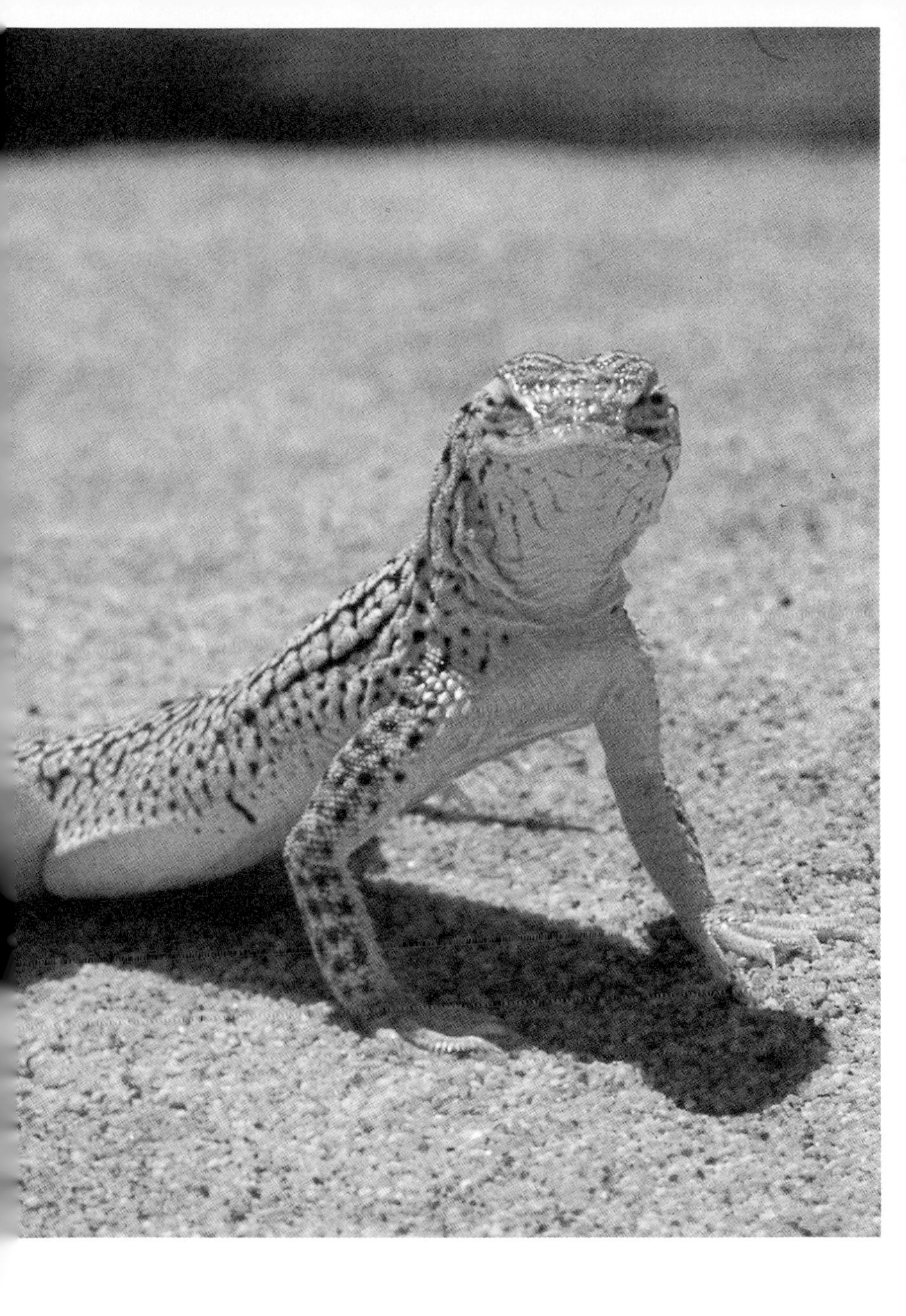

is on full, the full range of focusing is available. This switch affects both manual and AF operation.

Autofocus is not the most appropriate tool for shooting macro because the AF sensor is dead center. Many times the lens will have to search to find a focus point, and what it finds is often not the spot you had in mind. Macro focus is still better accomplished manually unless you are using the N90/F90. Remember that depth of field when working macro is very limited, so your focus had better be right on to make the most of what you have.

The 60mm has a depth-of-field distance scale for f/16 and f/32. Because f/32 means the lens is completely closed down (not recommended in most instances because of refraction), and f/16 generally does not offer enough depth of field for most 1:1 subjects, the depth-of-field chart leaves too much to the imagination. Most photographers shoot at f/22, and so devise their own depth-of-field chart to work with the 60mm. This can either be on a label placed on the lens or a chart that is held next to the lens barrel.

All of the legendary 55mm micros that preceded the 60mm incorporated Nikon's CRC (close-range correction) technology. The 60mm does not; instead, it achieves its tremendous edge-to-edge sharpness through the realignment of elements. This is probably the biggest departure from tradition for the 60mm and why it will probably be the most popular micro ever.

One other note—this lens works great at infinity as well. Do not pigeonhole this lens as "just a micro"—you will not be getting your money's worth out of it.

Nikkor 85mm f/2.8D PC Micro

Original release: 1999
Angle of coverage: 28°30'
Physical size: 4.3 x 3.3 inches (10.9 x 8.4 cm)
Weight: 27.3 ounces (775 g)
Filter size: 77mm
Lens hood: HS-7
M.F.D.: 1.3 feet (0.4 m)
Aperture range: f/2.8-f/45
Unique features: Tilt/shift mechanisms

The purpose of the 85mm f/2.8D PC lens is simple: to provide greater creative control over depth of field and perspective via the lens' tilt/shift in a 35mm format. While not being the sexiest lens around, it sure does deliver on its design purpose. First and foremost, this is one razor-sharp lens! But it is for the technically oriented. For example, this is not an AF lens, but the electronic rangefinder in the F5/F100 still functions.

Once the lens is mounted on the camera body, there is a locking lever near the base of the lens that, when depressed, permits the photographer to turn the lens to shoot horizontally or vertically. There are two click stops in between horizontal and vertical, permitting diagonal correction. Once you frame up your subject in the viewfinder, the next thing you need to do is take a meter reading. On the F5 (the F100 as well), the aperture control via the Subcommand dial on the body is gone; aperture control must be done using the preset aperture ring on the lens. There is a CPU in the lens, so aperture changes on the barrel can be communicated to the body and the correct shutter speed noted. Once you tilt or shift the lens, you can no longer use the TTL ambient light meter in the camera. All metering must be done prior to any lens movement.

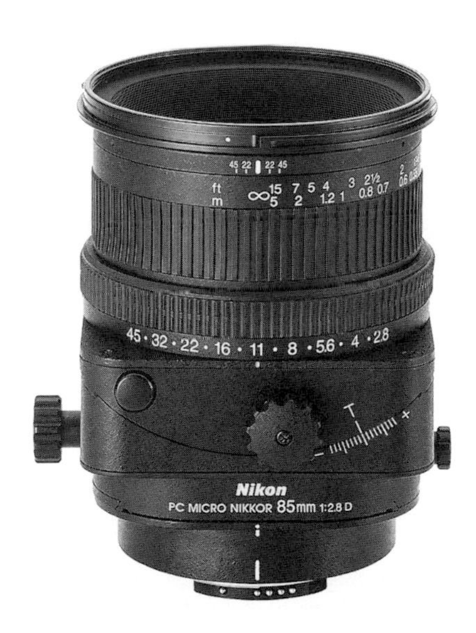

Nikkor 85mm f/2.8D PC Micro

The preset aperture on the 85mm f/2.8D PC can be held open for viewing/focusing via the aperture stopdown button (this is a cool feature!). This button holds the aperture open for viewing during focusing and composing but must be pushed, closing the aperture to the preset opening to take the actual photograph, to obtain the correct exposure.

The tilt mechanism in the 85mm f/2.8D PC is for controlling depth of field. There are two knobs for this action, one that actually tilts the lens barrel and another that locks the lens in place. The motion of tilting is silky smooth and you can easily tilt in full, horizontally and vertically, without fear of the image moving off the film plane. This can make a dramatic change in your plane of focus, vastly increasing your depth of field.

The shift mechanism of this lens is for perspective control. The instruction book that comes with the 85mm f/2.8D PC does an excellent job (via before and after photos) of giving the owner creative ideas on how this feature can be used. Basically, shifting the lens moves the lens barrel parallel with the film plane, moving the placement of the subject on the film plane while maintaining focus.

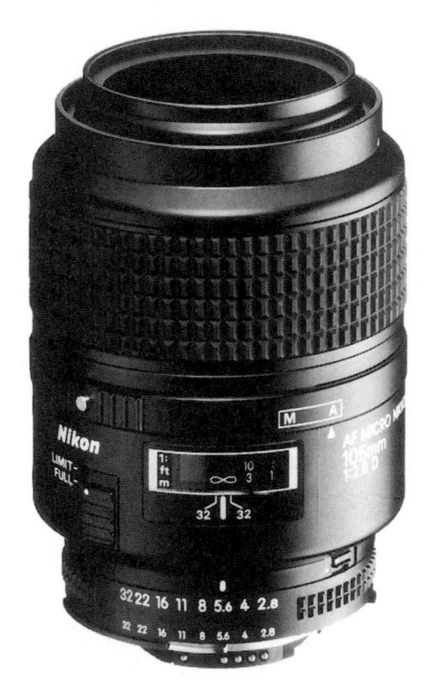

Nikkor 105mm f/2.8D AF Micro

Nikon created this lens with the macro/tabletop shooter in mind. This is why I believe the tilt and shift mechanisms are 90° from each other. You cannot use the shift mechanism to recompose after tilting, for example.

Where shooting with the 28 mm PC or 35 mm PC might seem confusing to the first-time user, the 85mm PC really isn't. The combination of today's camera bodies with a CPU on the lens for metering is a whole lot easier, making this lens literally a snap to use. It is particularly suited for the technically oriented photographer who is looking to squeeze every millimeter of depth of field out of an image. I'm very pleased to report that the lens delivers just that!

Nikkor 105mm f/2.8D AF Micro

Original release: 1993
Angle of coverage: 23°20′
Physical size: 4.1 x 3 inches (10.4 x 7.6 cm)
Weight: 19.6 ounces (549 g)
Filter size: 52mm
Lens hood: HS-7
M.F.D.: 1.2 feet (0.4 m)
Aperture range: f/2.8-f/32
Unique features: Focuses 1:1

Like the 60mm f/2.8D AF micro, the 105mm f/2.8D AF micro comes from a long line of micros. Beginning with the 105mm f/4 bellows lens, this current generation 105mm is by far the best. This is because it is able to focus 1:1 without extension tubes and because of its incredible image quality.

The 105mm employs the realigning element technology of the 60mm. In this way, the lens can focus 1:1 without the addition of 105mm of extension. This translates into not losing the normal 2 stops of light at 1:1, but instead having an effective f/stop of f/5 (1-2/3 stops). The free working distance at 1:1 is approximately seven inches (18 cm), less than the manual version but almost twice that of the 60mm.

This free working distance is the biggest factor to consider when deciding which micro lens to buy. This distance is important because of two factors: required distance from the subject and the use of auxiliary lights; shy or dangerous subjects require this extra distance for their and your safety. Adding flash or reflectors for lighting, which is common, can be a lot simpler with the extra free working distance. Trying to jam them in place when using the 60mm does not work well.

The 105mm is also a magnificent portrait lens, a testament to its tremendous flexibility. It can focus manually or automatically from 1:1 to infinity, and has a two-zone limit switch, same as the 60mm f/2.8D AF micro, to speed up AF operation.

If there is a drawback to the design of the 105mm f/2.8D AF, it is that its filter size is 52mm. As so many lenses are currently 62mm, this throwback to early Nikon means carrying either a second set of filters or a step-up ring. Neither is a great alternative.

Nikkor 105mm f/4.5 UV

Original release: 1988
Angle of coverage: 23°20′
Physical size: 4.6 x 2.7 inches (11.7 x 6.9 cm)
Weight: 18 ounces (504 g)
Filter size: 52mm
Lens hood: None
M.F.D.: 1.57 feet (0.5 m)
Aperture range: f/4.5-f/32
Unique features: Records UV band of light

The 105mm f/4.5 UV probably wins the "least known, least owned" prize because its use is so specialized. It looks a lot like the 105mm f/2.8 micro (manual version), but its similarity to normal camera optics ends there.

According to the Nikon dealer catalog, "UV rays are electromagnetic waves around 200-400nm. The human eye is sensitive only within a range of 380-780nm, though it is possible to get valuable information from UV photography which the human eye cannot catch, particularly in fields as medical and forensic science, criminal lab work, and examination of fine art and industrial works." This explanation sums up the purpose of the 105mm f/4.5 UV well.

This lens is a special-order item, and not one you're apt to find on your neighborhood dealer's shelf. As you might surmise from its description, it was not designed for the average photographer, but it's the best example of Nikon's continuing commitment to manufacturing optics for the scientific community. It is not a micro lens.

Nikkor 120mm f/4 IF Medical

Original release: 1981
Angle of coverage: 18°50′
Physical size: 5.9 x 3.9 inches (15 x 9.9 cm)
Weight: 31.4 ounces (879 g)
Filter size: 49mm
Lens hood: None
M.F.D.: 4 feet (1.2 m)
Aperture range: f/4-f/32
Unique features: Built-in ring light

Nikon throughout its manufacturing history has made optics with specific scientific applications. The Nikkor medical lens series is a good example of this; the Nikkor 120mm f/4 IF medical is the most current lens of their designs.

All medical Nikkors have a ring light flash incorporated into their design. Powered by either an LA-2 (AC) or LD-2 (DC) battery, the flash has enough power to illuminate subjects at 2:1 with

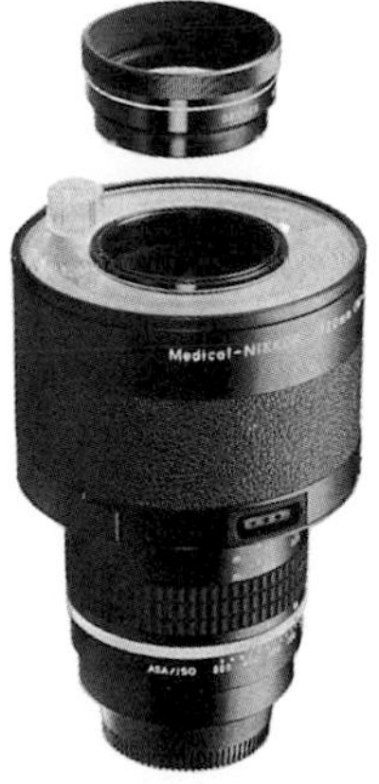

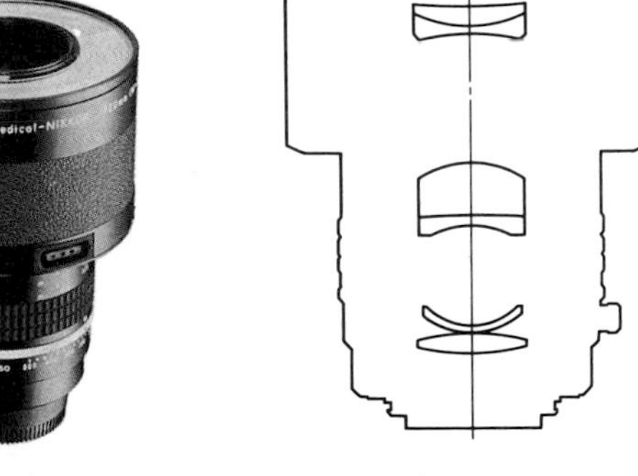

Nikkor 120mm f/4 IF Medical

maximum depth of field. The flash is built into the lens and encircles the front element. Two cords attach to the front of the lens barrel; one is the power cord and the other is the PC connection.

The flash does not have TTL technology. Instead, it uses a guide number system, such as the old 45GN. As the lens is focused at different distances, the lens automatically sets the aperture based on the focused distance. There are many drawbacks to this system, which current TTL technology handles better. Exposure compensation is best manipulated by changing the ISO on the camera. This makes for quick calculations and speedy return to zero compensation.

The 120mm f/4 IF medical focuses from 1:11 to 1:1 by itself (it cannot focus to infinity). By attaching its own special auxiliary close-up attachment, the lens focuses from 1:0.8 to 2:1. In addition, the lens has a built-in focusing lamp, so focusing can be easily performed. It also displays through-the-viewfinder magnification and ready light. The magnification can be imprinted on the film or turned off.

When first introduced, this highly specialized lens was very popular because it made many tasks easier. But in the almost twenty years since its introduction, innovations such as TTL have made its technology less desirable. Many lenses now use other optics with Nikon's SB-21, for example, rather than the 120mm f/4 IF medical, thus taking advantage of TTL while maintaining greater control over depth of field and exposure.

Nikkor 200mm f/4D ED IF AF Micro

Original release: 1993
Angle of coverage: 12°20′
Physical size: 7.7 x 3 inches (19.6 x 7.6 cm)
Weight: 2.6 pounds (1.2 kg)
Filter size: 62mm
Lens hood: HN-30
M.F.D.: 1.6 feet (0.5 m)
Aperture range: f/4-f/32
Unique features: CRC

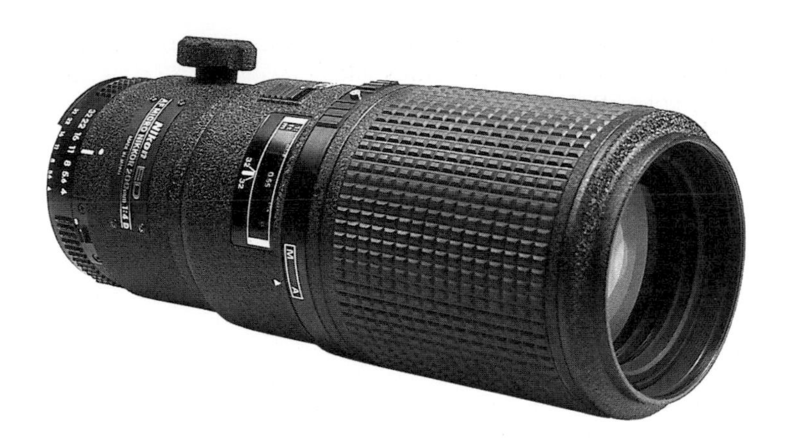

Nikkor 200mm f/4D ED IF AF Micro

The 200mm f/4D ED IF AF micro quickly rocketed to the top of the charts with its performance and flexibility. A completely new lens configuration, it demonstrates that Nikon lens designers continue to deliver the best. It still amazes me when I shoot with this lens to know just how small and light it is, with all the magnification and image power it delivers.

This amazing lens focuses from infinity down to 1:1 with a working distance (the distance between the front of the lens and the subject) of 10 inches (25.4 cm). It has an extremely sturdy built-in tripod collar, providing 360° rotation. Its ED glass and overall optical design deliver blistering sharpness throughout its focusing range. It has IF focusing, making focus quick while preventing the lens from expanding or contracting. The most amazing aspect of the 200mm f/4D ED IF AF micro is the fact it only loses 1-1/3 stop of light at 1:1. This is truly a gem of a lens. (The manual version is described in the oldies but goodies chapter.)

Nikkor 500mm f/8 Reflex

Original release: 1984
Angle of coverage: 5°
Physical size: 4.6 x 3.5 inches (11.7 x 8.9 cm)
Weight: 29.7 ounces (832 g)
Filter size: 39mm screw in
Lens hood: HN-27
M.F.D.: 5 feet (1.5 m)
Aperture range: Fixed
Unique features: None

Nikon has produced mirror lenses since it began manufacturing lenses. The company has constantly updated them throughout the decades, with the 500mm f/8 reflex the finest to date. There are many reasons for this, which tend to be overlooked as the stereotypes from previous versions still haunt this mirror lens.

The biggest improvement is in the mirror design. The catadioptric mirror of this 500mm f/8 reflex has been redesigned to virtually eliminate all chromatic aberration. Though the lens still produces the typical mirror lens "doughnuts" caused by out-of-focus background highlights, the sharpness of the lens is outstanding.

But the current version has more going for it than just sharpness. It is physically small, nearly 100% smaller than previous versions. This makes handholding the lens a snap, giving it added versatility. It can also focus down to five feet (1.5 m); the closest thing to it is the 500mm f/4 at 20 feet (6 m).

The drawback is that the 500mm f/8 reflex has a fixed aperture of f/8. Depth of field cannot be increased or decreased with this lens. A 39mm screw-in neutral density filter can be attached at the rear for manual exposure control (making the effective f/stop f/11), but this has no effect on depth of field. Other filters can be attached to manipulate color, but one filter must be in place at all times whatever the use.

The 500mm f/8 reflex works well with the 1.4x converter and marginally with a 2x. The TC-14B can be used with the 500 f/8 by removing the filter, which is the preferred method to achieve maximum sharpness. This creates a 700mm f/11 lens able to focus to five feet (1.5 m).

The mirror lens is commonly pooh-poohed by "serious" photographers because it is a mirror. This is a shame, as it can be very useful in many situations. In remote camera work, where a great deal of magnification is required and there is very little free working distance, the 500mm f/8N reflex's minimum focusing distance of five feet is a great option. When working from a canoe, where weight—as well as capsizing—is a concern, this relatively inexpensive lens is a great choice; this holds true for any situation where a super telephoto is required but where risking a multithousand-dollar lens is not advisable. Not that this lens is a throwaway, but it can be a problem solver where no other lens will work.

Nikkor 1000mm f/11 Reflex

Original release: 1977
Angle of coverage: 2°30′
Physical size: 9.5 x 4.7 inches (24.1 x 11.9 cm)
Weight: 4.2 pounds (1.9 kg)
Filter size: 39mm screw in
Lens hood: Built in
M.F.D.: 25 feet (7.5 m)
Aperture range: Fixed
Unique features: None

The 1000 f/11 reflex has been plagued with the same stereotyping as the 500mm mirror. In addition, its slow speed has dissuaded the majority of photographers from even trying the lens.

Though a sharp lens, the 100 f/11 reflex is a dark lens to focus, which hurts it. Only on bright days, when viewing is possible, does its sharp image shine through the viewfinder. Its long reach of 1000mm makes it a natural for wildlife photographers, but its doughnut-shaped highlights are very undesirable—not because they are unsightly, but because most photographers do not want others to know they use a mirror lens.

Will the current fast, high-quality films save the 1000mm f/11 reflex from oblivion? Doubtful, as the fixed f/11 is slow by any standard. Though it has a very narrow angle of view to isolate a subject, the f/11's deep depth of field lets in a lot of the world, nearly negating its isolating ability.

Nikkor 70-180mm f/4.5-5.6D ED AF Micro

Original release: 1997
Angle of coverage: 34°20'-13°40'
Physical size: 6. 6 x 3 inches (16.8 x 7.6 cm)
Weight: 34.9 (989 g)
Filter size: 62mm
Lens hood: HB-14
M.F.D.: 1.2 feet (0.4 m)
Aperture range: f/4.5-f.32
Unique features: None

Nikon introduced the 70-180mm f/4.5-5.6D ED AF micro as the "world's first autofocus zoom close-up lens," and from the first moment I connected it to my F5, I knew it was a great lens. Nikon further stated that "[From our] original idea of designing a new lens category—the zoom close-up lens—a lens has evolved that provides not just superb close functioning performance, but also a zoom range that is highly suitable for general photography." I have found this to be true.

The 70-180mm f/4.5-5.6D ED AF micro is a small, captivating lens that easily fits into any vest pocket. It has a tripod collar, providing extreme ease of use in the field. The ED glass delivers incredible image quality, shooting wide open whether it's a macro subject or a big-game species.

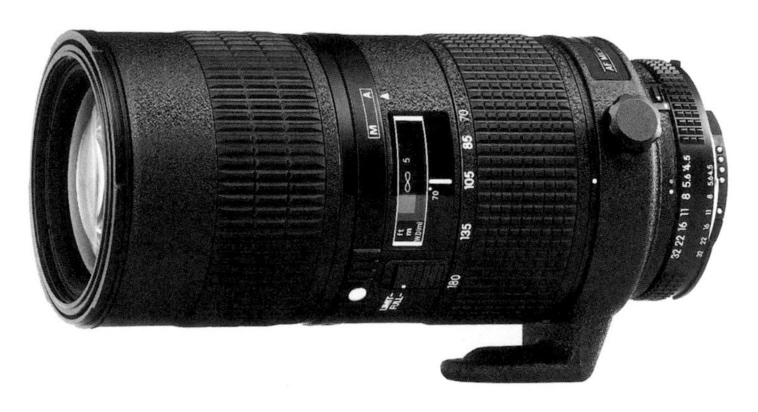

Nikkor 70-180mm f/4.5-5.6 ED AF Micro

The 70-180mm f/4.5-5.6D ED AF micro is a true zoom, meaning that once you focus the lens, the lens retains focus as you zoom. This is a two-ring zoom, one for focus and the other for zooming. The zoom ring is nice and wide, easy to work when wearing gloves. This is great when shooting macro and you want to crop the subject just so. The working distance with this lens when at 180mm and focusing to its closest distance (providing just slightly less than 1:1) is about five inches (12.7 cm). There is no macro setting, as there is in other zooms, but there is a true macro focusing capability. And if you want to get even greater magnification, you can attach the 6T filter, giving you nearly 2:1 magnification.

Just as you can go easily into Macro mode with this lens, you can slip into general shooting. This focal length is one of my favorites for shooting big game, such as elk and mountain goats. The lens' performance when photographing such subjects is tremendous, especially with the ease of use of filters. A lens so versatile, flexible, and of such incredible quality becomes a standout in my book.

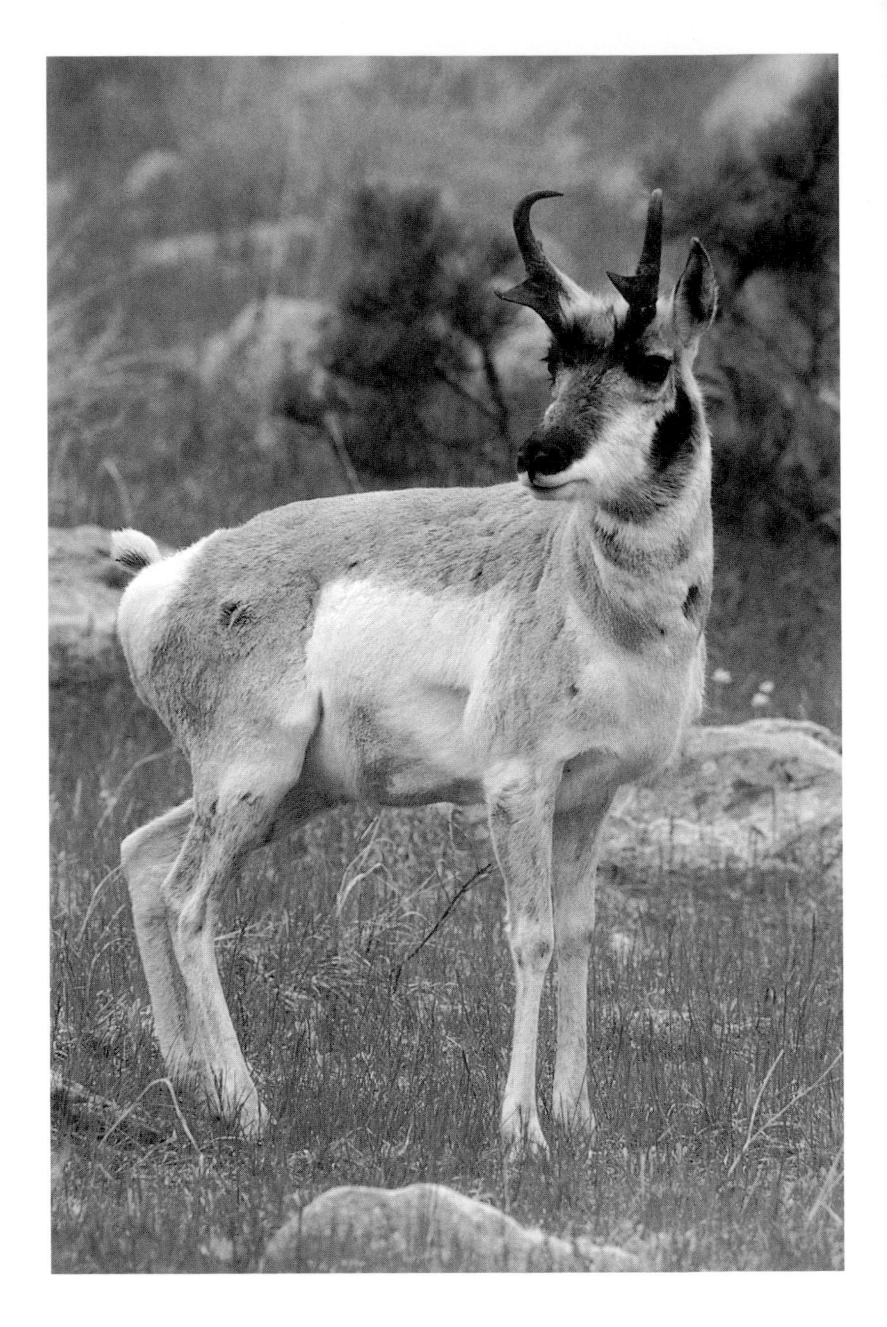

Teleconverters

Using the Tools

Teleconverters once had the stigma of being the poor man's telephoto. Quality and reliability were thought to have been sacrificed to save a buck. Though never true of Nikkor teleconverters, this stigma extended to them. It was not until Nikon introduced the 600mm f/4 with an accompanying TC-14 1.4x teleconverter did this all change. The TC-14 was not sold separately at first, but when demand grew, it was made available as an accessory.

The quality of the TC-14 was so good that Nikon's 2x teleconverters were finally taken seriously. Always expensive as far as teleconverters go, their optics matched their high price. Today, using a Nikon teleconverter is not only an accepted practice, but quite often a means of solving photographic problems that no other tool can solve.

Nikon produces only 1.4x and 2x teleconverters. The TC-14A and TC-14B are the 1.4x and the TC-201 and TC-301 are the 2x AI-type teleconverters. The lenses these teleconverters can be matched with have always been a confusing point. The rule of thumb that is generally used—TC-14A and TC-201 for lenses up to 200mm, TC-14B and TC-301 for 300mm and longer—is a loose fit at best.

The TC-14A and TC-201 have recessed front elements; the front element of the TC-14B and TC-301 protrudes out past the lens mounting flange. This is what you should go by when matching up converter and lens. A lens whose rear element is flush at its rear should be matched up with the TC-14A and TC-201. Lenses whose rear element is inset in the rear use the TC-14B and TC-301.

The 80-200mm f/2.8 AF-S is optically one of the finest zoom lenses available today. Coupled with the TC-14E, it is a killer combination that allows you to get in close while retaining near-perfect picture quality, as in this shot of a pronghorn.

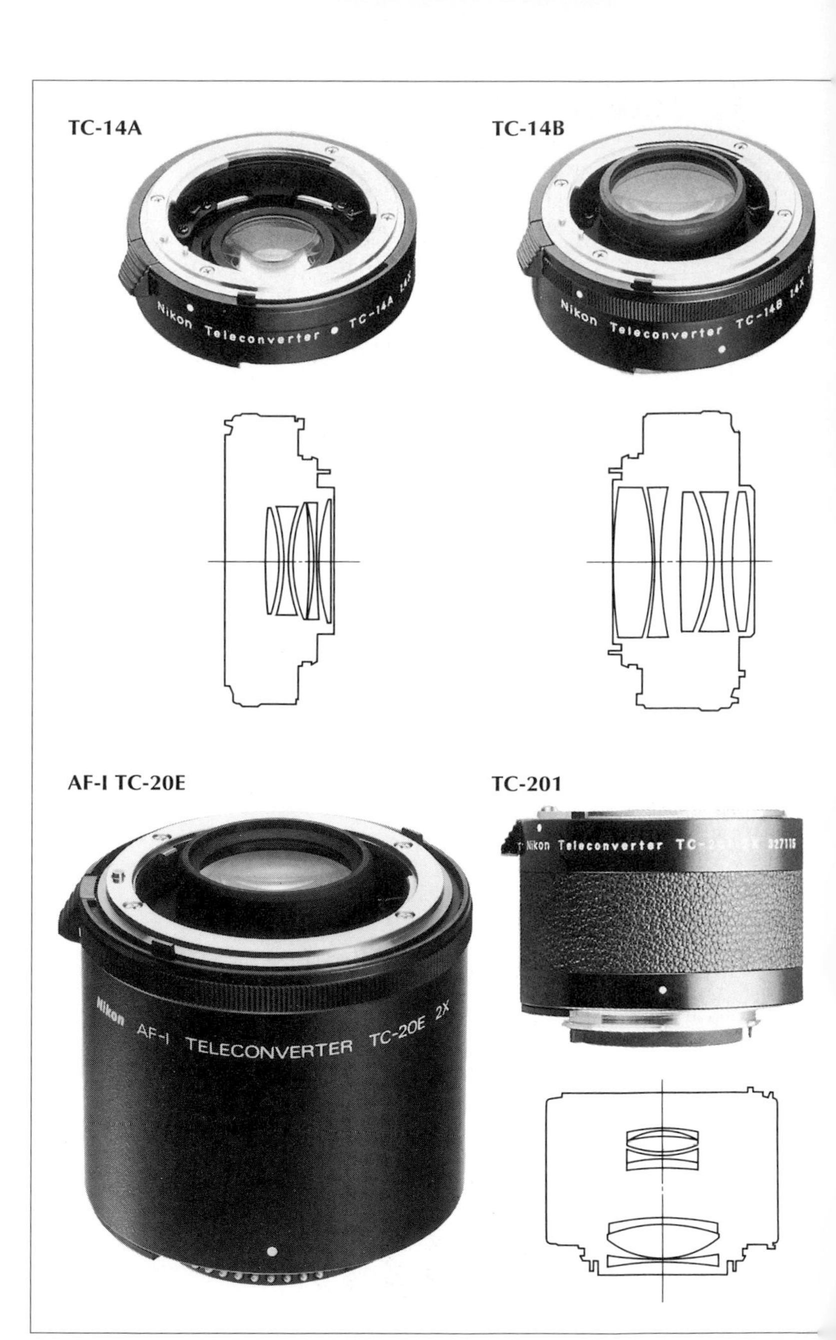
TC-14A
Nikon Teleconverter TC-14A
TC-14B
Nikon Teleconverter TC-14B
AF-I TC-20E
Nikon AF-I TELECONVERTER TC-20E 2X
TC-201
Nikon Teleconverter

TC-301

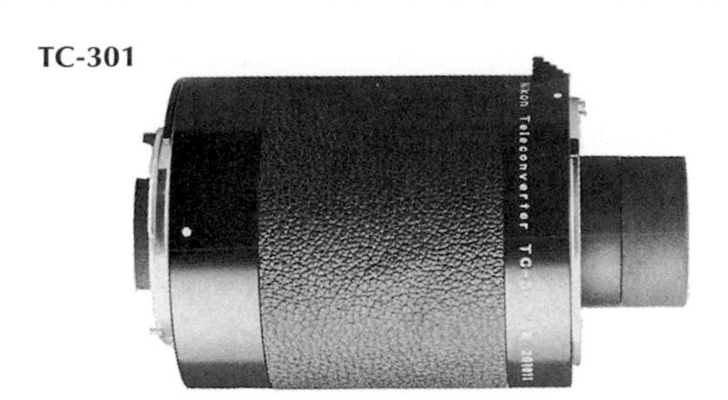

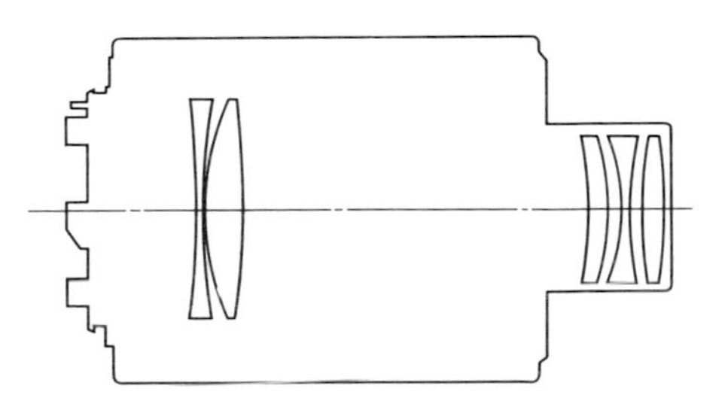

AF-I TC-14E

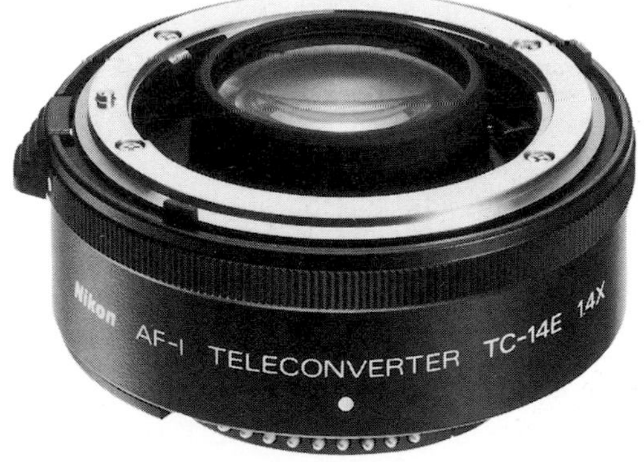

There are some exceptions to this. For example, the 200mm f/4 micro, which most photographers use with the TC-201, works best with the TC-301; the 500mm f/8N mirror lens works best with the TC-14B, with the rear filter removed; and the TC-14A and TC-201 can fit on and work with lenses whose rear element is inset, but often vignetting or loss of sharpness at the corners occurs.

Teleconverters do change the lens' effective f/stop. The TC-14A and TC-14B take up one full stop, while the TC-201 and TC-301 take up two. This means an f/2.8 lens will effectively be an f/4 with the TC-14A and B and an f/5.6 with the TC-201 and TC-301. The teleconverters also affect the lens' angle of view by 1.4x or 2x, corresponding to which teleconverter is in use; the reproduction (magnification) of a lens such as a micro is also 1.4x or 2x greater. The depth of field of the lens in use is decreased by 40% with the 1.4x, half with a 2x; it is not increased, nor is it the same as another prime lens equal in focal length to the lens and teleconverter combination.

This effect is one of the main reasons the teleconverter is used by pros. A longer focal length lens is acquired with greater isolation properties; a narrower angle of view and depth of field makes a super telephoto even more valuable as a tool. Such combinations as the 300mm f/2.8 with the TC-14B (becoming a 420mm f/4), the 500mm f/4 with the TC-301 (1000mm f/8), and the 600mm f/4 with the TC-14B (840mm f/5.6) are common throughout all disciplines of photography.

Are there any tricks of the trade to using a teleconverter? The isolating ability I just described is a biggie—it can apply to any lens and be used almost anytime. The exceptions are zooms. Except for the 180-600mm, 200-400mm, and other ED lenses, zooms do not perform well with a teleconverter attached.

And, except with the F4 camera, matrix metering is lost when using an AI-type teleconverter. This is because these teleconverters do not have electronics built into them to maintain communication between body and lens. AF-I lenses do not work with older teleconverters and must use only those matched to work with their electronics.

The TC-14E and TC-20E are the AF-I teleconverters. They are made specially for AF-I and AF-S lenses and are not meant for use with any other lenses. The TC-14E is the 1.4x and the TC-20E is the 2x. These teleconverters maintain full operation with all Nikon AF bodies and AF-I and AF-S lenses. The exceptions are the 600mm f/4 AF-I/AF-S and the TC-20E. AF operation requires an effective f/stop of f/5.6 or faster. The 600mm f/4, doubled, has an effective f/stop of f/8. This is beyond the range of the sensor, so it cannot work in AF with the TC-20E.

Nikkor TC-14A

Original release: 1984
Angle of coverage: 1.4x of lens in use
Physical size: 1 x 2.6 inches (2.5 x 6.6 cm)
Weight: 5.1 ounces (143 g)
Filter size: None
Lens hood: None
M.F.D.: Same as lens in use
Aperture range: f/2.8-f/45
Unique features: None

A marvelous teleconverter, the TC 14A works well on short-focal-length lenses. One of the best uses of this teleconverter is in macro work; when used with the 60mm f/2.8, for example, nearly 2:1 magnification is reached. It also works well with the 75-300mm zoom, an exception to the rule that teleconverters don't work well with zooms.

Nikkor TC-14B

Original release: 1984
Angle of coverage: 1.4x of lens in use
Physical size: 1.3 x 2.6 inches (3.3 x 6.6 cm)
Weight: 5.8 ounces (162 g)
Filter size: None
Lens hood: None
M.F.D.: Same as lens in use
Aperture range: f/2.8-f/45
Unique features: None

A very expensive teleconverter, the TC-14B is well worth every cent. This teleconverter is in wide use on every possible Nikkor

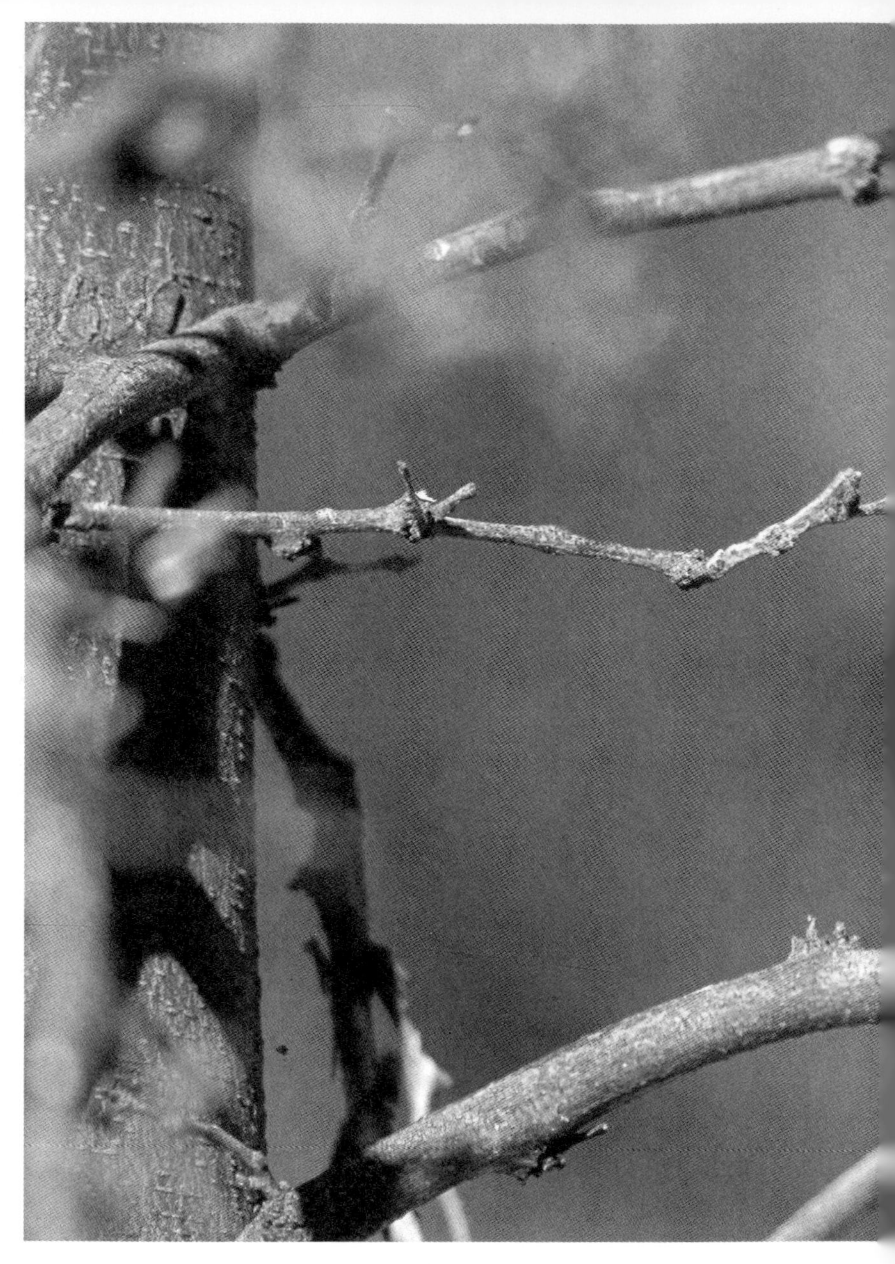

This portrait of the smallest owl in North America, the Northern Pygmy owl, was taken with an 800mm f/5.6.

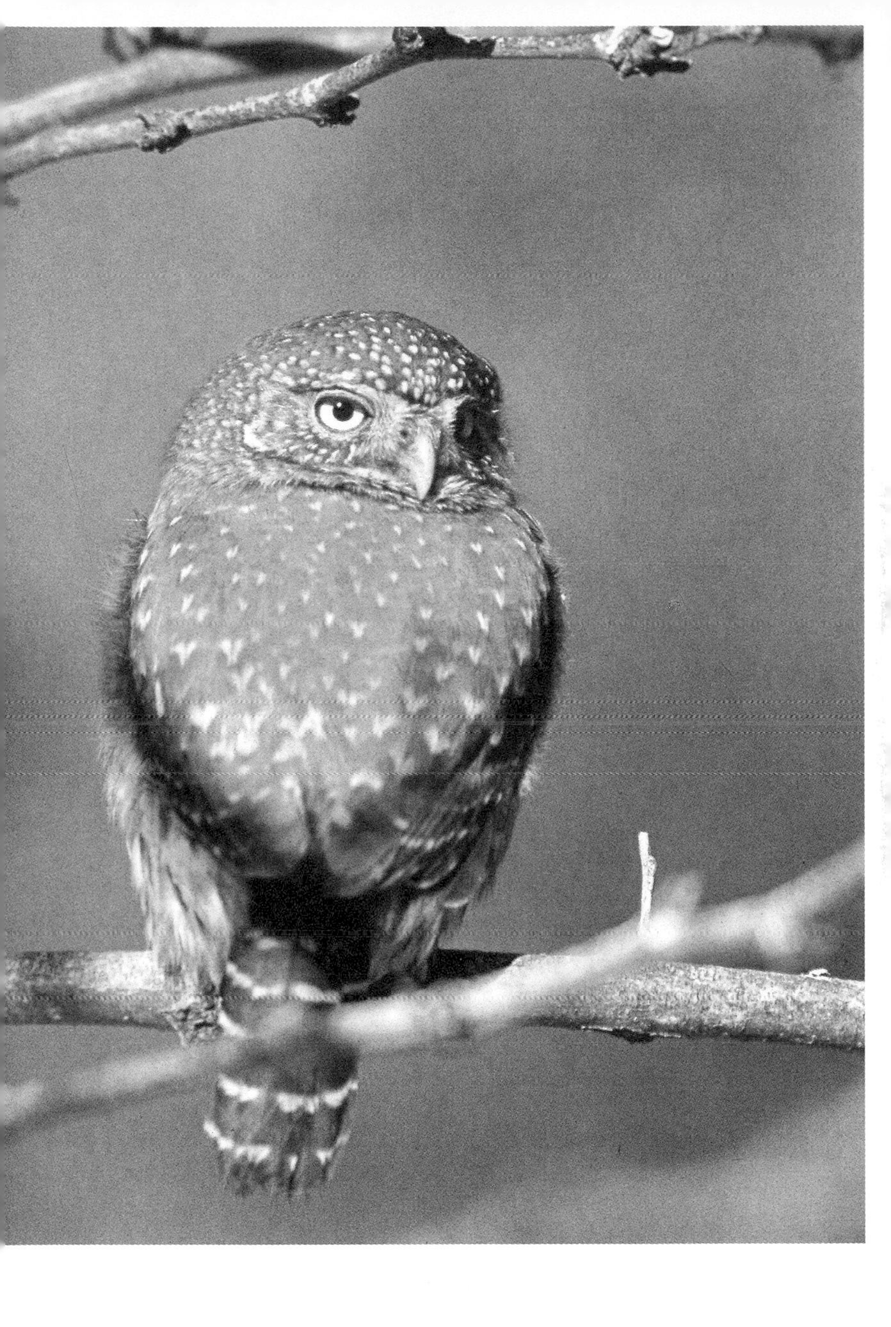

lens. Finding one—new or used—can be difficult because of its popularity. It improves every lens it works with.

Nikkor TC-14E

Original release: 1993
Angle of coverage: 1.4x of lens in use
Physical size: 1 x 2.6 inches (2.5 x 6.6 cm)
Weight: 7 ounces (196 g)
Filter size: None
Lens hood: None
M.F.D.: Same as lens in use
Aperture range: f/2-f/32
Unique features: Works only with AF-1 lenses

For owners of AF-I lenses, the announcement and then release of the TC-14E was music to their ears. Those owning the 300mm f/2.8 AF-I were probably the happiest, as the addition of the TC-14E makes it a killer 420mm f/4 AF-I that many photographers can hand hold.

Nikkor TC-20E

Original release: 1993
Angle of coverage: 2x of lens in use
Physical size: 2.2 x 2.6 inches (5.6 x 6.6 cm)
Weight: 12 ounces (336 g)
Filter size: None
Lens hood: None
M.F.D.: Same as lens in use
Aperture range: f/2-f/32
Unique features: Only with 300mm and 400mm AF-I

As few photographers have put the TC-20E to the test so far, not a lot of feedback is out on its popularity or performance. And, as doubling super telephotos is not as common as just adding a 1.4x, use of the TC-20E will be limited until other super telephotos, such as the 500mm f/4, are introduced as AF-I. Because the 500mm f/4 is one of the favorites to be doubled, its AF-I release will bring out great stories of the TC-20E's performance.

Nikkor TC-201

Original release: 1984
Angle of coverage: 2x of lens in use
Physical size: 2 x 2.5 inches (5.1 x 6.4 cm)
Weight: 8.1 ounces (227 g)
Filter size: None
Lens hood: None
M.F.D.: Same as lens in use
Aperture range: f/2-f/32
Unique features: None

One of the most commonly owned Nikkor teleconverters, the TC-201 has been used on every possible lens. And because it can work on every Nikkor lens, there really is no limit to the problems in photography it can solve. For many years, it was the way many got to 1:1 magnification with the 55mm micro. The TC-201 is a marvelous teleconverter, worthy of all the praise it receives.

Nikkor TC-301

Original release: 1984
Angle of coverage: 2x of lens in use
Physical size: 4.5 x 2.5 inches (11.4 x 6.4 cm)
Weight: 9.9 ounces (277 g)
Filter size: None
Lens hood: None
M.F.D.: Same as lens in use
Aperture range: f/5.6-f/64
Unique features: None

The TC-301 is probably the least owned of all Nikkor teleconverters because it is designed for super telephotos, whose owners normally do not double. The exception is the 500mm f/4, which is regularly transformed into a 1000mm f/8.

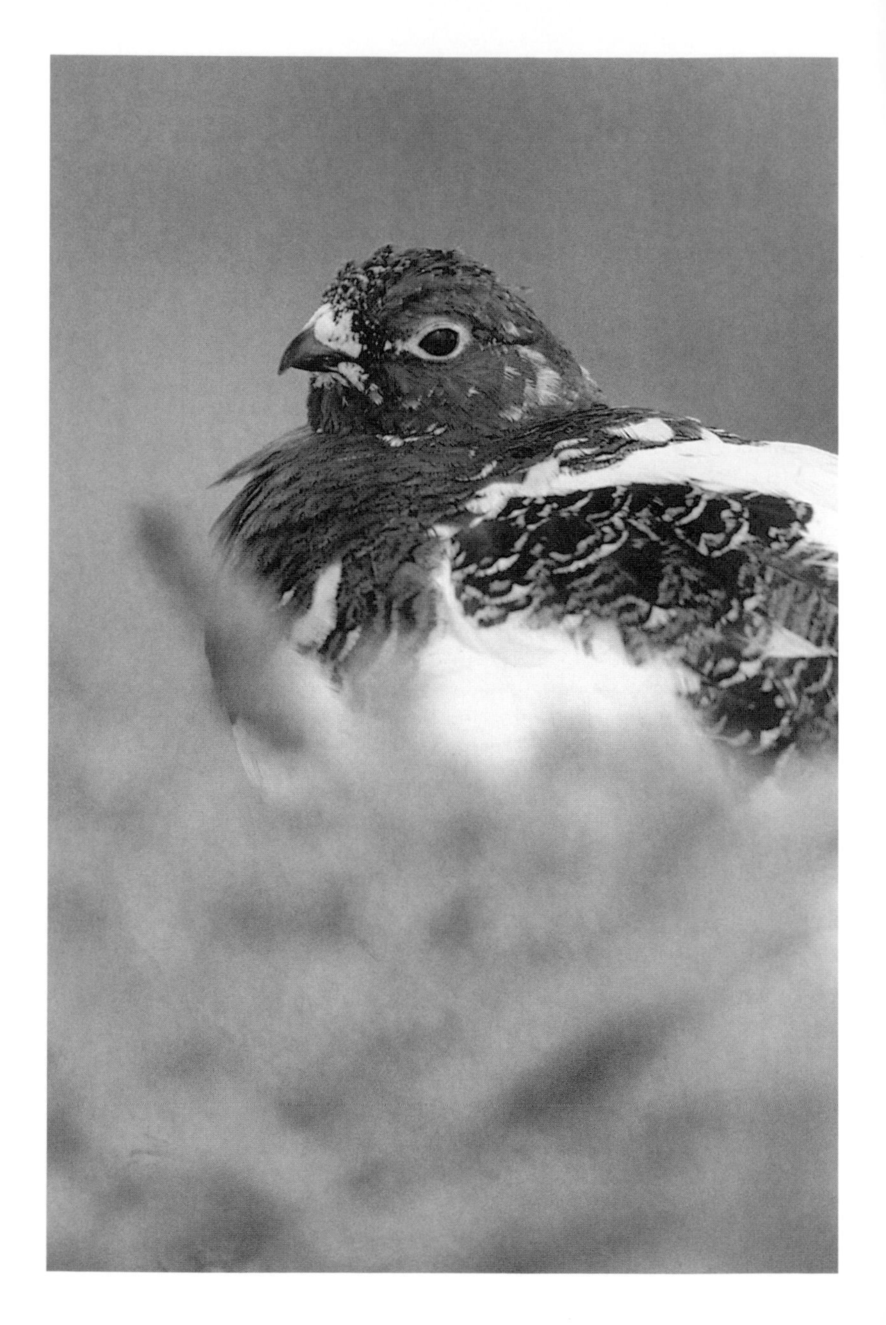

"Oldies but Goodies"

No one would argue that Nikon has always manufactured some of the world's finest optics. Many of its lenses, though out of production for a decade or more, are still found in photographers' bags. Some of these lenses are nearly impossible to find used and thus demand an incredible selling price when available. They are truly Nikon's "oldies but goodies."

Many of these now-classics are previous versions of current lenses written up in this book—including early manual lenses that are still extremely popular with today's photographers.

This list by no means covers all of the magnificent lenses in Nikon's past. Instead, it concentrates on those lenses still found in a majority of camera bags, or lenses still in high demand from the buying public. Others are lenses that have magnificent optics—and these, of course, can only be found used and at a high price. Finally, some of these lenses have been unfairly stereotyped, preventing many photographers from buying them. We'll argue these myths so that more photographers will be encouraged to try their incredible optics.

Nikkor 13mm f/5.6

Original release: 1976
Angle of coverage: 118°
Physical size: 3.9 x 4.5 inches (9.9 x 11.4 cm)
Weight: 2.7 pounds (1.2 kg)
Filter size: 39mm bayonet
Lens hood: Built in
M.F.D.: 1 foot (0.3 m)
Aperture range: f/5.6-f/22
Unique features: Rectilinear; CRC

Wildlife photographers love lenses like the 800mm f/8 ED IF because of its ability to isolate small subjects like this willow ptarmigan.

Nikkor 13mm f/5.6

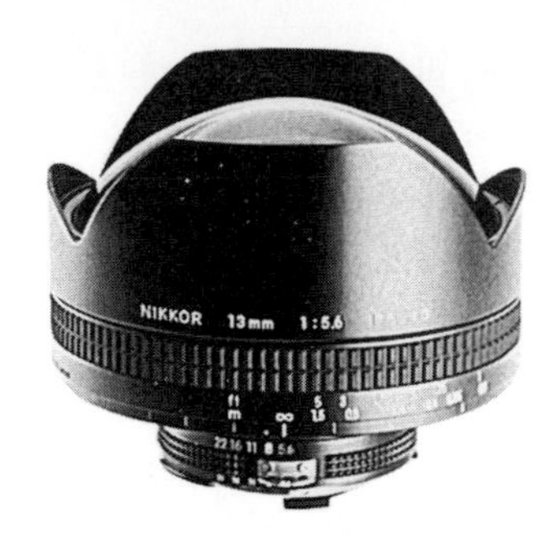

The 13mm f/5.6 is the widest lens in the Nikon line (excluding fisheyes). Along with the 15mm (see the chapter on fisheyes), it shares a common design feature—rectilinear correction—a fancy word for straight-line rendition. Where a fisheye of this coverage "bends" straight lines, making them curve, rectilinear design corrects for this barrel distortion. This design element makes the 13mm physically quite large, almost to the point of excluding it from being handheld.

The tremendous coverage and large front element (approximately 110mm) prohibits the use of front filters or accessory lens shades. Filters bayonet on at the rear element; Nikon provides four (A2, B2, L1B, O56) with the lens (hidden in the lid of the lens case). It is impossible without great expense to polarize or use a graduated neutral density filter on the 13mm; it must be custom made. The most common way to use other filters on the 13mm is by using gels taped to the rear element, and is the only way of employing a polarizing filter. It is a slow method as well, because the filter must be moved every time the direction in which the lens is pointed changes. Even then, the tremendous coverage of the lens might create uneven exposure because the polarization effect would not be the same across the entire 118° field.

Probably a bigger problem with this ultra wide is the shade. Built in and scalloped, it provides minimum coverage at best. Because of the lens' wide angle of view, though, a more adequate built-in shade would vignette into the frame. The extreme angle of coverage also produces tremendous flare problems if the photographer is not careful. These flares materialize in the form of purple or dark green "UFOs" (unidentified flare origins). They normally show up in the bottom of the viewfinder, and can occur even when the sun is not in the picture. Using a hand or small piece of cardboard as an auxiliary shade is the only option for ridding the photograph of this flare. You must be careful when doing this, because the auxiliary shade can cause vignetting—an excellent reason to use this lens on a camera with 100% viewing.

The front element must always be kept clean on the 13mm. Because the sun will quite often be in the photograph, any dirt or moisture rings on it will show up as a very bizarre type of flare. So cleaning the front element properly and keeping it clean is very important to getting a flare-free image.

With the 13mm's incredible angle of view and ability to focus so close, it is used most often to relate the subject to the background rather than just taking scenic shots. Getting close physically to the main subject, making it the largest element in the photograph, and then letting the tremendous depth of field of the 13mm bring in the background is one of the main applications of this lens. Many cover photographs are taken with this lens used in just this way. To take advantage of this technique, handholding—though difficult—is usually required. Because the focusing ring is very narrow and at the end of the barrel, proper handholding technique, described on page 53, must be followed. Special care must be taken that a dangling finger does not get in the photograph when handholding.

Because of its price and scarcity, the 13mm is rarely available for purchase. It is stocked at many lens rental houses—which is the best way to experience this magnificent lens firsthand.

Nikkor 16mm f/2.8

Original release: 1979
Angle of coverage: 180°
Physical size: 2.6 x 2.5 inches (6.6 x 6.4 cm)
Weight: 11.7 ounces (328 g)
Filter size: 39mm bayonet
Lens hood: Built in
M.F.D.: 1 foot (0.3 m)
Aperture range: f/2.8-f/22
Unique features: Full-frame fisheye

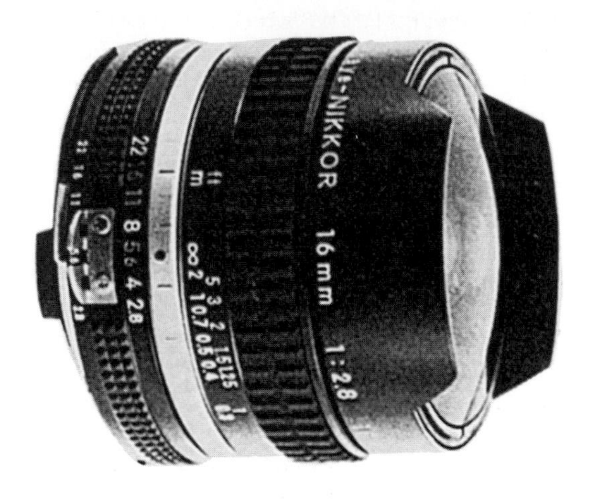

Nikkor 16mm f/2.8

The 16mm f/2.8 is a chameleon. More than any other lens in photography, changing the technique of using the 16mm f/2.8 can radically change the effect it creates in a scene.

Its full-frame, fisheye image, encompassing 180°, is its secret to being such a chameleon. The 180° is across the diagonal of the 24mm x 35mm film format. This produces its extreme barrel (fisheye) distortion, as well as its virtually unlimited, exaggerated perspective. Remember this is being "stretched," if you will, over the full frame rather than producing a circular image—and while providing even exposure over the entire frame. The 16mm f/2.8 is extremely well corrected for chromatic aberration, producing slightly higher contrast images that are assured, even when shooting wide open.

The 16mm f/2.8 has a built-in, scalloped lens hood that seems to be more than adequate. Even with its greater coverage than the 13mm, the 16mm tends to have less flare problems. This is partially because its front element is physically smaller in diameter than that of the 13mm. It still flares, but not as easily—which is good, as curing flare in the 16mm is nearly impossible, given its 180° coverage. Any hand or auxiliary shade is instantly in the photograph, no matter how much care is taken to avoid that happening.

The secret to using the 16mm f/2.8 is in understanding when and where to apply it. The barrel distortion is at its greatest when the lens is pointed either up or down (that is, if standing on a flat surface and shooting horizontally). When the horizon line is running through the dead center of the frame, this distortion is nil, affecting only vertical elements at the extreme edges of the frame. If there are no straight vertical lines in the photograph that would act as visual guides, the effect of the fisheye is negligible. Being above the scene—either on a cliff, ladder, or similar arrangement—masks the effect of the fisheye as long as the horizon line is running dead center through the frame.

This technique makes the 16mm f/2.8 great for photographing such subjects as scenic shots, as well as opening up possibilities in other realms in photography. For example, the 16mm is one of the most popular lenses to use for taking flight shots by remote. Attaching a remote camera on the end of a plane or hang glider wing can capture dramatic images. Because the wing is so long, any distortion of its lines is not noticeable. The added benefit is that the earth in the background will have a slight curvature to it. Because the earth is round, such curvature will be accepted as an accurate rendition; no one will think the photograph was taken with a fisheye. If the 16mm f/2.8 is used in a vertical format, or any of the parameters given above is not followed, the full-curve whammy of the lens comes out.

The 16mm f/2.8 can change as easily as the photographer's imagination will allow. Whether it's used to capture breathtaking scenic shots or making someone's tongue look miles long, the 180° view of the 16mm is virtually limitless.

This lens is now readily available on the used market for very little money, making it a great way to break into ultra-wide photography. Its updated, AF version is described in the chapter on fisheyes.

Nikkor 55mm f/2.8 Micro

Original release: 1982 **Angle of coverage:** 43° **Physical size:** 2.4 x 2.5 inches (6.1 x 6.4 cm) **Weight:** 18.2 ounces (510 g) **Filter size:** 52mm **Lens hood:** HN-3 **M.F.D.:** 3 feet (0.9 m) **Aperture range:** f/2.8-f/32 **Unique features:** Focus to 1:2; CRC

Probably no other lens is as responsible for getting photographers involved in exploring their natural world than the 55mm f/2.8 micro. Even those owning other brands know of the reputation of this lens. This reputation was not earned just in macro photography, but as an all-around lens delivering remarkable quality.

The 55mm f/2.8 incorporates Nikon's close-range correction (CRC) system, the key to its sharpness when focused at 1:1. This edge-to-edge quality is legendary, well known as "hair splitting." Although the CRC is not supposed to be in effect when the lens is focused near infinity, whether it is or not, the lens maintains the same edge-to-edge quality.

Getting to magnifications greater than 1:2 requires an extension tube of 27.5mm. Nikon makes the PK-13 specifically to match up with the 55mm f/2.8. The PK-13, which is exactly 27.5mm, maintains all meter and aperture couplings. To reach 2:1, adding either two more PK-13s or a 2x teleconverter is required. In either case, meter coupling is maintained—which

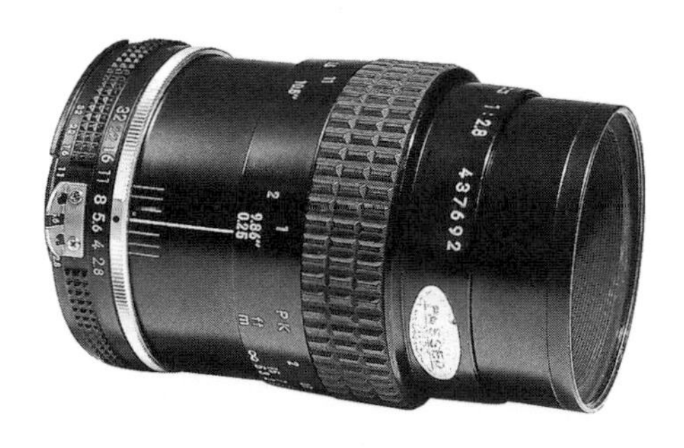

Nikkor 55mm f/2.8 Micro

is important, as two stops of light are lost for each 1x increase in magnification.

There is a scale on the lens barrel that could be confusing at first. When you look at the barrel, you will see "m," "ft," and "PK." The "m" is for meters, and is basically ignored by most U.S. photographers. The "ft" indicates distances in feet until getting down to 1:10 magnification, when it counts down to 1:2; it is relevant when the lens is in use directly mounted to a camera body. The "PK" scale, which start at 1:2 and works its way down to 1:1, indicates physical distance between the lens and subject when the PK-13 tube is attached to the lens.

Years after this lens has been discontinued, it still resides in hundreds of thousands of photographers' camera bags. This is even after the 60mm f/2.8 swept the current new-lens market. This is a testament to the quality and lasting ability of the 55mm f/2.8 micro—and in a fickle marketplace such as photography, that is saying a lot.

Nikkor 105mm f/4 Bellows Lens

Original release: 1969
Angle of coverage: 19°
Physical size: 2 x 2.5 inches (5.1 x 6.4 cm)
Weight: 8.1 ounces (277 g)
Filter size: 52mm
Lens hood: None
M.F.D.: 6 feet (1.8 m)
Aperture range: f/4-f/32
Unique features: Designed to work on bellows

This remarkable lens, the original 105mm micro, was designed specifically for use on the PB-4 and PB-5 bellows. On the bellows, the lens can be focused from infinity to 1.3x; on its own, it cannot be focused, as it has no focusing ring. It has a completely manual aperture, with no automatic diaphragm linkage. In 1969, it was high tech and very specialized, qualities that have kept it popular and in demand 30 years later.

The 105mm bellows lens (also referred to as the "short mount" 105mm) is extremely sharp. Even when used at high magnifications, it maintains sharp corners even though it is not a flat-field lens. Because it has no helicoid, it depends on the contractions and expansion of a bellows for focus. When used on a bellows, it is typically preset for a specific reproduction (magnification) size so the entire bellows/lens/camera setup is moved to focus on the subject.

Operating the aperture is the same as with a PC lens. Aperture readings can be taken anytime (if used with a bellows, add in the bellows factor) by manually stopping down the lens. The aperture on the 105mm bellows lens clicks on 1/3 stop increments (the only Nikkor lens to ever do this). A second ring can be turned and set at the predetermined f/stop so the aperture can be opened up for focusing. The lens must be manually closed down, though, when the photograph is taken.

On the bellows, the lens has an outstanding free-working distance of six feet (1.8 m) at a magnification of 1.3x. But the most popular use for the 105mm bellows lens is reversed on a telephoto lens, such as a 200mm f/4. Attached via a 52-52 adapter ring, this combination produces a magnification of 7x with a free working distance of four feet (1.2 m). The aperture on the 105mm bellows lens should be wide open for optimum results. Metering is accomplished by using the aperture on the main telephoto lens. It is recommended that this lens not be closed down past f/16.

Because of its tremendous flexibility and free working distance, few if any of these lenses can ever be found in a camera store; those that do show up normally cost four to five times the price of the lens when it was new. This is because it is a marvelous tool for the close-up photographer, surpassing many options available in today's modern lenses.

Nikkor 200mm f/4 IF Micro

Original release: 1981
Angle of coverage: 12°20′
Physical size: 7.1 x 2.6 inches (18 x 6.6 cm)
Weight: 28.3 ounces (558 g)
Filter size: 52mm
Lens hood: Built in
M.F.D.: 2.34 feet (0.7 m)
Aperture range: f/4-f/32
Unique features: Macro of 1:2

A magnificent lens, the 200mm f/4 micro was all the rage when it was first introduced. Due to the flurry over autofocus, it had been forgotten but now many photographers are finding the lens for the first time—and rediscovering just what a marvelous lens it really is. (The AF version is described in the chapter on specialty lenses.)

The 200mm f/4 micro is a small lens physically, its barrel diameter only slightly larger than its 52mm front element. It is very light weight, making handholding extremely easy. The tripod collar can be removed to further enhance using it handheld. And, because of its tremendous focusing range, it performs almost like a zoom.

The 200mm f/4 micro can focus from infinity to 1:2 without any additional accessories. The lens incorporates IF so it does not expand or contract when focused, resulting in its fast response to moving subjects. With the addition of a 1.4x converter, the lens becomes a 280mm f/5.6, able to focus nearly 1:1; with a 2x (TC-301 works the best), it's a 400mm f/8, focusing 1:1. All of this while maintaining a working distance of 2.3 feet (0.7 m)!

The original version (AI) had a narrow tripod collar with a wide aperture ring. The tripod collar was perfectly suited for the lens' weight and length. But with the introduction of AIS, the lens collar was made wider and the aperture ring made narrower. For those with large fingers, this could pose a bit of a problem.

Like all micros, the 200mm f/4 should not be pigeonholed and reserved just for close-up work. It is a great telephoto, especially for scenic photography.

Nikkor 300mm f/2 ED IF

Original release: 1984
Angle of coverage: 8°10′
Physical size: 13 x 7.2 inches (33 x 18.3 cm)
Weight: 16.6 pounds (7.5 kg)
Lens hood: HE-1
M.F.D.: 13 feet (3.9 m)
Aperture range: f/2-f/16
Unique features: Fast

At the 1984 Olympics, a new lens appeared on the track. There was no way it could be hidden; its 160mm front element

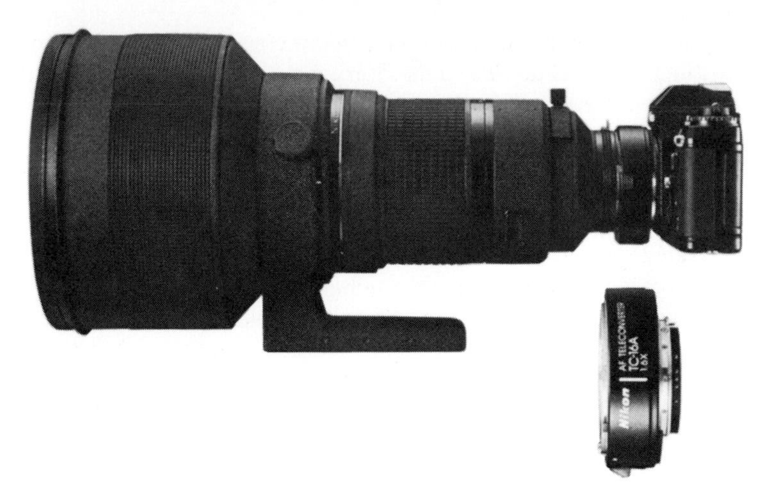

This Nikkor 300mm f/2 becomes a 480mm f/2.8 with the addition of the TC-16A teleconverter.

gleamed in the sun. The 300mm f/2 ED IF made its debut while photographers from around the world gathered with all their big super telephotos to capture the events. And for many photographers, the biggest event was the introduction of this lens.

At the time the 300mm f/2 ED IF was discontinued, it was a special-order item with a suggested list price of $22,000! Used, it still commands a high price, high demand, and high respect. This has a lot to do with the lens being so sharp, especially at f/2. It also has to do with its ability to isolate a subject better than any other lens. Most of all, it has the allure of being the fastest of the fast.

The lens is huge! At over 16 pounds, it weighs in as one of the top two heaviest lenses ever manufactured. Most of this weight is in the front element, making the lens extremely front heavy. This takes a little getting used to, which slows down its operation until the photographer gets into a set routine to handle the weight. Once a comfort level is reached in handling this lens, however, its very bright image makes operation extremely easy, even in quite dim light.

The 300mm f/2 was always sold with a dedicated teleconverter, the TC-14C. This teleconverter, which eats up 1 stop of light and increases focal length by 1.4x, converted the lens into a 420mm f/2.8 that focused down to 13 feet (3.9 m) and was tack sharp. The TC-14C was needed to preserve the edge-to-edge quality when the lens is shot wide open. The problem of uneven exposure due to vignetting is possible with all other Nikon teleconverters, including the TC-301.

Nikon states the use of the 300mm f/2 as "Ideal for indoor sports, action photography and all types of available-light shooting."

This is barely the tip of the iceberg for applications, however. Many wildlife photographers, fashion photographers, and other professionals have found this lens to be the only way to take photographs. Truly one of the rare Nikkor optics, shooting through it is a remarkable experience, with its very bright image and pinpoint focus.

The standard methods of using this lens include being able to afford it—that is, after finding one to purchase. Having large arm muscles to maneuver it and the imagination to make the most if its ability to isolate doesn't hurt, either. Think of it: the depth of field of f/2 with the angle of view of 300mm. The life of the 300mm f/2 as a new product might have been limited, but it will be in the field for as long as Nikon makes cameras.

Nikkor 300mm f/2.8 ED IF AF

Original release: 1989
Angle of coverage: 8°10′
Physical size: 9.8 x 5.4 inches (24.9 x 13.7 cm)
Weight: 5.6 pounds (2.5 kg)
Filter size: 32mm screw in
Lens hood: Built in and HE-6
M.F.D.: 10 feet (3 m)
Aperture range: f/2.8-f/22
Unique features: None

The manual version of the 300mm f/2.8 always overshadowed the 300mm f/2.8 AF (the latest version, the 300mm f/2.8D ED IF AF-S, is discussed in the chapter on super telephoto lenses). Though the optical quality was as good if not slightly better in the

Nikkor 300mm f/2.8 ED IF AF

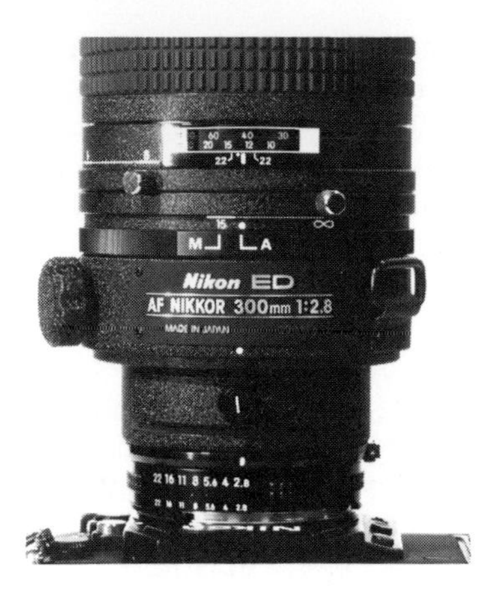

AF version, the general feel of the lens was not as rock solid as the manual version. The problem with this is that many photographers could be missing out on a great lens.

This is a remarkably sharp lens. It has a sexy front element that just glistens, but that large element makes the lens barely handholdable for most. Many sports photographers use the lens with a monopod; others have them attached to tripods. The f/2.8 permits shooting at fast shutter speeds, but the narrow angle of view demands a thoroughly practiced technique for getting sharp images.

This lens does not have fast AF speed; focus tracking is minimally effective with moving subjects. Most photographers use this lens manually, which is quite simple and can be quicker than the autofocus. The lens does not have a motor inside, it but it does have a CPU.

The lens has a rotatable collar, permitting 360° turning, indispensable when shooting vertically—much faster and sturdier than trying to turn a tripod head vertically. It also has the two-part shade system, one built in and the other reversible; combined, the two shades provide nearly seven inches (17.8 cm) of shade protection for the front element. The reversible shade is made of high-impact plastic, the permanent shade is metal.

The lens can easily work with the TC-14B, providing outstanding results as a 420mm f/4 lens. With a TC-301, the results are not as remarkable, with a slightly perceptible loss at the edges. The PK-11a works marvelously on the lens, reducing minimum focusing distance to a little less than nine feet (2.7 m).

The 300mm f/2.8 ED IF AF can be found used at fairly decent prices because of the introduction of the AF-I version. For those wanting to get into a fast 300mm lens, happening into one of these used is a great find. There is nothing optically or mechanically inferior with this lens. In fact, it is one of Nikon's sharpest—but don't let the secret out.

Nikkor 300mm f/4.5 ED IF

Original release: 1979
Angle of coverage: 8°10′
Physical size: 7.6 x 3.2 inches (19.3 x 8.1 cm)
Weight: 2.3 pounds (1 kg)
Filter size: 72mm
Lens hood: Built in
M.F.D.: 10 feet (3 m)
Aperture range: f/4.5-f/32
Unique features: IF

Until the 300mm f/4 ED IF AF came on the market, the 300mm f/4.5 ED IF was *the* 300mm to own. Its reign lasted over a decade, mostly because of its versatility. This has taken the lens into every possible arena of photography with great success. For this reason, thousands still find homes in photographers' arsenals of lenses.

The 300mm f/4 ED IF AF has a tripod collar that permits 360° rotation, and it's removable, which facilitates handholding; many photographers also use it on a gunstock for extra stability. In either case, its internal focusing—further enhanced by its small focus ring throw of just a little over 100°—gives a quick response to any subject.

Because of its lightweight, compact design, many photographers use the 300mm in conjunction with a TC-14B. This makes a handholdable 420mm f/7 with limited depth of field. Such isolation and portability has made it one of the preferred lenses for nature photography, but its versatility for the nature photographer goes beyond these attributes.

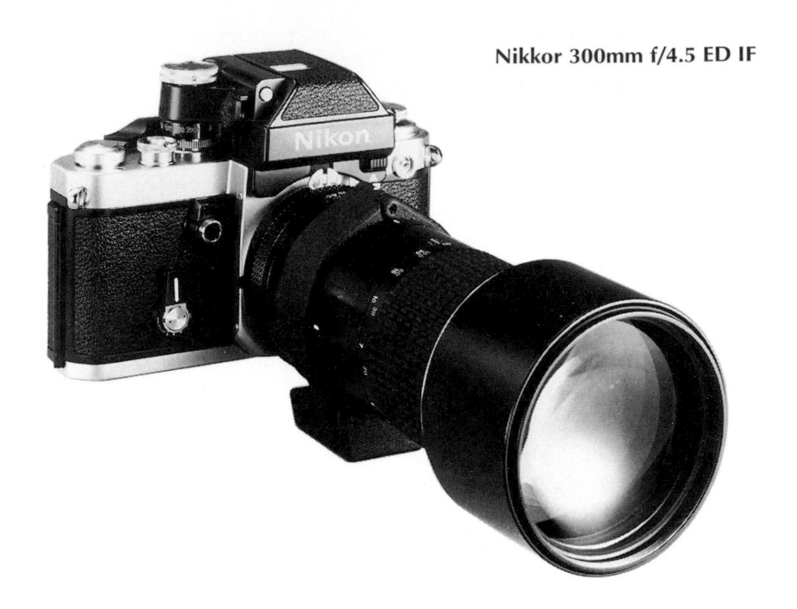

Nikkor 300mm f/4.5 ED IF

Another excellent application of this lens is with extension tubes. For example, by adding an PN-11 and PK-13 (80mm of extension) to the lens, it has the magnification of 1:2 with a three-foot (0.9 m) free working distance. Depth of field is a slight battle, as the extension tubes have moved the lens away from the film plane, but the image quality is outstanding. One application for this would be in photographing wildflowers.

With the introduction and wide acceptance of the 300mm f/4 ED IF AF, used 300mm f/4.5 ED IFs are available at reasonable prices. For the budget-minded photographer, this is an excellent opportunity to get a marvelous lens. The tradeoffs between the lenses are too few to even mention in one sentence; the benefits, though, are greater than can be described.

Nikkor 500mm f/4 P ED IF

If any lens has broken the mold of super telephotos, it is the 500mm f/4 P ED IF. It has been a hot lens since the day of its release—and not for a moment has it ever looked back.

What immediately attracted so many to this lens is its physical design. The weight of its 122mm dustproof plate and front element group are balanced over the entire length of the lens.

Original release: 1988
Angle of coverage: 5°
Physical size: 15.5 x 5.4 inches (39.4 x 13.7 cm)
Weight: 6.6 pounds (3 kg)
Filter size: 39mm screw in
Lens hood: HK-17
M.F.D.: 20 feet (6 m)
Aperture range: f/4-f/22
Unique features: "P" chip

Because it's relatively short and so well balanced, it does not take a mega tripod to give this lens the proper support. It is easy to wheel about when shooting, and can respond quickly to a fast subject.

For those photographing moving subjects, whether it's cars, planes, or birds, the 500mm f/4 P is marvelous for panning because of its maneuverability. The main thing to remember is to continue to pan even after the exposure to make sure the shutter has completely closed. Anything less and the subject will be out of focus.

What sell the 500mm f/4 P are its quality and flexibility. It is razor sharp! This still applies when using a TC-14B (700mm f/5.6) or TC-301 (1000mm f/8), extremely common with this lens. It is also used quite often with an extension tube. Though the lens focuses down to a respectable 20 feet, many photographers use it with a PK-12, bringing the minimum focusing distance down to a little over 16 feet (4.8 m).

The 500mm f/4 P has an internal CPU, which communicates with cameras having matrix metering. This has further endeared the lens with N8008/F-801 users, who are left out of matrix metering with nearly all super telephotos within a reasonable price range (reasonable for a super telephoto, that is).

The 500mm f/4 P has one of the deepest lens shades around. It reverses when in use, providing nine inches (252 cm) of shade protection; this is great for the sport photographer who gets plowed into by a football player. For the nature photographer, this extra shade might keep that flinging branch from hitting the front element. In addition, because the shade is so deep, shooting backlit subjects is slightly easier, thus opening up other photographic possibilities.

There is one last big selling point of the 500mm f/4 P—its focal length. If there were such a thing as an ideal focal length for super telephotos, this would be it. For many photographers, 400mm is too short, and for others, 600mm too long. The 500mm fits right in between these focal lengths, satisfying the needs of the majority of photographers.

Nikkor 800mm f/8 ED IF

Original release: 1979
Angle of coverage: 3°
Physical size: 17.8 x 5.3 inches (45.2 x 13.5 cm)
Weight: 7.7 pounds (3.5 kg)
Filter size: 39mm
Lens hood: Built in
M.F.D.: 35 feet (10.5 m)
Aperture range: f/8-f/32
Unique features: None

An obscure lens, the 800mm f/8 ED IF is one of Nikon's better kept secrets of all time. The optics of the lens, which are quite sharp, have been overshadowed by its f/8 speed. It is also haunted by the previous 800mm f/8 lenses, which were not ED IF, and physically very long and slow. The original 800 f/8 was a two-part lens with a tremendously long focusing throw and very dark view. The majority of lenses that made the trek from a two-part system to ED IF also got faster, but somehow the 800mm f/8 didn't.

The 800mm f/8 is a remarkably well-balanced lens. This is important, as the focusing ring is behind the tripod collar, where a hand should rest for correct long lens technique. The lens is basically a narrow tube, with only the front element end diameter a little larger than 122mm. The elements take up very little room in the barrel, which is mostly air space. This is what makes the lens so well balanced.

With fast lenses so important, 800 f/8 lenses can be found at almost give-away prices. It might take a little looking to find a used one, though, as those who own the lens rarely let go of it. Many of these are wildlife photographers who use the lens on a gunstock. Its balance and weight make it easy to use, especially

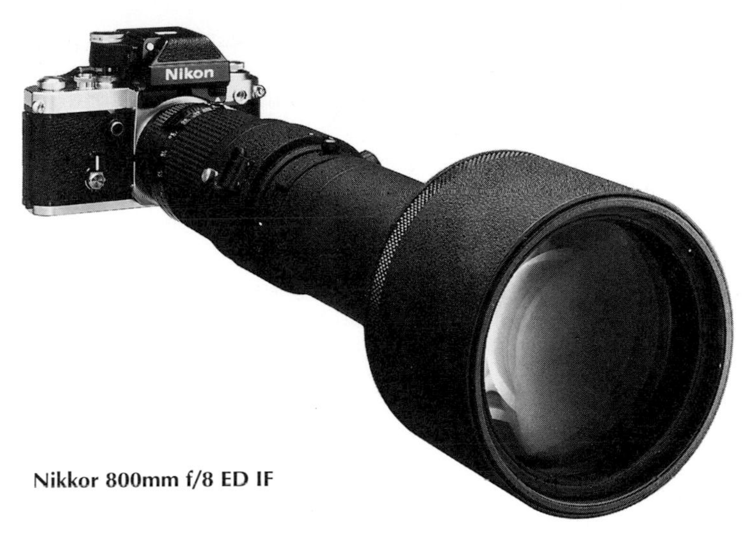

Nikkor 800mm f/8 ED IF

when stalking wildlife; its light weight also makes it an excellent choice for close-up photography. The lens works great with extension tubes with the PN-11, reducing the minimum focusing distance to 27 feet (8.1 m).

One recommendation is to get rid of the case supplied with the 800mm f/8. It's the same case used for the 1200mm f/11 and is really oversized for this lens. Long Lens Bags by Domke® work much better, not taking up as much space while providing lots of protection and quick access.

Nikkor 1200mm f/11 ED IF

Original release: 1982
Angle of coverage: 2°
Physical size: 22.4 x 5.3 inches (56.9 x 13.5 cm)
Weight: 9.1 pounds (4.1 kg)
Filter size: 39mm
Lens hood: Built in
M.F.D.: 45 feet (13.5 m)
Aperture range: f/11-f/32
Unique features: None

The secret weapon in many prominent wildlife photographers' arsenals, few of the 1200mm f/11 exist in the marketplace today. Its predecessor, a two-part lens, though extremely slow, was very popular—due, in part, to the tremendously long reach of the lens and its very narrow angle of view. The longest lens in its day, its reach had a romantic appeal as well as problem-solving abilities. Other than the 2000mm f/16 mirror, this is the longest lens Nikon has ever made.

The 1200mm f/11 is basically a tube with glass at the front element and then one other group just in front of the tripod collar; the rest of the lens is an air gap making up the focal length. With the element group right in front of the collar, the focusing ring cannot be near it. Consequently, the focusing ring is at the rear of the lens, which makes using correct long lens technique difficult. The lens is well balanced, though, which aids greatly in operation.

Nikon wrote of the 1200mm f/11, "The king of super-telephotos. . . . ideal for sports, wildlife, and frame-filling shots of the sun or moon itself." With a staggering 24x magnification compared to a 50mm lens, the 1200mm can pull in and isolate like no other. The fact that this lens has been totally absent on the used lens market—even though it's been discontinued since 1988—almost defies the odds. This is because not only were few of these lenses manufactured, but those who own them never get rid of them. This is the highest tribute a lens can receive.

Nikkor 25-50mm f/4

Original release: 1980
Angle of coverage: 80°10'-47°50'
Physical size: 4.1 x 3 inches (10.4 x 7.6 cm)
Weight: 22.5 ounces (630 g)
Filter size: 72mm
Lens hood: HK-7
M.F.D.: 2 feet (0.6 m)
Aperture range: f/4-f/22
Unique features: None

This is an amazing zoom. It fits that magic comfort range of 25-50mm f/4 in a nice small package. At its introduction, fast lenses were not in high demand; this is reflected in its constant f/4. It is a two-ring (two-touch) lens—one ring zooms and one ring focuses. This was one of Nikon's first two-ring zooms, in fact, and the big selling point was that the focus would not be accidentally changed during zooming.

The 25-50mm f/4 also was Nikon's first wide-angle zoom, which made it very popular from the start. The price, though, kept it out of reach of many general photographers. It was not until Nikon closed out the lens when it was discontinued that the masses got to see what the few owned.

The 25-50mm f/4 is incredibly sharp from corner to corner. Whether focused at its minimum focusing distance or at infinity, the edge-to-edge sharpness rivals prime focal length lenses.

The lens is a marvelous tool for scenic photographers. Whether shooting overall grand views or close-ups, this is a one-lens arsenal. Its 72mm filter size accepts Nikon 72mm polarizers; rear filtration for color correction is a simple operation. It also works marvelously with extension tubes, the PK-11 creating a magnification of 1:4.

With the advent of autofocus, many manual lenses have been abandoned. The 25-50mm f/4 was one of the first to go, but smart photographers snatched it up so that today it is almost impossible to find. This is a lens' biggest tribute and a sure sign that it is something special.

Nikkor 35-200mm f/3.5-4.5

Original release: 1986
Angle of coverage: 62°-12°20'
Physical size: 5 x 2.7 inches (12.7 x 6.9 cm)
Weight: 25.9 ounces (725 g)
Filter size: 62mm
Lens hood: HK-15
M.F.D.: 1 foot (0.3 m)
Aperture range: f/3.5-f/22
Unique features: Macro mode

The 35-200mm f/3.5-4.5 has been lost in the conversion to AF systems. This remarkable lens was one of the first zooms to be introduced with variable f/stops, but at a time when manual

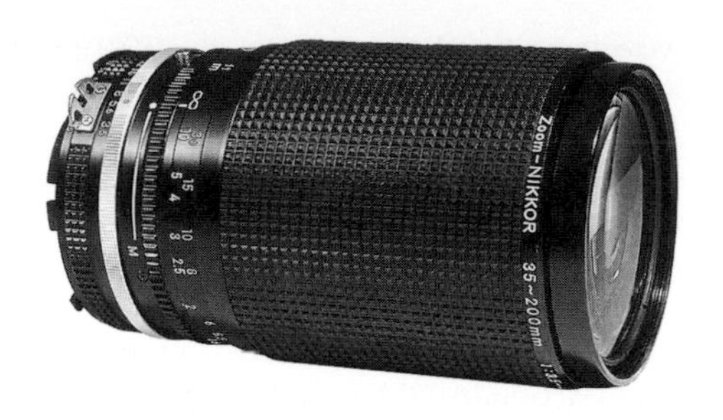

Nikkor 35-200mm f/3.5-4.5

everything was so big this lens never really caught on—a loss to photographers, because the 35-200mm delivers extremely sharp images in a compact and easy-to-use push-pull zoom.

Like many zooms, it has a Macro mode, delivering 1:4 magnification. This can easily be increased with the use of extension tubes, delivering excellent edge-to-edge quality, and further enhanced with Nikon's close-up lenses, 5T and 6T. Because of its small size, it can be easily handheld, lending itself to many applications where a larger 200mm lens would be difficult; this includes macro subjects. It has no tripod mount, but because the lens is small a tripod can be attached to the body.

With the upgrading of many photographers' systems to autofocus, the 35-200mm can often be found on the used-lens shelf. With the exception of its slower lens speed, it has a greater range and smaller size than the 80-200mm f/2.8 AF. Its filter size, 62mm, is also smaller, fitting the norm for most of the current AF lenses. The 35-200mm is one of the best examples of a great lens being passed by because of speed rather than performance.

Nikkor 50-135mm f/3.5

Original release: 1984
Angle of coverage: 46°-18°
Physical size: 4.9 x 2.8 inches (12.4 x 7.1 cm)
Weight: 26.2 ounces (734 g)
Filter size: 62mm
Lens hood: HK-10
M.F.D.: 2 feet (0.6 m)
Aperture range: f/3.5-f/32
Unique features: Macro mode

A zoom with a limited range, the 50-135mm f/3.5 has always had a big fan club. There are numerous reasons for this. The biggest is the fact that the lens is extremely sharp throughout its entire range; another is its rather compact design. These virtues were wrapped up in an affordable price range, making the lens accessible to all photographers.

The 50-135mm f/3.5 fits a range that was temporarily lacking coverage by a zoom. Its minimum focusing distance instantly made it a big hit, especially when coupled with a 5T or 6T, and photographers were quick to buy it, finding extreme versatility in its compact range. The lens is capable of 1:2 magnification with two feet (0.06 m) of free working distance. Its image quality, when used in this way, is remarkable, especially as that quality is achieved with a zoom.

Another charming characteristic of the 50-135mm f/3.5 is that its front element does not turn. This is an advantage when using a polarizer—along with its f/32 minimum f/stop, a particularly important feature for scenic photographers.

When Nikon announces that it has discontinued a lens, there is a feeding frenzy to buy any remaining stock. The 50-135mm f/3.5 was one of the biggest of these frenzies; some photographers stocked up on multiple units. Today, even with faster, greater range and smaller zooms, the 50-135mm is rarely found used in a camera store. It is one of those legends Nikon is known so well to produce.

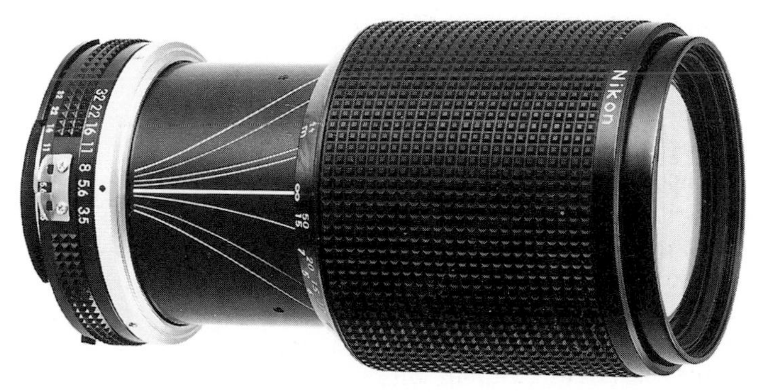

Nikkor 50-135mm f/3.5

Nikkor 75-300mm f/4.5-5.6 AF

Original release: 1989
Angle of coverage: 31°40'-8°10'
Physical size: 6.8 x 2.6 inches (17.3 x 6.6 cm)
Weight: 30 ounces (840 g)
Filter size: 62mm
Lens hood: HN-24
M.F.D.: 5 feet (1.5 m)
Aperture range: f/4.5-f/32
Unique features: Macro mode

The 75-300mm f/4.5-5.6 AF, an incredible lens, has a home in many nature photographers' camera bags because of its amazing versatility, with excellent to outstanding optics at a very economical price.

Its range is also excellent, providing a lot of reach in a small package. At the 300mm setting it is an f/5.6, which is slow. But it is small, which makes handholding at this range easy. The lens incorporates a tripod collar, endearing it to most of its owners. The collar, though, is not like those found on the super telephotos. Because of this, using it requires practicing long-lens techniques. Using the lens mounted to the tripod remotely can result in less than satisfactory images because of the weak tripod collar.

The 75-300mm's Macro mode allows it to focus down to five feet (1.5 mm). This holds true through the entire zoom range, making it one of the closest focusing 300mm lenses. For photographing subjects such as a rattlesnake, this is good, but it is also good for taking pictures of nesting birds or of people. The lens readily accepts and works magnificently with extension tubes, increasing its versatility.

The 75-300mm's AF speed is about as fast as its f/stop. To help increase the AF speed, it has a limit switch, but the switch really has a minimal effect. The focusing of the lens is probably its only drawback. With the focusing ring at the end of the lens near the filter ring, when the lens is zoomed out to 300mm, some photographers have difficulty handholding it properly.

The 75-300mm's 62mm filter size makes it perfect for scenic work. Because there are so many filters—such as polarizer and

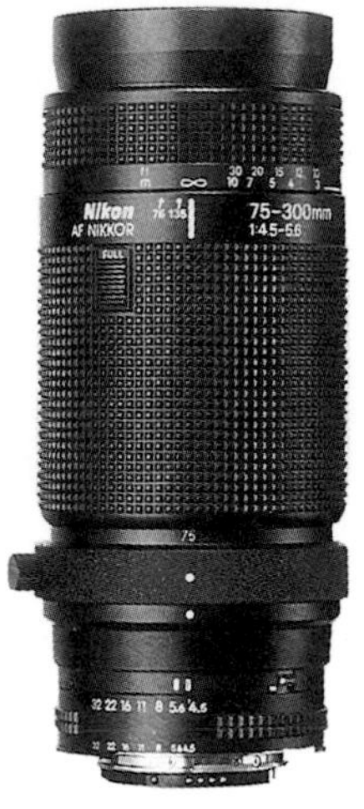

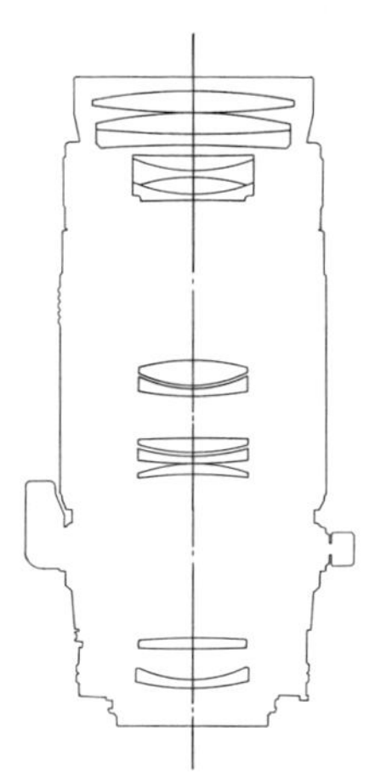

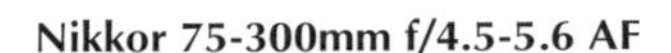
Nikkor 75-300mm f/4.5-5.6 AF

graduated split neutral density—available in this size, the zoom is a natural. This is especially true at the 300mm range, as other 300mm lenses have 72mm or larger front elements.

Nikkor 80-200mm f/4.5

Original release: 1970
Angle of coverage: 25°-10°
Physical size: 6.4 x 2.8 inches (16.3 x 17.1 cm)
Weight: 29.3 ounces (820 g)
Filter size: 52mm
Lens hood: HN-7
M.F.D.: 4 feet (1.2 m)
Aperture range: f/4.5-f/32
Unique features: None

No other lens was as responsible for making zooms a useful photographic tool than the 80-200mm f/4.5, which went through a number of optical refinements through its eight-year run. The final version was probably its finest, but this is a judgment that splits hairs at best, because the changes have mostly been small precision ones in the element coatings.

The 80-200mm f/4.5 is a one-touch, push-pull zoom. It is a true zoom, with focus not changing during the zooming action.

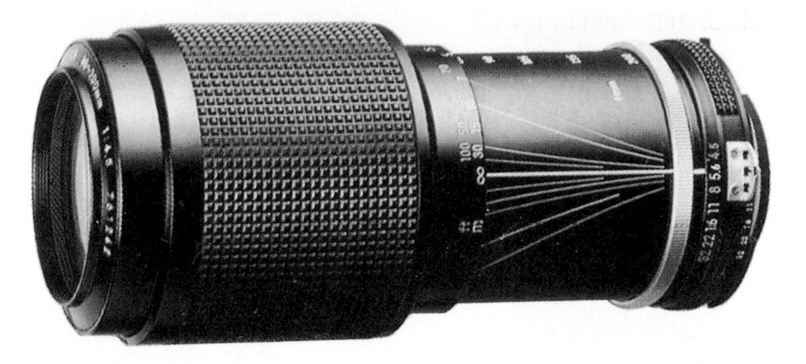

Nikkor 80-200mm f/4.5

This is an important characteristic, as many lenses focus at the 200mm setting, then zoom back for the proper framing. Because the 80-200mm is so well balanced, its zoom action is not a problem, fitting the hand perfectly. All of this, combined with its remarkable optics, made the 80-200mm one of the most popular zooms ever manufactured.

It did not fare well with teleconverters, though. The combination of all the glass caused a dropoff in quality, especially at the edges. The lens was also hardly ever used with extension tubes, as that was not a common practice in its heyday; today, though, many photographers use it in this manner with excellent results.

The number of 80-200mm f/4.5 lenses that was produced was staggering. Even so, very few can now be found on store shelves. True, its use by photographers is a fraction of what it once was, but most photographers lucky enough to have one refuse to let it go. Whether it's a connection with a glory time in photography, loyalty to a trusted friend, or backup when the modern stuff breaks, the 80-200mm f/4.5 has a hold on photographers enjoyed by few other lenses.

Nikkor 200-400mm f/4 ED

Original release: 1984
Angle of coverage: 12°20'-6°10'
Physical size: 13 x 5.7 inches (33 x 14.5 cm)
Weight: 8.6 pounds (3.9 kg)
Filter size: 122mm
Lens hood: HE-2
M.F.D.: 13 feet (3.9 m)
Aperture range: f/4-f/32
Unique features: None

A lens that came and went quickly, the 200-400mm f/4 ED is more popular today than when it was available new. I remember camera stores with this lens just received in stock, selling it at cost just to get rid of it because it wouldn't sell. In 1984, dealer cost was $2470, but today some have bought this lens used for just under $10,000!

The 200-400mm f/4 ED is a great lens, producing beautiful images that are tack sharp. Its flexibility and bright image have made it a mainstay for wildlife photographers. In fact, 90% of the 200-400mm f/4 ED lenses are used by wildlife photographers; these professionals have found these lenses to be one of the best for big game, with the focal length and f/stop isolating and complementing the mighty giants of our landscape.

The 200-400mm f/4 ED is commonly used with the TC-14B—making the lens into a 280-560mm f/5.6 zoom; in this configuration, the lens becomes a great tool for bird photography, especially nesting birds. Its flexibility is so tremendous and its quality so good that the lens is still able to command a high price.

Nikkor 200-400mm f/4 ED

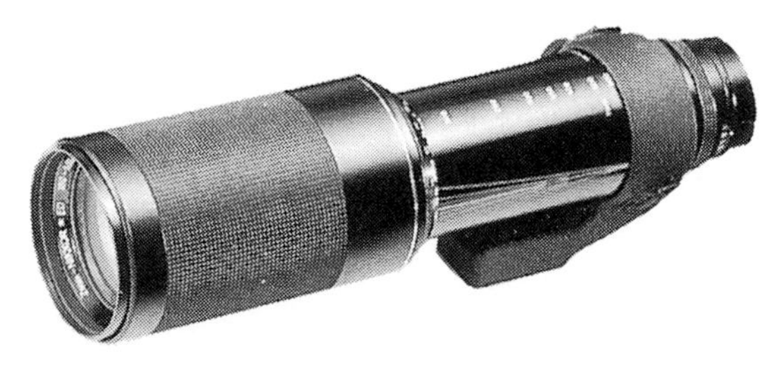

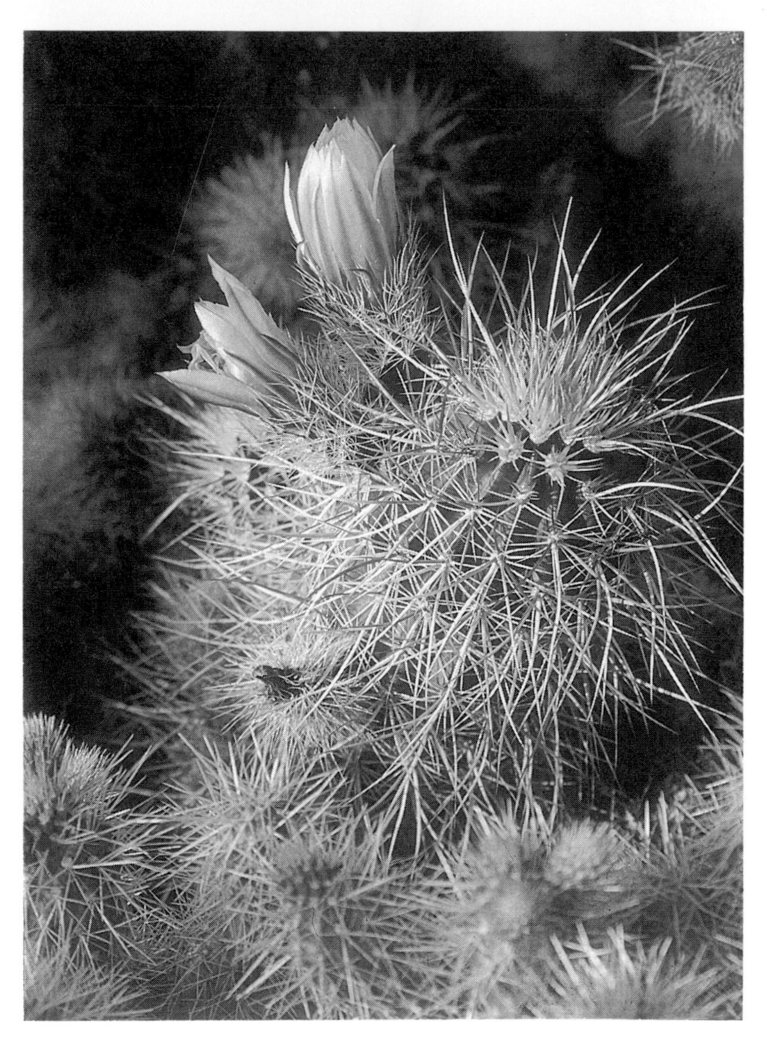

The rising sun and a 300mm f/2.8 caught this Simpson's Hedgehog cactus blossom opening for the first time.